Undercurrents

Queer Asia

The Queer Asia book series opens a space for monographs and anthologies in all disciplines focused on non-normative sexuality and gender cultures, identities and practices in Asia. Queer Studies and Queer Theory originated in and remain dominated by North American and European academic circles, and existing publishing has followed these tendencies. However, growing numbers of scholars inside and beyond Asia are producing work that challenges and corrects this imbalance. The Queer Asia book series – first of its kind in publishing – provides a valuable opportunity for developing and sustaining these initiatives.

Editorial Collective
Chris Berry (Goldsmiths, University of London)
John Nguyet Erni (Lingnan University)
Peter Jackson (Australian National University)
Helen Hok-Sze Leung (Simon Fraser University)

International Editorial Board
Dennis Altman (La Trobe University)
Tom Boellstorff (University of California, Irvine)
Judith Butler (University of California, Berkeley)
Ding Naifei (National Central University, Taiwan)
David Eng (Rutgers University)
Neil Garcia (University of the Philippines, Diliman)
David Halperin (University of Michigan, Ann Arbor)
Josephine Chuen-juei Ho (National Central University, Taiwan)
Annamarie Jagose (University of Auckland, New Zealand)
Kam Louie (University of Hong Kong)
Lenore Manderson (Monash University, Australia)
Fran Martin (University of Melbourne, Australia)
Meaghan Morris (Lingnan University, Hong Kong)
Dédé Oetomo (University of Surabaya, Indonesia)
Cindy Patton (Simon Fraser University, Canada)
Elspeth Probyn (University of Sydney, Australia)
John Treat (Yale University)
Carol Vance (Columbia University)

Helen Hok-Sze Leung

Undercurrents
Queer Culture and Postcolonial
Hong Kong

香港大學出版社
HONG KONG UNIVERSITY PRESS

Hong Kong University Press
14/F Hing Wai Centre
7 Tin Wan Praya Road
Aberdeen
Hong Kong

© UBC Press 2008

ISBN 978-962-209-950-0

This softcover edition published by Hong Kong University Press is available in Asia.

Printed in Canada on ancient-forest-free paper (100% post-consumer recycled)
that is processed chlorine- and acid-free, with vegetable-based inks.

I fear tragedy will recur

I am fated in my fate

To be out of touch with what's beautiful

History repeats itself

In this bustling city

It is not possible

To love without undercurrents

What use is there for me to go on cherishing you?

If I hold you tight this time

Will it not be another empty embrace?

Still quietly waiting

For you to say I'm too sensitive

I have a sense of foreboding about everything

And then I cannot open my eyes to see fate arrive

And then clouds gather around the skies

– Lin Xi, "Undercurrents"

Contents

Illustrations

Ho Check Chong at Ko Shing Theatre

Preface

The seed of this book was likely sown a long time ago, by an old photograph in my mother's haphazardly arranged and endlessly fascinating family album. Taken in 1955, the photograph shows my late grandfather playing the role of Princess Ping Yeung at a charity performance of the Cantonese opera *The Dream Encounter between Emperor Wu of Han and Lady Wai*. Although he died when I was only four, my grandfather had remained a legendary figure in my imagination. His bold but short-lived career in theatre and in film – first as an actor and later as a producer – was invariably considered a failure by the family, but his *joie de vivre*, generosity, and creativity left lasting impressions on my young mind. I have always felt inexplicably drawn to that photograph – to my grandfather's evident pleasure in cross-gender performance and to the mysterious world of theatre and film where this pleasure could be freely indulged. It was not until much, much later that I connected my affinity with the photograph to other snippets of gossip that drew my empathy: my grandmother's tales about the "self-combed" women who loved each other; the news of a great-aunt's daughter who transitioned from female to male during the 1980s; my mother's whispers about a young cousin's curiously frequent visits to the public bathhouse. I would later come to appreciate these drifting fragments of family lore as a form of queer knowledge, one that – unlike in adult life – was acquired not from theory, activism, or subcultural participation but unknowingly from stories half-heard and dimly remembered that circulate in the nooks and crannies of daily life. What follows is inspired by this knowledge.

Acknowledgments

This book grew out of a project initially undertaken during my tenure as a Killam Postdoctoral Research Fellow at the University of British Columbia (UBC) from 1999 to 2001. I gratefully acknowledge the Killam Trusts for the valuable opportunity to develop a new research project in relative peace and with ample resources. An Endowed Research Fellowship and a President's Research Grant from Simon Fraser University (SFU) provided subsequent funding for the project.

A big thank you goes to Emily Andrew, my editor at UBC Press, who pursued this project with enthusiasm and facilitated the entire process with more efficiency and grace than I could have imagined possible. My appreciation also to Ann Macklem, who handled all the production details with care. I am indebted to the two anonymous readers for UBC Press, whose perceptive comments helped me improve the manuscript. Thanks also to Lee Ka-sing for generously allowing me to reproduce an image from his impressive project *Dot Hong Kong* for the book cover.

The collegial environment at both UBC and SFU has greatly benefitted my work. Kate Swatek was my postdoctoral supervisor and the first to warmly embrace the idea of the book. Numerous colleagues at the Department of Asian Studies and the Institute of Asian Research at UBC provided a regular source of friendly banter and intellectual exchange. I am grateful to my past and present colleagues at the Department of Women's Studies at SFU for their day-to-day support and camaraderie, especially Lara Campbell for our lively conversations in the car and Cindy Patton for intellectual and personal guidance. Peter Dickinson generously shared professional advice that was invaluable for a first-time author.

I learned a great deal from all the students I have had the pleasure to work with over the years, especially Anisha Abdulla, Usamah Ansari, Leah Allen, Sam Bradd, Jillian Deri, Cole Dodsley, Trish Garner, Emma Kesler, Marie-Geneviève Lane, Byron Lee, Colin Medhurst, and Tara Robertson. I am deeply grateful for their questions, insights, and the generous interest they took in my work.

In the course of writing this book, I have met many colleagues whose works have profoundly enriched mine. An incomplete list of those who offered feedback and encouragement includes: Chris Berry, Chu Wei-cheng, David Eng, Leslie Feinberg, John Erni, Richard Fung, Gayatri Gopinath, Judith Halberstam, Ho Sik-Ying, Lucetta Kam, Travis Kong, Lim Song Hwee, Iona Man-Cheong, Fran Martin, Nayan Shah, Shih Shu-mei, Mirana Szeto, Denise Tang, Daniel Tsang, and Audrey Yue.

The vibrant queer Asian community in Vancouver is a source of strength for both my work and my well-being. My thanks go to everyone I met through Monsoon and worked with closely during Lotus Roots 2002, especially Eleanor Cheung, Ritz Chow, Yuuki Hirano, Eileen Kage, Shahaa Kakar, Sook Kong, Laiwan, Desiree Lim, Cynthia Lowe, Debora O, and Rita Wong for their friendship and queer solidarity.

I have been spoiled by the hospitality of friends who filled my travels with excellent food and conversation: Chow Yiu-Fai and Jeroen de Kloet in Amsterdam; Karin Ann, Lusina Ho, Joe Lau, and Yau Ching in Hong Kong; Susan Stryker in San Francisco; Kiko Benitez and Chandan Reddy in Seattle; Nuzhat Abbas in Toronto; and Leung Ping-Kwan in whichever city we happen to find ourselves. James Keefer lent me his eye for detail by proofreading parts of the manuscript. Jeff Shalan remains my best friend and best interlocutor. My teacher Mary Layoun continues to be a source of inspiration even from afar.

I can never thank my parents enough for their affection and unwavering support. My father encouraged me from an early age to be a diligent learner and an independent thinker. My mother never stops sharing her love of movies with me, and my fondest memory while growing up remains our many, many trips to the cinema together. Finally, my love and thanks always to Kam Wai Kui for sharing all of life's joys with me.

Portions of this book have previously been published. An earlier draft of one section in Chapter 1 appeared as "Let's Love Hong Kong: A Queer Look at Cosmopatriotism," in *Cosmopatriots: On Distant Longings and Close Encounters,* ed. Jeroen de Kloet and Edward Jurriens (Amsterdam: Rodopi, 2007), 21-40. A short version of Chapter 3 appeared as "Unsung Heroes: Reading Transgender Subjectivities in Hong Kong Action Cinema," in *Masculinities and Hong Kong Cinema,* ed. Laikwan Pang and Day Wong (Hong Kong: Hong Kong University Press, 2005), 81-98. The "Undercurrents" lyric quoted on p. v is used with permission, © 1997 EMI Music Publishing Hong Kong/Go East Music Publishing Co Ltd, music by Chan Fai Young, lyric by Lin Xi.

Note on Romanization

This book uses the Hanyu Pinyin system of Romanization for Chinese words, names, and phrases, except in instances when a preferred alternative spelling exists (for example, most Hong Kong and Taiwanese personal names). The Pinyin and Chinese equivalents of these exceptions are given in the bibliography, filmography, and appendices. All transliterated Chinese names are ordered first by surname, followed by first name.

In Hong Kong films the characters' Chinese names are often rendered in English forms in the subtitles. For the sake of clarity, I refer to the English versions in the book and list their Pinyin and Chinese equivalents in the Glossary. Names that do not appear in the Glossary are originally rendered in English in the films. Hong Kong films also have official English titles that are not literal translations of their Chinese titles. I refer to the English versions in the book and include the Chinese titles in the filmography.

All English translations from Chinese material that appear in this book are mine unless noted otherwise.

Undercurrents

Introduction

This book began as an examination of gay and lesbian images in contemporary Hong Kong cinema but quickly became a very different kind of study. I was struck early on by the restrictive nature of "gay and lesbian" as a category of analysis. Its association with specific trajectories of identity formations, coupled with the political dynamics of the gay and lesbian movement in the West, means that its "application" to Hong Kong culture would in effect "disqualify" many representations as simply not gay or lesbian *enough*. When I was interviewed at the 2001 Lesbian and Gay Film Festival in San Francisco after speaking at a panel on Asian films, the interviewer asked me how gay and lesbian Hong Kong filmmakers would feel about San Francisco. "They see us as a model of their own future, don't they?" he added confidently. The interviewer's unknowingly condescending attitude derives not only from his pride in San Francisco's liberated self-image but also from a belief in the universality and linear progression of gay and lesbian liberation. San Francisco represents an ideal to which more "backward" societies must aspire. Frustrated by the inability of my original framework to challenge such attitudes, I duly abandoned "gay and lesbian" as a rubric in my study. At the same time, I became fascinated by everything that did not "fit" into the project before: all the representations that seemed too closeted, too ambiguous, or too understated now appeared to me in all their nuance and complexity. In stories of illicit sexual encounters, nebulous relationships, and magically sex-changed bodies, I found undercurrents of anxiety over identity crisis, family conflict, and the failed heterosexual promise. I saw forms of desire that resist the bounds of sexual orientation and saw relational bonds that escape categorization. My interest in the cinema also led me down related but distinct paths of cultural inquiry to explore cinema's relation to urban space, literary and operatic traditions, stardom and iconicity, and community-driven subcultural practices.

As I am interested in the ways that these works resist assimilation into the representational logic of heterosexuality *and* homosexuality, my inquiry demands a reading practice that is attuned to what is not quite intelligible in normative conceptions of gender and sexuality. Grounded in a body of theoretical works that challenge dominant sexual and gender norms, "queer" provides me with an analytical framework to look for what denaturalizes, disrupts, or resignifies the relation conventionally drawn between gendered embodiments, erotic desire, and sexual identities. In Michele Aaron's discussion of the New Queer Cinema movement during the 1990s, she draws particular attention to this critical aspiration of "queer": "Queer represents the resistance to, primarily, the normative codes of gender and sexual expression – that masculine men sleep with feminine women – but also to the restrictive potential of gay and lesbian sexuality – that only men sleep with men, and women sleep with women. In this way, queer, as a critical concept, encompasses the non-fixity of gender expression and the non-fixity of both straight and gay sexuality."[1]

While the practitioners of New Queer Cinema deploy this anti-normative tactic to produce consciously queer films, the same critical intention and political commitment are not always present in the works that I discuss in this book. Furthermore, the sexual identity of the filmmaker/author, the actual content of the work, and the work's reception among queer audiences are not necessarily aligned. In other words, while New Queer Cinema may be characterized as films with a queer aesthetic that were made by queer artists for a queer audience, what I refer to as "queer culture" in this book rarely meets all of the above criteria. Rather, these works fall somewhere within the range of what Henry Benshoff and Sean Griffin, in their study of queer film history in Hollywood, have suggested as possible definitions of a queer work: works that contain queer characters and that engage with queer issues in some meaningful ways; works made by queer artists that are inflected with a queer sensibility; works viewed from a queer spectatorial position, sometimes against the grain of the text; genres that may be considered queer forms; and finally, the inherent queer potential of spectatorship (i.e., of the process of identifying with and desiring characters).[2] Ultimately, what I have come to name "queer" in the book should best be thought of as an *effect* of my queer reading. These texts are queer not because they represent certain sexual minorities or particular sexual practices (although some do just that); rather, they have a potential to enable a queer critique of sexual and gender normativity that queer reading practices realize.

There is, however, a tension between the anti-normative aspiration of "queer" and the common usage of the term outside of theoretical discourse as a shorthand for lesbian, gay, bisexual, and transgender (LGBT) identities. Queer critiques of the normalization of gay and lesbian politics have not always resulted in a challenge to identitarian formations but instead in a proliferation of minority identities. In film festivals, campus student organizations, and community centres, "queer" more often functions as an umbrella term for sexual minorities: an open-ended category for a rainbow coalition of (currently known and future potential) identities. In this sense, "queer" bears an affinity to the Chinese term *tongzhi.* Literally meaning "comrade," *tongzhi* was coined by Hong Kong playwright Edward Lam in the late 1980s when he used it in the Chinese title of the Lesbian and Gay Film Festival in Hong Kong. The term became popularized when Lam used it as a translation of "New Queer Cinema" for a film festival in Taiwan in 1992. Thereafter, *tongzhi* caught on quickly in both Hong Kong and Taiwan, first as a preferred term of self-identification that replaces the more clinical term *tongxinglian* (homosexuals) and later as a widely accepted umbrella term of reference to sexual minorities. In its original conception, *tongzhi* shares the appropriative and irreverent spirit of "queer": it is a superbly ironic re-articulation of the serious political address of "comrade" used in recent history by both Nationalist Party and Communist Party members. At the same time, the term's invocation of unity and solidarity implies a coalitional approach to sexual identity. In Taiwan another term, *ku'er* (literally "cool child"), came into circulation in the 1990s among a group of writers who adopted it as a transliteration – and local mutation – of "queer."[3] *Ku'er* was conceptualized in explicit contrast to *tongzhi:* while the former approximates the theoretical and deconstructive stance of "queer," the latter is associated with LGBT identity politics. In some ways, the bifurcation of *ku'er* and *tongzhi* in Taiwan serves to resolve the tension within "queer": the theoretical sense is disentangled from the identitarian sense. By contrast, because *ku'er* never caught on in Hong Kong, the tension in "queer" – between deconstructive critique and coalitional identity politics – is retained in the notion of *tongzhi.* In this book I use *tongzhi* and "queer" in this "tense" way – to theorize what escapes, exceeds, and resists normative formations while acknowledging the very real lure of identity politics conceived in plural and coalitional terms.

Working and writing in Vancouver, a city with a large diasporic population from Hong Kong and ready access to many aspects of Hong Kong culture, I sometimes find it easy to forget that I am *not* located in Hong Kong and am in fact writing from the perspective of an outsider, albeit an involved outsider with various ties to the city. In her book *Sexing Shadows,* Hong Kong filmmaker and critic Yau Ching observes a contrast between the attitudes of overseas and local critics in writings on queer issues. Yau notes that while overseas scholars often read against the grain of ambivalent representations to mine their radical potential, Hong Kong-based scholars seem more invested in exposing their ideological limits and veiled homophobia.[4] As a reflection on my own reading practice, which certainly bears affinity to the position Yau attributes to overseas scholars, I am led to examine the different pressures that produce these critical positions. As a diasporic critic,

I often come under the pressure of the "global gay" narrative that assimi-lates non-Western queer expressions into its own trajectory and image (ex-emplified by the attitude of my interviewer in San Francisco). Many of the works analyzed in this book, for instance, would appear in this trajectory to be backward, pre-identitarian expressions that are still playing catch-up with the West. The imperative of the diasporic critic to resist such a model of analysis leads to reading practices that look for textual openings to tap a different kind of queer potential than what is anticipated by the "global gay" imperative. For the queer critic working in Hong Kong, the day-to-day struggle against heteronormative pressures in the city at large and in the culture industry in particular gives rise to a far more cautionary attitude toward the ideological limits and potentially injurious effects of ambiva-lent representations.

Furthermore, the distinction that Yau observes may also reveal an inter-nal tension within Hong Kong's cultural space that solicits two distinct modes of interpretive inquiry: a generally hostile atmosphere for *tongzhi* social ac-tivism, on the one hand, and a long cultural tradition that accepts or at least comfortably accommodates gender and sexual variance, on the other. The social and political activist movement organized under the banner of *tongzhi* has had a predominant focus on legal reform – from efforts to decriminalize consensual homosexual acts in the late 1980s to the success-ful recent attempt to challenge the age of consent for sodomy as well as ongoing efforts to include sexual orientation in anti-discrimination laws.[5] These activist efforts are often met with vocal mainstream opposition and receive very little political support even from the most progressive politi-cians. In contrast to what Chu Wei-cheng has called a "civic turn" in Tai-wan, where mainstream political parties competed (if ultimately only perfunctorily) to appear *tongzhi*-friendly in a bid to cultivate an image of political enlightenment,[6] Hong Kong politicians – including those who are in fact *tongzhi*-friendly in their political platforms – often compete to ap-pear *less* so.[7] Against such an inhospitable political atmosphere, it may be surprising to *also* find a long tradition of culturally visible forms of gender and sexual variance – from the numerous instances that Stanley Kwan docu-ments in his film *Yin ± Yang: Gender in Chinese Cinema* (see Chapter 3) to mainstream icons like Yam Kim-Fai in the 1960s and Leslie Cheung in the 1990s (see Chapter 4). It may not be an exaggeration to suggest that non-normative gender embodiments and homoerotic desire have long been mainstays in Hong Kong's cultural imaginary despite the lack of social and political support. This curious ambivalence between hostility and accept-ance is explored throughout the book.

If, like a film, a book can have a theme song, then Faye Wong's 1997 hit "Undercurrents" – an excerpt of which serves as the book's epigraph – would be playing through a good part of this work. The titular image illuminates not only the song's theme but intriguingly also the process of its circulation and reappropriation. Ostensibly an uncertain expression of love (the speaker desires to "hold tight" a lover but fears what may turn out to be an "empty embrace"), the song deftly entwines this personal anxiety with the political uncertainty of the city's postcolonial transition ("history" – both individual and collective – repeats itself in this "bustling city"). A year after the song's initial release, it was covered by Anthony Wong in a version rearranged by Keith Leung and used on the soundtrack of the film *Hold You Tight* (Stanley Kwan, 1998). The sexually ambivalent character of both Wong's music (see Chapter 4) and Kwan's film (see Chapter 1) unmoors the song from its initial context while trailing other undercurrents: the political subtext has now acquired a sexual undertone (the uncertainty of national belonging parallels the unpredictability of desire). Echoing the song, this book makes an implicit proposal that contemporary queer culture in Hong Kong is paradigmatic of the city's postcolonial experience. In contrast to the typical course of other postcolonial narratives, the putative "end" of colonialism in Hong Kong has not led to national independence but rather to a "handover" from one power to another without any process of self-determination among the people most directly affected. The handover is justified by a nationalist discourse of "return" *(huigui)* that leaves very little room for challenge or dissent. The dictum of Hong Kong's postcolonial governance – "One Country, Two Systems" – and the promise of "Fifty Years of No Change" have fuelled the city's collective aspiration for regional autonomy, political democratization, and continuation of its cultural distinctiveness. Yet, as President Hu Jintao quipped on the Tenth Anniversary of Hong Kong's handover/return: "Two systems must never be allowed to override one country."[8] The challenge for Hong Kong society to remain as such thus involves a struggle for intelligibility in a discursive regime that gives credence to its difference only on condition that such difference does not disrupt national "harmony." This sense of "difference" can never be reproduced as a counter-narrative of nationalism (as Taiwanese or Tibetan nationalism have more controversially attempted to do). Devoid of any political possibility of an alternative nationalist claim, Hong Kong's self-narrative of difference is far more nebulous: it is often perceptible only as an undertow of unease that refuses to allow the surface calm to settle. It is no wonder that the preoccupation with representation (or more precisely, with the unrepresentable) has remained a powerful critical current in Hong Kong cultural studies. At the beginning of his study of Hong Kong culture during the 1980s and 1990s, poet and critic Leung Ping-Kwan asks this question:

Why is the story of Hong Kong so difficult to tell? Many people have tried. Some have told it through a fishing harbour, a junk, skyscrapers, and the neon lights. Others tell it through the mist at Lei Yu Mun, or the bars at Lan Kwei Fong. The more you tell the story, the simpler it seems to get, but then again it also starts to look more complex. Every time you tell the story of Hong Kong, it becomes the story of some place else. Every time you tell a story about some place else, it becomes the story of Hong Kong. The story becomes longer and more chaotic as it gets told. How ultimately should we tell the story of Hong Kong?[9]

The story that cannot quite get told is also a queer story – a tale of "difference" that is palpable only as an undercurrent. It resists the logic of the norm and risks oblivion under its representational pressure. As I will explore in the rest of the book, it is perhaps no coincidence that some of the most creative tales about the postcolonial city, and the most visionary stories of survival under its crisis-ridden milieu, are told through a queer lens.

Another undercurrent that runs throughout this book is a conscious effort to weave insights from major theoretical works in English seamlessly into Hong Kong's local Chinese-language debates. In contrast to the practice in Taiwan, Chinese-language publications do not "count" professionally as much as their English counterparts within the current academic structure in Hong Kong. As a result, there is no Chinese-language academic scene that is comparable to that in Taiwan. Yet, many of Hong Kong's most thoughtful writers on gender and sexuality still prefer to write in Chinese. Most often, these works are disseminated through nonacademic venues (such as newspaper columns, nonacademic publishers, Internet sites) and adapted to the stylistic demands of these media. While not always written in orthodox academic formats, many of these writings advance sophisticated theoretical positions and are in implicit or explicit conversation with major formal academic works in the field. Writers like Anson Mak and Yau Ching, among others, often occupy multiple positions as creative artist, community activist, and academic. Their multivalent experiences and multiple perspectives are frequently reflected in the richness of their works. Too often in the past, critical works on Hong Kong culture written in English have glossed over or completely ignored local discussions, giving the false impression that they are merely derivative of the theoretical debates in the West. In this book I try to return some of the spotlight to these discussions, which are themselves a kind of undercurrent in the global critical scene.

The book is organized around five themes with numerous interconnections between them. Chapter 1 examines Hong Kong's urban culture and the relation between queer and postcolonial space through a detailed analysis of six films that imbricate queer themes with specific locales of the postcolonial city. I show how these cinematic representations of sexual and erotic relations privilege everyday experiences of the city's "small places" over those mapped by the grand narrative of nation and identity. Chapter 2 examines a tradition of erotic culture between girls that frequently appears in modern Chinese literature. I trace the fragmented recurrence of this tradition in recent Hong Kong cinema and examine the impact that such lingering traces of queer girlhood may have on our understanding of temporality and adulthood. Chapter 3 examines the recent emergence of transgender studies in Hong Kong and its lack of theoretical and cultural inquiries. As an alternative to the predominantly identitarian conception of transgender in current work in Hong Kong, I propose an approach to transgender as "bodily effects" and as "a term of relationality" in analyses of cultural texts. I examine two films that have hitherto been interpreted as failed representations of homosexuality and show how signifying transgender in these films complicates our understanding of gender and sexual formations. I also make a case for why cultural work should matter to activism and social research. Chapter 4 looks back at the career of late singer and actor Leslie Cheung and suggests that the current narrative of his legacy elides the extremely ambivalent relation that he cultivated with *tongzhi* communities over the course of his long career. I track and analyze key moments of paradox in Cheung's life and career to argue for a more complex way of remembering this queer icon. Chapter 5 explores several recent "do-it-yourself" projects of queer self-writing and examines how each negotiates the boundaries between global and local, private and public, and individual and collective discourses of identity. I argue for the importance of marking and sustaining these ephemeral forms of queer self-inscription.

1
Sex and the Postcolonial City

City Views: From the Peak to the Rooftop

Victoria Peak at night is the most celebrated viewpoint in Hong Kong. Once touted by the Tourism Board as a "multi-million-dollar light show," what runs dangerously close to becoming a tourist cliché is transformed, in the words of literary historian Lu Wei-Luan, into a metaphor for a way of seeing the city, its people, and its culture. Recalling the sudden sensation that she experiences when the Peak Tram starts to move along the precipitous slope and the vertiginous vision of the city unfolds before her as the tram slides slowly upward, Lu writes:

> The scenery of Hong Kong at night is most enigmatic. The glistening lights transform into infinite layers, overlapping and varying in depth. I love looking with half-closed eyes at the lights gleaming all over the hills, so much like an intricate piece of embroidery. It's seductive precisely because you cannot see it too clearly. Visitors don't have to give it too much thought. Keep this scene in mind and it's enough to remember Hong Kong by.
>
> I always tell friends from abroad that Hong Kong is an opaque city and those who inhabit it also inherit this quality ... Love in a fallen city: a love that is opaque and entangled. This is the story of Hong Kong and its people.[1]

Forgoing the vocabulary customarily used to describe the famous view ("dazzling," "glittering," "splendid"), Lu remarks on the "opaqueness" of the scenery and of the city's character. For Lu, it is not so much the beauty of what is seen but the incompleteness of the vision – the inability for anyone to *really* see the city clearly from here – that defines the perspective as one belonging quintessentially to Hong Kong. The fleeting reference to Eileen Chang's *Love in a Fallen City*, a novella published in 1943 and set in Hong Kong around the time of the Japanese occupation during the Second World War, subtly explains the sentiment behind this opaque vision. In the novella, the protagonist Liu Fanyuan utters this famous line to his lover Bai

Liusu while they are standing in front of a wall: "If one day civilization has been destroyed ... and everything is finished: burnt, bombed, fallen, perhaps with only this wall standing. Liusu, if we meet each other then, at the foundation of this wall ... Liusu, perhaps you will feel something real for me and I will feel something real for you."[2] Subsequently in the story, after the city has indeed fallen to war and devastation, the two fall in love and marry each other. The irony lies, of course, in the knowledge that "true love" itself is only a by-product of calamity, contingent on the vicissitude of the fallen city. The sentiment of love that is triggered by Lu's view of Hong Kong from the Peak is also intimately linked to the fate of a fallen city. It owes its fate not to the destruction of war but to the many crises precipitated by the postcolonial moment: the conflict-ridden political transition, rapid mutation of the city's economic role in the region, incessant urban development, and constant pressure from the Chinese state to value "harmony" over democratic aspirations.

Understood in this way, the view from the Peak provides a metaphor for a way of (not quite) seeing Hong Kong that bears close resemblance to a particular *cinematic* perspective on the city. In their introduction to *Between Home and World,* an anthology of critical essays on Hong Kong cinema that attempt to "give the cinema a name," Esther M.K. Cheung and Chu Yiu-wai argue that Hong Kong cinema is best understood as a "crisis cinema." Rather than locating Hong Kong cinema as part of a "national cinema," which runs the danger of glossing over Hong Kong culture's numerous points of disidentification with Mainland China, the notion of crisis more specifically "takes into account the complexity of the various kinds of mutation that Hong Kong is caught up with."[3] One crisis illustrated in the anthology stems from the *urban* character of Hong Kong cinema and its negotiation between a perpetual sense of dislocation and a desire to "re-enchant a sense of belonging."[4] As demonstrated in the works of several prominent cultural critics writing on Hong Kong cinema, the lens through which a city in crisis is most interestingly viewed tends to be self-reflexively opaque. Leung Ping-Kwan's historical study of urban representations in Hong Kong cinema from the 1950s to the 1990s traces the mutation of the city on screen over a half-century – from the dichotomized image of the urban as a polar opposite to the rural in the 1950s, to the Westernized depiction of a government-designed city of modernity in the 1960s, and finally to the increasingly complex formation since the 1970s of an urban space that cannot be apprehended in any singular, straightforward fashion but is rendered by a new generation of filmmakers through contradictions, irony, multiple perspectives, and continual experimentation with visuality.[5] Ackbar Abbas's study of Hong Kong cinema suggests even more explicitly that the most prominent cinematic perspective on the city during the transitional period in the 1980s and 1990s approaches visuality as a *problem*. Abbas's formulation of the *déjà disparu,* or the "space of disappearance," understands the self-aware visual complexity of Hong Kong cinema to be a result of the time-space compression that David Harvey has famously argued to be characteristic of the postmodern city.[6] More important, it also represents the "(negative) experience of an invisible order of things, always just teetering on the brink of consciousness."[7] This "opaque" perspective on what is barely seen can thus signify what is not intelligible – in other words, what eludes the normative logic of seeing.

The studies cited above focus on issues of visuality and deal primarily with films made in the period leading up to the handover in 1997. More recently, discussion about the "post-97" sensibility in Hong Kong cinema has drawn critical attention to issues of *temporality*. The very notion of "post-97" is fraught with irony, as it is in effect a *pre*-1997 formulation and, as such, remains a part of the teleological narrative of 1997. In *Post-97 and Hong Kong Cinema,* film critic Longtin discusses this contradiction: "'Post-97' expresses a hope to move beyond '97,' a hope to begin again from zero. Yet, that is merely what it says and not how it functions. The more we are intent on ending an era, the more we are extending that self-same era."[8] Longtin coins the deliberately awkward term "post-post-97" to describe a moment when Hong Kong has truly moved *beyond* the political transition – that is, when it is no longer possible to hold out for any of the hopes or fears of what Hong Kong will become after 1997. In 2003, at the time of Longtin's writing, the future looked particularly bleak: the persistent economic downturn, the ineffectual postcolonial government, the constant stalling of political reforms in a thoroughly politicized society that seems poised for full democracy, the traumatic experience of SARS (Sudden Acquired Respiratory Syndrome) all seem to signify an interminable present time when dates and periodization do not carry any real meaning. "Post-post-1997" Hong Kong is a city fallen not to invasion or attacks but to its own inability to define what it will become or to control when it will no longer be recognized as itself. This sensibility finds a powerful outlet in the hugely successful *Infernal Affairs* trilogy (Andrew Lau and Mak Siu-Fai, 2002-03). The Chinese title of the trilogy literally means "the interminable hell" *(Wujian dao),* a dimension in Buddhist cosmology where everything, from time to space to suffering, is interminable. The theme of being undercover runs through all three films: almost all the major characters are living with secret identities ostensibly for the good of a collective (be it the Hong Kong police force or a Triad gang), but in effect each character is irreparably split between multiple demands of loyalty and betrayal. The titular "interminable hell" refers to the burden of this double identity. Longtin ends his discussion of "post-97" with a provocative image from the first film: the rooftop. The protagonist, Chan Wing-Yan, a cop who has been working undercover as a Triad gang member for seven years, regularly meets his boss, Lieutenant Wong, on the rooftop. During the course of the film, Chan gradually becomes aware that fewer and fewer people actually know of his undercover status. Eventually, Wong is the only one left with the knowledge. Since the rooftop is the only place where they meet, it has become the only place where Chan's "real" (or "past," as it soon turns out) identity is intelligible. The glorious height of the rooftop provides a panoramic view of the city but also heralds danger. Wong has cautioned, "Don't screw around here; people can die." These turn out to be prophetic words as Wong is subsequently pushed off the rooftop by enemies and falls to his death, leaving Chan stranded interminably with his "false" (or at this point, "new") identity. Longtin states: "*The rooftop provides secret meetings that acknowledge the ambivalence of identity.* A secretive action conducted in broad daylight. There is darkness in light, and the secret mission is supposed to be a light in darkness. Yet, the audience will be tempted to ask: Which really is light? And which is darkness? At the same time, if the only person who knows your real identity will soon die, doesn't that 'real' identity cease to exist?"[9] The rooftop signifies for Longtin a frightening apprehension of the speed of mutation as it starts to overtake one's sense of historical memory and identity. Moreover, as the prequel *Infernal Affairs 2* reveals, Chan is in fact the illegitimate son of a Triad boss and was assigned an undercover assignment in the Triad for this very reason: to betray his own blood family. What renders an identity "real" thus seems to be contingent on its relation to the moment and to an interminably layered *process* of identity formations. Much like Victoria Peak, the rooftop seemingly offers a bird's-eye view of the city, but its actual vantage point is far more complicated and tenuous. While the Peak provides a safe viewpoint from which to apprehend the beauty of the city shrouded in mist and layers of lights, the rooftop affords a perspective of the city that simultaneously involves an acute awareness of one's own ambivalent and precarious location in it – threatened with forgetfulness, burdened with life-or-death decisions, and with few viable exits in sight. The time at the rooftop is moreover interminable: one begins to lose track of when it all began or when it will end.

This Way Out: Postcolonial Space as Queer Space

The *Infernal Affairs* trilogy has struck such a chord in the popular imagination that references to the films are now commonplace in Hong Kong's political lexicon. While the metaphor of the rooftop may seem an unduly pessimistic way of apprehending the city's predicament, the films also offer other, less obvious, ways out of the problem of identity crisis in postcolonial Hong Kong. Of particular interest from a queer perspective is the theme of being undercover and its significance for the controversial politics of "passing" and of "coming out." At the height of the "outing activism" in the United States during the 1990s, high-profile public figures were "outed" by activists like Michelangelo Signorile, who argues throughout his book *Queers in America* that it should be the "responsibility" of queer public figures not to pass themselves off as straight.[10] Even those who reject outing activism, like Urvaishi Vaid, explicitly describe being in the closet as "immoral behavior."[11] The moralistic overtone of the narrative of "coming out" implies that passing (i.e., not continually marking oneself as visibly and knowably different from heterosexuals) is an act of betrayal. More recently, the categorical certainty that "being out" is an ethical necessity and existential possibility is challenged by renewed considerations of bisexuality,[12] transsexuality,[13] queer femininity,[14] and sexual practices outside of the West,[15] all of which initiate a rather different set of debates regarding passing. In myriad ways these works and the debates that ensue in their wake show that the teleological narrative of "coming out" can remain blind not only to sexual and gender difference that is not reducible to homosexuality but also to the instability of identity itself. Coming out embraces a previously repudiated identity and in effect concedes that the identity now fully articulates who and what one is. Such reassurance forecloses a sense of what Judith Butler in *Undoing Gender* terms being "beside oneself."[16] In a discussion of the role of "rights" discourse in the LGBT movement, Butler cautions against the language that understands minorities entitled to rights as "bounded beings, distinct, recognizable, delineated subjects before the law." While such language bestows legal legitimacy, it fails to do justice to "passion, grief and rage, all of which tear us from ourselves, bind us to others, transport us, undo us, and implicate us in lives that are not our own."[17] It is rather the vulnerability – the "dispossession" of one's sense of self through feeling desire or grief – that, for Butler, yields transformational possibilities. In a similar way, the *knowledge* of passing, which in the *Infernal Affairs* films is an anxiety-ridden form of "unknowing" oneself, exposes the fundamental uncertainty of identity. The tense build-up of suspicion throughout the films climaxes in the final sequel, where virtually every character is revealed to be, or to have been, working undercover, often for more than one side. Suspiciously, identity itself appears to entail another form of passing.

This paradoxical relation between identity and passing provides an intriguing premise for filmmaker Stanley Kwan to explore the connection between queer and postcolonial contexts. *Still Love You after All These* (Stanley Kwan, 1997), a short film made during the months leading up to the handover in 1997, splices together a performance piece that Kwan did for the experimental theatre group Zuni Icosahedron, clips from his early films *Love unto Waste, Rouge,* and *Full Moon in New York,* and Kwan's meditation on his childhood, the city, and the impending political change. Kwan describes Hong Kong people's identification in this way: "In Hong Kong, we know that we are 'Chinese' but also that we are distinctly different from

Chinese in other places." Kwan recalls how neither the Cantonese nor English folk tunes that were taught to him in schools give him a sense of belonging. The closest approximation of "folk music" for his generation, Kwan suggests, is the "blurry but intense connection with Cantonese opera." In particular, a scene from one of the most popular operas, *Princess Cheung Ping,* resonates for Kwan:

> "Encounter at the Nunnery" takes place after Princess Cheung Ping has gone into hiding in a Daoist nunnery. When her husband comes to look for her, she initially dares not reveal her identity to him. In the lyrics, there is a classic line: "Deny, deny … yet in the end there is no more denial." This single line of lyric was like a constant mirror for me when I was growing up, especially in relation to my sexual orientation. Now, after changes upon changes, the line has come to be connected to this moment, and to Hong Kong people's identification. This line, and the identity crisis with which it is entangled, seem to have caught up with me again, twice in half my life.

Kwan seems to be implying that it is time for Hong Kong people to stop denying their Chinese identity, just as he had to stop denying being gay in the past. Yet, paradoxically, what Kwan lovingly evokes in the film is *not* his "liberation" from denial and the reassurance of coming into identity, be it sexual or national. Rather, Kwan seems to cherish precisely *the experience of denial*. Why is there such a palpable sense of loss in the film? Is Kwan mourning for the closet and the colonial era? To understand this apparently "treacherous" (at least in the eyes of nationalists and outing activists) response, we must pay attention to the sentiment of *place* that is also a crucial part of *Still Love You*. In the film, Kwan mentions the colonial flavour of many of Hong Kong's street names: Nathan Road, King's Road, Princess Margaret Road. Yet, as Kwan goes on to say, there are also streets that "very casually borrow names from other places for their own use." An example is Tonkin Street, where Kwan grew up. Tonkin Street is literally "Tokyo Street" *(Dongjing jie)* in Chinese: a random borrowing of the name of another place for local usage, with a casual disregard for the "accuracy" of its origin, hence the nonstandard (mis)spelling of its name in English. Tonkin Street, like so much of Hong Kong itself, results from the hybrid forces of globalized influences, on the one hand, and from local (mis)appropriation, on the other. Kwan films Tonkin Street as a unique site where place and memory intersect. The camera lingers on images such as the water drainage that Kwan grew up thinking was a "river," the list of shops and neighbourhood personalities that he "could recite with his eyes closed," and the men's washroom in the cinema outside his bedroom window, where he first witnessed shadowy scenes of illicit sexual activities. These are the neighbourhood sights, smells, and sounds of a closeted boy's experience in a colonial city. *Still Love You* expresses an affection for this time-space, which the advent of a nationalist narrative of "return" – much like the "coming out" narrative of identity – claims to *supersede* and consequently renders irrelevant.

What comes across as queer in *Still Love You* is thus not Kwan's certainty of being gay (or Chinese) but his loving evocation of a disappearing time-space that is not bound to such reassurance. Queer space, in such a context, is not an integral and distinct zone of difference. Rather, as exemplified in Gordon Brent Ingram's understanding of "queerscape," queer space is better understood as a "locality of contests" between normative constitutions of identity and less acceptable forms of identification, desire, and contact. Ingraham understands queerscapes to be "larger than a closet" but smaller and more locality-specific than communities.[18] Ingram's emphasis on locality draws particular attention to local uses of space, to social transactions and interactions at the level of neighbourhood, and to erotic and affective relations to locales and a city's "small places." In *Still Love You*, Kwan attempts to map, through his camera, this queerscape as Hong Kong's postcolonial space – the hybrid everyday locales, caught up with speedy changes and traces of half-remembered histories, that contribute to their inhabitants' sense of being somehow "distinctly different" from people whose identity they otherwise share. Kwan pointedly narrates the entire film in Mandarin, the decreed national dialect, rather than in his native Cantonese. He is "passing" linguistically as "Chinese" while ironically evoking the emotional particularity of his experience of growing up in Hong Kong, which can never be completely encapsulated in the distinctly "foreign" dialect in which it is articulated.

The film's reference to passing practices and to the overlap of queer space with heteronormative space in an *urban* setting like Hong Kong goes against the grain of the theoretical tendency that associates such ambivalence with nonmetropolitan areas. Judith Halberstam has self-critically addressed queer theorists' (including her own) tendency to project the city as a liberated place that is more conducive to the formation of queer identities, thus resulting in a "metronormative" narrative that equates "the physical journey from small town to big city with the psychological journey of closet case to out and proud."[19] To critique metronormativity, Halberstam calls for cross-cultural studies of queer lives in nonmetropolitan areas. She suggests that there may be similarities between alternative sexual communities in North American small towns or rural areas and those in non-Western regions, such as practices of "distinct gender roles, active/passive sexual positioning, and passing," and notes their "proximity to, rather than ... distinction from, heterosexualities."[20] Such a critical direction should not, however, lead us to concede that there is a distinctive "metropolitan" sexuality to which the above characteristics are no longer relevant. It is important to remember that metronormative delineation of gay space not only projects a devalued and homogenized picture of rural communities but *also* glosses over vital differences in urban formations, especially those outside of the West. Many of the world's teeming cities are, after all, both metropolitan *and* non-Western (or variously Westernized in different and complicated ways). Although the queer spaces of these cities have been influenced by a plethora of global forces, they often bear little resemblance to presumed "global gay" models like San Francisco and Amsterdam. Just as the globalization of sexuality results not in homogenization but in intricate processes of transcultural exchanges, translations, and appropriations, urban queer spaces that are produced by a confluence of global and local forces do not necessarily replicate a predictable metropolitan sexuality but more likely result in hybrid spaces that retain varying degrees of local traces.

The character of Hong Kong's urban space is tied both to the administrative reach of its colonial boundaries and to the pressure of globalization on these boundaries. The rigorously regulated border between Hong Kong and Mainland China has delimited the finite territorial reach of the city in order to allow for its administrative distinction as previously a British Crown Colony and, now, a Special Administrative Region of China. At the same time, the city's aspiration to be a cosmopolitan "world city" that reaps the spoils of globalization demands an incessant circulation of capital, enabled by ceaseless urbanization, large-scale infrastructural transformations, and the congregation of both an elite group of high-paid professionals and large numbers of low-paid labourers imported from beyond the territory (like the domestic workers from South East Asia). As a result of these conditions, Huang Tsung-Yi suggests, the living space available in Hong Kong has become "more and more congested, expansive and limited."[21] Huang describes Hong Kong as a "dual city" where "the cramped living conditions in pigeon-hole high-rise residential buildings articulate local hyper-densities against the backdrop of an arresting global capitalist showcase."[22] The "expansion" of the city is thus more accurately experienced as an implosion that sustains the social and aesthetic "values" of the financial districts through the functionalist destruction of old neighbourhoods to maximize profitable land use. Ackbar Abbas has characterized Hong Kong's urban development as a form of "self-replication": "new districts repeat the structures of the city centre, producing not suburbia (spaces designed to be different) but exurbia (which is a repetition of the same)."[23] Abbas goes on to observe that Hong Kong's city space is not planned "like a work of art."[24] Rather, planning is susceptible to unpredictable outcomes, and the "zoning" of difference is often overridden by squeezed boundaries and overlapping regions. It is no coincidence that some of the most interesting cinematic representations of the city's oldest and oft-rebuilt neighbourhoods in the Western District (Hong Kong's earliest area of development) appear in ghost films, most famously in *Rouge* (Stanley Kwan, 1987) and, more recently, in *Visible Secrets* (Ann Hui, 2001). The city is inevitably haunted by itself: what becomes contracted, squeezed, destroyed, and erased by the ceaseless rebuilding and consolidation of space can remain or return only spectrally as barely perceived vestiges of what is half-remembered and vaguely felt. In distinction from the "gay ghetto" in some cosmopolitan cities, which has become a way of masking class-specific consumption of space, Hong Kong's queer space can be understood as a part of this spectral dimension of the city. Animated by illicit desire and unacknowledged relations that remain temporary, fluid, and susceptible to instant annihilation, this spectral space does not exist on its own and must, as Jean-Ulrick Désert describes, be activated and "made proprietary by the occupant."[25] It comes and goes during transitory moments of spontaneity and haunts a space that is always already in use as something else by someone else.

Whether from the Peak or from the rooftop, the nebulous view of the postcolonial city is its most enduring face. What remains unseen and not immediately perceptible is as much a part of the city as what dominates the glittering skyline. What follows is an exploration of these elusive and textured spaces as they (dis)appear on screen.

The City in Secret: Cruising and Community

Cruising as a way of erotically inhabiting and imagining the city has a long lineage in urban culture. While women's cruising has remained either virtually undocumented, except in fleeting fictional fragments, or mired in controversy over its range and meanings,[26] gay males' cruising has left enough social and cultural traces to inspire more than a handful of studies on its history, geography, and representations in culture. In his study of cruising on the streets of New York and London, Mark Turner suggests that the gay cruiser succeeds the nineteenth-century figure of the *flâneur* as the emblem of the ephemeral, alienating experience of urban modernity.[27] One of the most documented cruising sites in Chinese communities is Taipei's New Park (now renamed the 228 Peace Park), a cruising ground of immense historical importance to Taipei's gay male community.[28] New Park has also been etched in broader cultural memory by its iconic depiction in Bai Xianyong's 1983 novel *Niezi* (Crystal Boys) and by the many subsequent literary, cinematic, and television works that it has influenced or inspired. Like other public sexual spaces facing prospects of redevelopment, New Park served as an ideological battlefield between competing visions of citizenship, modernity, and what constitutes "appropriate" sexual subjects during the 1990s, while other cruising venues in Taipei proliferated in its stead.[29] Across the strait in Mainland China, gay cruising spaces have been only scantily documented.[30] More vivid depictions can be glimpsed *fictionally* in films like *East Palace West Palace* (Zhang Yuan, 1996), which portrays the public toilets behind the Forbidden City as a cruising area, or in Cui Zi'en's underground films, which offer idiosyncratic portrayals of queer subcultural lives in Beijing.[31] Explorations into Hong Kong's gay-cruising grounds are just as few and far between. In a study of Hong Kong's urban style, the writer and architect Mathias Woo recalls how a graduate student who proposed a project to research the history of cruising in Hong Kong was turned down by professors in Hong Kong University's Department of Architecture.[32] In Woo's own chapter on saunas and bathhouses, he makes no mention of the existence of a queer clientele.[33] Cao Minwei's popular history of Hong Kong's erotic culture devotes only one page and a brief allusion to gay cruising out of nearly two hundred pages of documentation of heterosexual sexual practices and erotic sites in Hong Kong.[34] The cinema, once again, provides a fictional lens through which these underdocumented spaces may be imagined. In his study of gay masculinity in Hong Kong cinema, Travis Kong categorizes three types of cinematic representation of gay cruising: as something done "out of pain," or "out of curiosity," or simply as a "fact of life.[35] Kong puts *Bishonen* (Yonfan, 1998) and *Hold You Tight* (Stanley Kwan, 1998), two films that came out immediately after the handover, in the latter category. The signature melodramatic excess of Yonfan cannot be more different in style from Kwan's subtle and distancing approach. Even so, their films share one thing in common: each of their intricate plots is instigated by a scene of cruising during the first five minutes of the film. How does this "fact of life" unfold, and what does it reveal about community, conflict, and specific locales in the city?

Inspired by the Japanese *shojo manga* tradition, which portrays relationships between beautiful boys, *Bishonen* tells a sentimental tale about a group of young men, their experience of sex work, and their relationship with each other.[36] Most of the story is set in a neighbourhood in Central. Even though Central is Hong Kong's downtown core and houses the financial district and the Legislative Council, its official and glamourous quarters blend almost seamlessly into more complex, colourful, and hybrid spaces. One such space is Lan Kwei Fong, the name of a single street that has now become synonymous with an extended area of gay bars, dance clubs, and hip restaurants. This idiosyncratic neighbourhood with long, narrow streets is flanked in the north by the towering, harbour-side skyscrapers, slopes uphill in the south toward the luxury residential area of Mid-Levels, and winds westward toward the old areas of Sheung Wan and the Western District. Farther west, passing the "world's longest outdoor escalator system" (used most memorably as the neighbourhood's signature in Wong Kar-Wai's *Chungking Express,* 1994), antique shops and art galleries mingle with family-run print shops, traditional rice dealers, and street stalls selling everything from preserved shrimps and dried vegetables to used clothing and antique trinkets. The neighbourhood is a place where genuine historical traces overlap with fabricated "antiquity," while local consumption of quasi-Western goods cheerfully blends with touristy faux-Chinese ostentation. The character of the inhabitants also undergoes a daily makeover, as the white-collar suit-clad set during the day gives way to the young, the transient, and the queer at night.

This neighbourhood is revealed in the opening sequence of *Bishonen* to be a latent erotic zone where queer desire is always lurking just beneath the surface. The camera follows the young and confident Jet as he saunters along the narrow streets and alleys with a narcissistic air of self-admiration. He soon senses that he is being cruised and, with a knowing smirk on his face, takes his prey on a leisurely chase around the block. A series of shots stages their mutual awareness of each other: the camera fixes on Jet's knowing pause, showing a view of his back, cuts to the older man's hungry, intent look, and then cuts back to Jet as he turns and glances back at the man. The mutual recognition is then translated into a playful movement across the neighbourhood: a repeated sequence depicts Jet leisurely walking along the street, while the older man enters the frame seconds later in hurried pursuit. Finally, a tracking shot follows Jet through a winding alley and into the public toilet, with the camera dramatically freezing on a close-up of the gender sign indicating the men's washroom. The older man then takes Jet home, and the sequence ends with a close-up of Jet looking directly into the camera, admonishing his client to pay "cash on delivery." The focus of these scenes is the coded exchange of glances and the spontaneous, stealthy, and sure-footed movement of the cruising men rather than their actual sexual act, which is not shown on screen at all. As Turner emphasizes, cruising is a "*process* of walking, gazing, and engaging another (or others)" that affords pleasure in and of itself, whether or not it ends in sex.[37] In these opening sequences, the pleasurable and elaborate movement of the cruising men activates the latent queer space of the neighbourhood and, right there in broad daylight and amid everyday activities, transforms it into a sexual playground and a site of erotic and financial transaction.

The film then goes on to unravel more layers in this eroticized space. As Jet resumes his laidback saunter through the narrow streets after his profitable sexual encounter, a *second* exchange of glances takes place, this time between Jet and a seemingly heterosexual couple. Jet first notices them when he is admiring his reflection in the window of an art gallery but finds himself confronted by the couple's cheerful, teasing look. As Jet walks away, embarrassed, he also becomes more and more intrigued. In contrast to the previous sequence, Jet is no longer being pursued but has himself become a pursuer of sorts: he is shown walking into the camera frame, curiously searching the street corners and alleys for another glimpse of the couple. Later, as Jet walks through the bustling streets, he sees the couple again at an outdoor café beckoning him to join them. Looking unsure, Jet nods in

Jet's "backward glance," in
Bishonen (Yonfan, 1998)

recognition but walks away pensively as he heads toward the bar-brothel where he works. In contrast to the opening sequences, which stage the exchange of glances and physical movement within the recognizable codes of cruising, the significance of this second exchange is ambivalent. Jet at first appears to belong in a separate universe from the couple, inhabiting mutually exclusive aspects of the neighbourhood. Yet, this seeming discrepancy between heterosexual couplehood and queer cruiser, between open-air romance and underground sexual transaction, will later be dramatically overturned. Much like the quotidian hustle and bustle of the neighbourhood, which veils its latent eroticism, the apparent normalcy of the "couple," later revealed to be Sam and Kana, hides their activities in the queer underbelly of the neighbourhood.

When Sam appears again, he is in police uniform, apparently an upstanding citizen and a dutiful son to his family. His "back story" is revealed only step by step in a series of flashbacks, the first of which is initiated by an incidental scene. Two young policemen are "walking the beat" in the neighbourhood, gleefully exercising their authority by issuing parking tickets. Through their chit-chat, we find out that easy money can be earned if young policemen are willing to pose for erotic pictures at the home of a man named Gucci. After a photo shoot with these young men, Gucci calls Jet's employer and asks him to find him some new boys while reminiscing about the "cool" young man who once posed for him, who was willing to do anything while never changing his fiercely proud demeanour. As Gucci's nostalgic voice trails off, the camera cuts to a medium shot of Sam in a police uniform. As the camera pulls away, revealing Gucci's studio setting, the police uniform – previously associated with order and authority – is now transformed into the fetishized object of a lecherous gaze. This slyly staged sequence pokes fun at the authoritative veneer of the police force at the same time that it reveals another layer of the neighbourhood's secret spaces. Beneath the façade of the well-ordered city are hidden enclaves where illicit erotic transactions are happily carried out by the enforcers of the law.

While Sam turns out to be rather more complicated than he has initially appeared, so does his companion Kana, although her "back story" is only fleetingly suggested in a short bar scene. This brief spotlight on Kana's sexual foray is important not only because it belies her apparent heterosexuality but *also* because it disrupts what, by this point in the film, is emerging as an exclusively gay male sexual landscape. Kana reasserts, at least momentarily, a queer female presence that suggests the existence of an erotic terrain beyond gay male space. On a night when Jet has failed to score any clients, he goes to a bar to see whether he can restore his self-confidence. There, standing and smoking nonchalantly in the middle of the bar, is a stunningly attractive and androgynously dressed Kana. Jet catches her eyes but does not recognize her to be half of the seemingly heterosexual couple he has previously encountered. The editing stages a triangular relay of gazes between Kana, Jet, and a good-looking butch sitting on the other side of the bar. Unlike the opening sequence, where the series of gazes within the cruising game succeed one another without uncertainty or interruption, the triangular game of seduction here remains more tantalizingly uncertain. Who is looking at whom, and why? In her reworking of Eve Sedgwick's "epistemology of the closet" from bisexual perspectives, Maria Prammagiore theorizes "epistemologies of the fence" as "ways of apprehending, organizing, and intervening in the world that refuse one-to-one correspondences between sex acts and identity, between erotic objects and sexualities, between identification and desire."[38] In cinematic terms, Prammagiore illustrates her notion with examples of films that present a "spectatorial difficulty of clearly distinguishing between wanting to 'be' a character ... and wanting to 'have' a character" and where "any character is a potential ego-ideal as well as a sexual object for other characters and for spectators."[39] In this scene the

Kana in a relay of gazes, in
Bishonen (Yonfan, 1998)

traditional shot/reverse shot that was used to code the certain and seamless exchange between the cruising men on the street is replaced by a triangular structure of looks that deliberately confounds monosexual expectations. Up to this point in the film Jet has shown sexual interest only in men, while Kana has appeared to be in an apparently heterosexual couple. In this scene Kana's androgynous appearance replicates the boyish beauty accentuated in the film's title. She may be attractive to Jet because she is "like" him, much as Jet's male lovers outside of his trade also tend to be young and boyish like himself, as opposed to the older men he services. At the same time, Kana's elegant androgyny would signify "femme" under the butch gaze, forming an attraction that is based on difference rather than identification. The bisexual spectatorship produced in this relay of gazes suggests that there are more complicated sexual topographies amid the film's predominantly gay male space. Moreover, it shows that queer female desire exists in a wide and often unpredictable range of gendered configurations. Eventually, Jet goes over to Kana and whispers into her ear, asking whether he has "seen her before" and whether she "wants to fuck." Kana answers both questions with a coy "I'll think about it" and then cheerfully goes off with the butch, who has by now also made her way over, leaving Jet bemused and a little crestfallen. Kana's rejection of Jet is at the same time only a deferral (she'll "think about it") – a coy play on the fence that keeps the spectators (and Jet) wondering what erotic possibilities exist between her and Jet. It also leads, in retrospect, to a much more suggestive interpretation of Kana's relation to Sam in the initial scene when they appear as a couple. In contrast to the more common portrayal of the desexualization of women in their intimate relation with gay men, Kana's relation to Jet and Sam – which is both erotic and decidedly not heterosexual – proves far more intriguing.

Bishonen is most interesting when it uncovers latent queer spaces of the neighbourhood and shows in unexpected ways how they become activated by sexually adventurous inhabitants. The film's dénouement, however, opposes these queer spaces absolutely and tragically to the domain of the family. After Jet befriends Sam he often visits him at his home and, in time, strikes up a close relationship with Sam's parents, who remain oblivious to the sexual attraction between the two young men. Scenes of domestic intimacy in the stable, enclosed space of the home are contrasted with the spontaneous, uncertain, and layered existence on the streets and in the bars. At the end of the film, Sam kills himself in shame after his father accidentally walks in on him having sex with Jet at home, collapsing the hitherto neatly separated worlds. The way the suicide is shot calls particular attention to the dying man's perspective rather than to the physical violence of his death. Sam is shown crying on the rooftop of a building with a splendid view of the financial district's towering skyscrapers. The camera

does not show Sam jumping but tracks his falling perspective in slow motion with a vertiginous, downward-moving shot of the skyscrapers. As an
emblem of the tragedy that is taking place, the shot suggests that the veneer
of the city's worldliness and modernity collapses under the weight of its
own contradiction. In this way, *Bishonen* recontains the city's queerscape in
a space of perpetual conflict – where the streets are always opposed to the
domestic interior and where the spontaneity of cruising runs counter to
the stable structure of the family.

In contrast to *Bishonen's* ultimately pessimistic resolution, *Hold You Tight*
more radically imagines the postcolonial city *as* a kind of queer space. In
this film familial or domestic relations do not exist within an unchanging
structure that remains in conflict with queer sexuality. Rather, relational
structure itself is subject to various kinds of queering and mutation. The
film tells an intricate story about five people who are haphazardly linked
together by random events: a gay real estate agent, Tong, befriends a com-
puter programmer, Fung Wai, whose wife, Moon, has recently died abroad.
Before her death Moon had an affair with a young Taiwanese lifeguard,
Xiao Zhe. When Xiao Zhe returns to Taipei in grief over Moon's death, he
meets a divorced boutique owner, Rosa, a Hong Kong woman with an uncanny resemblance to Moon. After listening to his story, Rosa prompts Xiao
Zhe to think about whether his attraction to Moon is not in part a displaced
attraction to her husband. Prior to sleeping with Rosa, Xiao Zhe makes a
long-distance phone call to Wai. Eventually Wai hears Xiao Zhe's (off-screen)
"confession" on his answering machine, and the film ends in an intimate
conversation between Wai and Tong on a beach facing the Chinese border.

A cruising scene also takes place very early on in the film, when Tong has
an enjoyable sexual encounter with a stranger in a sauna. In a study of the
emergence of queer spaces in European and American cities during the twen-
tieth century, Aaron Betsky characterizes the space of cruising in this way:
"It was a space that could not be seen, had no contours, and never endured
beyond the sexual act. Its order was and is that of gestures. What makes this
space of cruising so important is that it shows that you don't have to make
spaces to contain and encourage relations between people, because they
will just appear exactly at the moment where they are least expected – or
wanted. These spaces, moreover, have a sudden sensuality that belies that
anonymous emptiness of the modern city."[40] The sauna scene, which is
followed by a shot of Tong smilingly throwing away a piece of paper (presumably a phone number) as he makes his way out into the street, is staged
very much in the spirit of Betsky's formulation – as a place where connections are made and terminated spontaneously, a place that is contained
within and yet belies the loneliness of the city. Sandwiched between scenes
set in two of Hong Kong's most important sites of transit, Tong's cruising

activities also take on particular significance. The preceding scene, which opens the film, takes place in Kai-Tak Airport on the eve of its closure just prior to the handover in 1997. A group of Japanese tourists are taking pictures of the airport "for the last time," as the new Chek Lap Kok Airport, the last large-scale infrastructural transformation overseen by the British colonial administration, will open imminently. The camera cuts from Moon, as she unwittingly embarks on her last journey, to Rosa, whose life will soon intersect Moon's via a relation with Moon's lover, although at this juncture the two women (played by the same actress) remain totally unaware of each other. While the old airport signals a space caught up in the flux of change and the passage of a departing era, it also provides the anonymous ground on which perfect strangers are open to unexpected forms of future connection. Immediately following the sauna scene, the film moves from the old airport to the Mass Transit Railway (MTR). Completed in 1979, the MTR remains one of Hong Kong's most identifiable symbols of colonial modernity. Its construction has radically remapped how the city's time-space is experienced by its inhabitants, facilitating direct links between previously unconnected areas and expanding reachable spaces in ever-shortening amounts of time. In this scene the trains provide the alibi for a fragmenting city life as well as new possibilities of connection. While Tong rides on the MTR, the camera follows his random, wandering gaze. He first notices two men, obviously lovers, quarrelling. The well-dressed, middle-class man talks about his plans to emigrate to Vancouver, while his younger, materially less privileged lover bitterly reproaches the older man for abandoning him. Then Tong listens to the conversation between two women who sit next to him, apparently either mother and daughter or mother-in-law and daughter-in-law. The old woman, who has recently moved from Mainland China, sits in stone-faced silence while the middle-aged woman incessantly complains in acrimonious anger that the old woman has effectively ruined her life by coming to Hong Kong. These two incidental shots effectively convey the stressful and disintegrating effects on families and relationships caused by large-scale emigration out of Hong Kong (to cities like Vancouver) and immigration into Hong Kong (from Mainland China). At the same time, as Tong's train passes through a station, Wai is standing on the train platform while Xiao Zhe watches him in the background. Unbeknown to the three characters, as well as to the spectators at this time, all three people will soon become involved in each other's lives in unforeseeable ways.

Juxtaposed with these scenes, Tong's cruising is both metonymically a part of the postcolonial cityscape and metaphorically *like* this cityscape. Much like the space of cruising, the alienating and rapidly changing space of the postcolonial city reflects a loneliness that prompts unanticipated intimacies. The relationships that unfold in the rest of the film erupt, like spontaneous sexual encounters, out of unexpected and contingent spaces, weaving queer connections amid anxiety and crisis. These relations are further mapped onto the city's urban development. If the old airport and the MTR are indisputable markers of the colonial city, then the newly built bridges and highways, linking the urban core to the new airport and the numerous "new towns" that have been developed in outlying areas, are clear landmarks of the postcolonial city. The film quite pointedly conjures up this cityscape by locating Wai and Moon's new home in Tin Shui-Wai, a newly developed area close to the border with Mainland China. In his study of urban cinema, Leung Ping-Kwan specifically points out this detail as an example of filmmakers' attempts to explore "marginal and alternative spaces of Hong Kong."[41] This plot detail motivates the cinematography's movement through the city via its newly mapped trajectories. In particular, as Tong's friendship with Wai flourishes, he is frequently shown to be driving Wai home and moving across the new bridges and highways, signalling that this movement across newly linked spaces parallels the emotional and erotic intrigue of the film.

New and often unexpected emotional connections, often arising from a previous loss, are woven between all the characters. Fung Wai and Xiao Zhe both mourn the loss of Moon, and their grief propels them toward a desire for new intimacies. In turn, the people who take care of them have also mourned the loss of loved ones and desire new connections. In a touchingly understated scene, Tong sits forlorn in his apartment after receiving a fax with the news that the current partner of his former boyfriend has recently died in London. Tong immediately makes arrangements to send help anonymously to his former lover. This incidental scene reveals a community that maintains care and connection beyond the bounds of a committed sexual relationship but, at the same time, also depicts the emptiness in Tong's immediate life despite such a community. Another incidental scene illustrates Rosa's painful decision to give up custody of her only daughter when she leaves Hong Kong for Taiwan after her divorce. Tong's and Rosa's respective acts of kindness and generosity toward Wai and Xiao Zhe are thus ways of redeeming their own lives from loneliness.

The erotic connections between the characters are similarly intricate. When Xiao Zhe is seducing Moon before her death, he gives her a bottle of his favourite cologne because he wishes to "smell himself on the person he loves." One night after Moon's death, Wai becomes very drunk and has to be driven home by Tong, and Xiao Zhe offers to help Wai to his bedroom. Alone with Wai in the apartment, Xiao Zhe finds the cologne that he gave Moon in the bathroom and sprays it on the unconscious Wai before leaving. When Wai wakes up in the morning, he mistakenly believes that it was Tong who sprayed the fragrance on him, and the thought pleases him. Later, after hearing Xiao Zhe's shocking "confession," presumably both about his affair with Moon and his attraction to Wai, he turns to Tong for advice and solace. As the two friends sit talking on a beach directly facing Mainland China, they negotiate the not quite clearly established borders of their friendship/relationship. The ambivalence of the relationship between Xiao Zhe and Wai as well as between Tong and Wai does not necessarily suggest the film's timidity in imagining a full-blown sexual relationship between men. In fact, these (as yet) unconsummated relationships unhinge what is arguably a heterocentric fixation that categorically demarcates sexual from nonsexual relationships. Like the fragrance that wafts in the air heedless of boundaries, eroticism permeates these characters' lives, crossing the boundaries conventionally drawn between friendship, sexuality, love, jealousy, and guilt while fostering new modalities of intimacy in a world where strangers (always possibly becoming friends) need to, and do, take care of each other.

The film's last scene, which shows Tong and Wai in a car crossing one of the spectacular new bridges that link outlying new towns to the city core, offers a parable about change through an implicit reference to the film *Days of Being Wild* (Wong Kar-Wai, 1990). Although less well known internationally than Wong's later films, *Days of Being Wild* is, for many Hong Kong film critics, *the* most influential Chinese-language film of the 1990s.[42] In the film's opening the protagonist, Yuddy, asks the woman he is seducing to watch the clock for a minute, after which he delivers what has now become a classic line in Hong Kong cinema: "One minute before 3 p.m., on April 16, 1960. We have now been friends for one minute. Because of you, I will always remember this minute." The film's obsession with time, dates, and memory – a theme that recurs in all of Wong's subsequent films – mirrors a collective fixation in Hong Kong during the time leading up to the handover. Almost parodying Yuddy, Tong asks Wai whether he remembers what he was doing on 16 September 1984. In pointed contrast to Wong's film, in which Yuddy *does* remember the significance of the date even at the time of his death (although he would like others to think he has forgotten), Wai remarks on the absurdity of the question and simply claims that he does not have much memory associated with the date. Tong, who likewise cannot remember, tells this story in response: "It's strange. We lose and gain things for no apparent reasons. It's like waking up in the morning and find that a burglar has taken away all your belongings, and replaced them entirely with new things." Incidentally, 1984 was the year in which the Sino-British Joint Declaration, which formally established the fact and timeline of Hong Kong's sovereignty transfer, was signed. Tong's ad hoc parable suggests that the predicament of forgetfulness need not be crippling, while loss may paradoxically be an enabling condition. The film ends in a series of shots following the car's movement on the spectacular bridge in the faint light of daybreak. The passage into an uncertain future may be anxiety-ridden, but it also makes possible a new survival tactic, whereby the longing to "hold tight" or to "never forget" gives way to resilience in the face of change.

The City Otherwise: Cosmopolitan Allegories

Compared to Central or even the new towns, Lamma Island may at first appear to be *least* representative of Hong Kong's urban space. Located a half-hour by ferry southwest of Hong Kong's main island, Lamma was once a fishing village, and it remains one of the least developed areas in the territory. The small island's relative isolation, sparse population (less than six thousand over an area of around thirteen square kilometres), and lack of amenities (there are no roads and consequently no cars) result in attractively low property values that, over the years, have lured political dissidents from Mainland China, expatriates, students, artists, and environmentalists to make their home on Lamma. The writer and film critic Bono Lee even describes Lamma Island as a combination of Berkeley in California and the Santorini Islands in Greece.[43] Lee's flight of fancy may not be entirely accurate, but his comparison highlights Lamma's progressive and laidback atmosphere, a quality not so easily found in other parts of Hong Kong. Lamma is also associated with erotic freedom and experimentation. Lee mentions an urban legend that describes the last ferry to Lamma as a free-sex zone,[44] while the 1996 film *Love and Sex amongst the Ruins* (Cheung Chi-Sing, 1996) portrays Lamma Island as a bisexual playground where an impotent man relearns his sexual parameters. This air of alterity, combined with the island's hybrid makeshift community, renders Lamma a particularly powerful setting for imagining Hong Kong *otherwise*. In a widely circulated critique of Hong Kong's urban policies, Taiwanese scholar Long Yingtai has pointed out that the incessant drive of Hong Kong's urbanization persistently imposes the aesthetic and values of the middle class throughout the city.[45] Hong Kong's much touted aspiration to be "Asia's world city" has thus served as a justification for a class-specific form of urban development, ceaselessly pursued at the expense of neighbourhood preservation, environmental protection, and historical memory. In *Island Tales* (Stanley Kwan, 2000) and *The Map of Sex and Love* (Evans Chan, 2001), Lamma Island is imagined as a queer space where a different kind of cosmopolitanism may flourish.

Filmed entirely on location on Lamma Island, *Island Tales* tells the story of one day in the lives of seven people who find themselves quarantined on the fictional Mayfly Island when the rumour of a deadly plague breaks out. The photographer, Marion, has come to try out her new digital camera, accompanied by her close friend Sharon. The young porn star, Hon, has escaped to the island for a day of relaxation. Haruki writes for a Tokyo literary journal and has been recuperating from tuberculosis on the island. The

Taiwanese woman, Mei-Ling, is waiting for her lover – an English bar-owner whom she has met at a party the night before – to return. Aunt Mei is the Englishman's business partner, while the lonely gay man, Bo, owns the boarding house where Hon is staying. During the course of the night, Marion dies of a heart attack, while these strangers drift across the island and encounter each other, finally ending the evening in a spontaneous dance party at the bar. The quarantine is lifted the next day.

Showing an uncanny prescience about the epidemic occasioned by SARS, which, three years after the film's release, did turn Hong Kong into a city under siege by a plague, the film uses the allegorical situation to explore the dynamics of a society where mobility is prized. Early on in the film, the writer, Haruki, imagines a triangular relationship between three elements: "Boat, island, people ... none exists independently of the other two. Together, they form an unbreakable triangle." This "unbreakable" relationship is momentarily broken when the quarantine is declared and the boat – the means of escape as well as return – is eliminated from the equation. Much has been written about Hong Kong's historical role as a port city and about the sense of transience that this role inspires in the city's inhabitants:

> Hong Kong has up to quite recently been a city of transients. Much of the population was made up of refugees or expatriates who thought of Hong Kong as a temporary stop, no matter how long they stayed. The sense of the temporary is very strong, even if it can be entirely counterfactual. The city is not so much a place as a space of transit. It has always been, and will perhaps always be, a port in the most literal sense – a doorway, a point in between – even though the nature of the port has changed.[46]

Anxieties over the 1997 handover prompted a significant new wave of emigration out of Hong Kong during the late 1980s and early 1990s, creating a sizable class of what Aihwa Ong calls "flexible citizens"[47] who shuttle back and forth between Hong Kong and cities like Vancouver, Toronto, and Sydney. What distinguishes this new breed of emigrants from their predecessors is their privilege of mobility: they demand an escape route out of Hong Kong but retain the right to return. This mentality is best illustrated by the logic behind the Hong Kong government's encouraging attitude during the decade prior to the handover toward various immigration schemes proposed by countries like the United Kingdom and Singapore, which grant the right of abode without demanding that the applicant take up residency immediately. In a study of this migration system, Ronald Skeldon describes the logic in this way: "The logic of these schemes was that, if people knew they had a fallback position and right of abode in another place, this would discourage them from emigrating now in search of foreign passports. These schemes were, in effect, *de facto* anti-immigration policies."[48] In other words, people will not stay unless they know that they can leave some time in the future. From another perspective, it also means that people who move abroad to acquire foreign passports do so with the prospect of returning in mind. Indeed, many who emigrated in the 1980s did return with their foreign passports in hand during the 1990s while maintaining close family and business ties in their destination countries.

By taking away the element of the boat, *Island Tales* asks an intriguing question of Hong Kong's cosmopolitans: what if one is not able to leave for unexpected reasons? As Marion remarks to Sharon when Sharon worries about missing the ferry: "The boat, the boat! There'll always be another boat!" Yet, unbeknown to her at the time, there will not be another boat for Marion, who will die of a heart attack shortly after making this remark. The film does not return to the pre-1997 obsession with the search for "belonging" or for some definite sense of a "Hong Kong identity." The motley crew on Mayfly Island comprises strangers who, in Haruki's words, "have accidentally drifted into each other's territories." Once the option of leaving has been taken away, there is little else for the characters to do than to give in to spontaneous and accidental encounters. The philosophy behind such an impetus offers an alternative perspective on Hong Kong as a community. It does not presuppose the familiar ideologies of shared history, culture, language, and so forth. It simply honours a principle of mutual service at a time of need. On that one chaotic evening on Mayfly Island, the characters have abandoned themselves to what the political theorist William Corlett, in his formulation of a "community without unity," has theorized as "gift-giving": "To give ourselves to a practice with such intensity that our subjectivity becomes a function of the practice (instead of the other way around), is to give a gift. During gift-giving something mysterious takes over, the practice seems to determine the identities of the giver and the receiver. The gift charts its own destination ... The gift is accidental, cannot be calculated, comes and goes, multiplies differences."[49] Corlett's study attempts to bridge a deconstructive critique of identity, on the one hand, and a communitarian understanding of ethics and mutual service, on the other. His notion of an "accidental" community, forged by relations that are not predicated on a predetermined discourse of identity that would inevitably demand a suppression of difference, approximates the fable of community in *Island Tales*. The fable proposes that those always thinking about leaving give in to the community at hand – *not* because they are bound to it by blood and patriotism but because survival may depend on the unpredictable relations they forge with the strangers they chance to encounter.

There is one important aspect of the various encounters in *Island Tales* that is not explicitly accounted for in Corlett's notion of community: eroticism. Yet, the erotic is surely one of the most appropriate expressions of gift giving. In her study of bisexual eroticism, Marjorie Garber draws attention to the ways eroticism cannot be predicted or controlled according to the dictates of sexual identity.[50] Eroticism is accidental, spontaneous, extravagant, and without reassurance. It comes and goes without warning; it traverses unexpected terrain and crosses unlikely borders. There is not a single sex scene in *Island Tales,* but the camera draws attention to an erotic energy that traverses the screen in unexpected ways. Viewers are trained by heteronormativity to decode the trajectory of a character's gaze according to their sexual orientation, and mainstream cinema usually encourages such a habit, leaving little room for erotic ambiguity except in instances of comic misunderstanding. In *Island Tales* such erotic "reassurance" is absent in a very striking way. Most of the important encounters that take place on the island – between Haruki and Hon, Sharon and Marion, Mei-Ling and Hon, and finally, Haruki and Marion – are erotically charged. For instance, in the seaside scene where Haruki encounters Hon for the first time, the camera directs Haruki's gaze to the muscular body of Hon while showing Hon's body moving confidently into intimate proximity with Haruki. In a scene after Marion's death, Sharon confesses that she wishes Marion had been her lover. This scene is filmed in blue filter and (literally and figuratively) shows Sharon in a rare light. When the erotic erupts between a man and a woman, it is *also* steered in a queer direction. For instance, when the two most sexualized characters – Mei-Ling and Hon – lie together on the beach, thus creating some expectation of heterosexual intimacy, Mei-Ling touches Hon's face and gently addresses him as her dead brother, thus permeating their sexuality with an incestuous dimension. In the penultimate scene, where Haruki lies down next to Marion's corpse, a touch of necrophilic eroticism passes between Haruki and the serene body of the dead.

The film also projects a queer time where linear chronology is partially abandoned in favour of a temporality that loops back and forth, recalling events not in the order that they take place but as they would appear in imperfect memory – augmented by delayed knowledge and unexpected discoveries. In the opening sequence of *Island Tales* shots of a helicopter flying, cameras flashing, journalists speaking into microphones, and crowds milling about the pier create the atmosphere of an aftermath. The unexplained image of a dead body recalls the typical opening of the detective story and heralds a retrospective narrative that will eventually come full-circle back to the scene of the aftermath while disclosing its full significance. Yet, the rest of the film is edited in a way that detracts from this narrative expectation. The frequent insertion of anachronistic events creates a radical disjuncture between story time and narration time. Scenes are often edited together because of their *emotional* proximity to each other. For instance, after Haruki bids Hon good-bye at his house before either learns about the quarantine, a shot of Hon running freely toward the ocean in the early morning light is inserted. In story time, this scene does not take place until much later. The insertion of the scene at this point stalls rather than advances the plot, but it illustrates the precise qualities in Hon that both attract and repel Haruki at this moment. Similarly, the scene of Marion's death is broken up into several pivotal moments that are placed separately at various revelatory points of the narrative. Instead of representing the physical event of Marion's death, which takes place in one scene, the film tracks its delayed and disseminated impact on other characters. Most effectively, the film ends with an incidental scene that occurs very early on in story time: Marion accidentally runs into Haruki at a fruit stand and whispers to him, "What a nice day!" Ending the film with this apparently trivial scene skews the entire narrative away from the supposedly central allegory (the plague, the quarantine, the media attention) and toward a spontaneous, haphazard encounter between two strangers. The film points us to what Haruki calls "the other side of reality." Instead of the elaborate, sumptuous, and sorrowful look backward that is typical of nostalgic narratives, the ending of *Island Tales* proposes a quiet *sidelong* glance at trivial, accidental, and spontaneous moments that can nonetheless become sites of revelation.

The most important of these moments occurs almost exactly half-way through the film when the photographer, Marion, who is about to die suddenly of a heart attack, recites in her native Japanese a long passage from the Bible to her friend Sharon. The passage from *Deuteronomy*, which speaks of a temporal order whereby everything occurs at a proper time, appears to Marion curiously similar to certain parts of the *I-Ching*. Sharon, who understands only Chinese and English, affectionately tells her friend that she has no idea what she's talking about. The camera lingers on this pivotal moment, filming in slow motion Sharon's tender caress on her friend's face as Marion recites the long catalogue of human activities – laughing, crying, dancing, mourning, and dying, among others – that will take place in their own proper order. The scene portrays a moment of exchange and a fleeting passage across cultural, emotional, and erotic borders. In her effort to comfort Sharon (who tries to maintain control even in the face of an uncontrollable crisis), Marion has forged a surprising link between two radically different belief systems. Unwittingly, she also reveals a flash of prescience about her own impending death, which will have unforeseen significance for other characters. Marion's effort has also sparked a rare emotional response from the habitually cold and rational Sharon, whose sudden display of physical affection betrays a hint of the erotic attachment that we later learn she has to Marion. Yet, Sharon does not actually understand the significance of Marion's recitation. The shifts between mutually unintelligible languages – which occur with pointed frequency in a film that alternates between Cantonese, Mandarin, English, and Japanese – serve here as a reminder that crossing borders is not an easy or immediate matter. It does not happen through sheer acts of will. When its seeds are sown (as in this scene of exchange between Marion and Sharon), flowers will bloom and fruits will be borne in their own proper time. *Island Tales* offers an allegory of postcolonial Hong Kong that rewrites the city's dominant conception of time-space. The film imagines a communal space that is structured through spontaneous care giving rather than charted by identity bonds. It displaces the linear narrative of progress and nostalgia with detours through the accidental and trivial, which the film shows can be moments of unexpected importance.

While Mayfly Island offers an imaginary projection of what the city could be otherwise, *The Map of Sex and Love* (hereafter *Map*) understands the island space as a respite from the city and a place to recuperate memory. Also filmed on Lamma Island, the film tells the story of three young people who drift into each other's path. Wei-Ming is a filmmaker who, after his mother's death and his father's confinement to a nursing home in Macau, has returned from New York to his family's first home on the island. Larry is a dancer who harbours secret guilt about an act of revenge that he thinks he inflicted on a high school teacher who tried to "cure" him of his homosexuality. Mimi is looking after a friend's crafts shop and hides her traumatic experience of mental illness. It is on the island that Wei-Ming recalls how his mother used to burn incense on the ancestral altar, and Mimi attempts a time-consuming recipe of a fish dish her mother used to cook for her, while Larry choreographs ballet to Cantonese opera music. Recalling the past, as all three characters will find out, propels them toward a surprising discovery of transnational interconnections, overlapping oppression, and intersecting complicity. Furthermore, as the title suggests, the film tries to "map" this journey of discovery across the terrain of sex and love. As the three friends negotiate their desire and affection for each other, they also negotiate their desire and affection for their city, its trauma, and its future.

In the film's opening sequence Wei-Ming takes the airport express into the city. The scenery courses across the screen as it would outside the moving train, giving us a glimpse of the passages from the outlying Lantau Island (where the airport is located) into the city. The new airport that opened in 1997, along with the Tsing-Ma Bridge, through which the airport express travels, are the most prominent architectural markers of Hong Kong's postcolonial era. As Wei-Ming films himself talking into the camera, he asks: "People say this is the postcolonial era. How do we love this postcolonial Hong Kong? How do we protect its democracy and its laws?" Then, turning to the subject of new immigrants from Mainland China, Wei-Ming suddenly points his camera at what he calls "the most popular new immigrant in the future," and the image cuts to Mickey Mouse, sitting on the train and waving playfully. Much later in the film, this shot of Mickey will take on different significance when a newsreel announces the Disney theme park project underway on Lantau Island. As Wei-Ming watches the news, we

Wei-Ming asking Mickey how we should love Hong Kong, in *The Map of Sex and Love* (Evans Chan, 2001)

catch in the background snippets of an activist angrily asking how many jobs one-tenth of the budget of the Disney project would create if it were used instead on environmental preservation of Lantau Island. Thus, already in the short opening sequence and captured in Wei-Ming's film project, we are introduced to the twin forces of change in Hong Kong's postcolonial era: the city's rapid integration into the Chinese state and economy, symbolized by the daily influx of new immigrants from Mainland China, and Hong Kong's own complete integration into the global capitalist economy, symbolized by projects like the Disney theme park that threaten to urbanize the last of Hong Kong's remaining countryside. What does it mean to love Hong Kong in such times? This is the question that Wei-Ming ponders and that the film attempts to answer.

Wei-Ming's film project is also intertwined with his own sexual landscape, which is precariously perched between his New York boyfriend, linked to him throughout the film only by phone and becoming increasingly distant, and Larry, whom he encounters by chance at a pier and later sleeps with in the sauna that Larry frequents. Unlike the films discussed in the previous section, where cruising can evoke spontaneous connections and an eruption of intensity, *Map* associates cruising with the city, an environment that is fraught with distance and deception (Larry is in the habit of giving out fake phone numbers, and Wei-Ming runs out before conversations get too personal). It is only on Lamma Island – where Wei-Ming and Larry meet again, this time in the company of Mimi – that their relationship, both erotic and emotional, is able to flourish. As the three become closer, their traumatic memories also begin to intersect in interesting ways. In his youth Larry confessed his homosexual impulse to a high school teacher whose response was to give him a bunch of rubber bands so that he could put them on his wrist and inflict pain every time he felt such desire. Mimi

Wei-Ming, Mimi,
and Larry on Lamma
Island, in *The Map
of Sex and Love*
(Evans Chan, 2001)

has a history of mental problems and had a recent breakdown while travelling in Belgrade. While researching for a film project, Wei-Ming has come across rumours concerning the laundering of Nazi gold through Macau, and he begins to question whether his father, who worked as a goldsmith in Macau after the Second World War, might have handled such gold. In Ann Cvetkovich's study of trauma culture, she examines the interconnections between "private" traumas such as sexual abuse and "national" or "public" traumas such as experiences of war and catastrophe. More important, Cvetkovich suggests that trauma need not be understood in shaming and pathologized terms as something to "get over." Rather, trauma can be recognized as the creative ground on which many forms of queer culture are forged. Furthermore, such cultural formations, in bringing trauma to the public sphere, are in effect transforming our very understanding of the "public."[51] By interweaving these three friends' memories, *Map* intersects personal with historical trauma: Mimi's very private breakdown takes place in a city recently scarred by war; Wei-Ming's historical inquiry forces him to confront his personal relations to his father; Larry's painful encounter with homophobia reminds Wei-Ming of the parallel fates of homosexuals and Jews during the Holocaust. As the friends' search for answers takes them from Hong Kong to Macau, they also become aware of the parallels between the two former colonies. Recalling and telling their memories of trauma thus results in creating unexpected connections between the private and the public, between Europe and Asia, between sexual and racial oppressions. Woven together, the three friends' pasts become a kind of cosmopolitan memory that sustains attachment through a knowledge of *interconnections* between places, peoples, and histories. Their intensified love for each other also exemplifies a cosmopolitan form of rootedness, one borne not of detachment from places but of entangled roots that spring from multiple locations and temporalities. It is this kind of love that the film advocates for postcolonial Hong Kong and as an answer to its initial questions.

There is, however, one blind spot in the film's complex vision of relationality. Evans Chan, the film's writer and director, has acknowledged in an interview that feminist critics have found Mimi's relationship with the two men somewhat problematic, especially toward the end when she is "spurred on" by the men to befriend a Malay Chinese performance artist, as though the triangle is becoming too unbalanced.[52] Referring to the film's last shot, which shows Larry with a new companion and Mimi by herself while viewing a video that Wei-Ming has sent from New York, Chan says he intended the scene to "suggest that [Mimi's] new-found relationship, which we saw earlier, may or may not be a stable one."[53] Chan's explanation tries to ameliorate feminist objections to Mimi becoming an emotional transaction between men. From a queer perspective, however, the problem lies elsewhere. The triangular friendship could have had enormous erotic potential, yet the film seems able to imagine only Mimi as a sexual outsider in the trio. In a scene where Mimi comes close to having a breakdown, she forces herself to witness her friends having sex with each other and then runs out of the room in pain, while wondering on the voiceover how these two bodies whom she loves can lose themselves in each other with such abandon. Yet why is Mimi allowed to apprehend gay desire only as an outsider and with so much pathos? If the friends' emotions and memories can intersect in such provocative ways, why can't their bodies and their desires? As my earlier discussion of the character Kana in *Bishonen* illustrates, the intimacy between women and gay men can be far more complex and erotically challenging. The desexualization of Mimi may be symptomatic of a tendency in queer cinema to eroticize only gay male bodies. It is thus fitting that one year after *Map*'s release, another independent feature, *Ho Yuk: Let's Love Hong Kong* (Yau Ching, 2002), returned the queer spotlight to women and explored questions about the postcolonial city through their erotic connections.

Our City of Nowhere: Surviving the Future

Ho Yuk: Let's Love Hong Kong (hereafter *Ho Yuk*) is set in the not-too-distant future when overurbanization has shrunk and cluttered Hong Kong's cityscape while turning it into a hostile and lonely living environment. In this imaginary future, cosmopolitan Hong Kong, "Asia's world city," has become an urban wasteland with no more potential for "development" except into cyberspace. The frequent use of cramped, staged, indoor sets gives the feeling that the city's "locales" have shrunk into claustrophobic artificiality. The film's plot revolves around three women: Chan Kwok-Chan, a melancholic cyberporn actress; Zero, a Jill-of-all-trades who hustles numerous odd jobs; and Nicole, an executive who conducts a global business but spends her free time worrying about the *feng shui* of her abode. It is uncertain whether these women are actively moving through the city's hyper-density or simply being carried along by its unrelenting rhythm of change. This ambivalence is already resonant in the film's title. *Yuk (yu)* – a verb in Cantonese meaning "to move" – is here colloquially used as an adjective to describe a perception of movement. The verb, which signifies an active will to move across space, is displaced by the adjective, which signifies a passive perception of movement around one's stagnant, nonmoving self. Chan Kwok-Chan expresses this anxiety when she complains to her mother after feeling an earthquake that is imperceptible except to those who stay perfectly still: "Why is it that I feel movement around me and yet I stay still, unmoving?" Such anxiety, however, is itself displaced by another, less explicit, shade of meaning in the title. The adverb *ho (hao)*, meaning "very," can also be understood as an adjective meaning "fond of." The anxious perception of movement can be playfully transformed, by a mere change of tone in pronouncing the first character, into a fondness for movement. Thus, in contrast to Chan Kwok-Chan, Zero actively pursues her desire and livelihood with humour and enthusiasm. She does not feel the anxiety of movement around her but becomes herself a subject pleasurably on the move. Finally, the title echoes one other important element in the film. One of the opening shots draws our attention to the character *yuk (yu)*, which is made up of two parts, each of which forms a character on its own: *nui (nu)* and *dzi (zi)*. *Nui dzi (nuzi)* put together signifies "women." *Ho Yuk* is about women's space – where women desire each other across the extremely difficult emotional and physical terrain of Hong Kong's urban life.

Hong Kong is one of the most densely populated cities in the world, and living space is one of the most hyper-inflated commodities in the city.[54] Owning a flat of one's own is the quintessential Hong Kong dream. While intense real estate speculation over the years has made millionaires of many middle-class homeowners, the collapse of the housing market after the Asian financial crisis in 1997 has left just as many in dire straits, and their recovery has depended on the vagaries of government policies and the global economic climate. For other more disenfranchised groups, home ownership remains a distant and elusive goal. *Ho Yuk* takes a poignant, satirical look at this predicament. Zero is a squatter in an abandoned movie theatre, where she tries to maintain the illusion of a home, complete with house decorations and two cats, all in the space of a single theatre seat. Chan Kwok-Chan lives with her parents in a one-room flat in a housing estate, where the family shares the same space for everything from cooking, eating, and watching television to sleeping. Chan's dream is to earn enough money in the next decade to move into a bigger house with her mother. Her regular forays into the rental market highlight the squalid conditions of the city's living space. In the sugar-coated speech of the slick rental agent, any window that looks outside has a "view," while crumbling old buildings offer

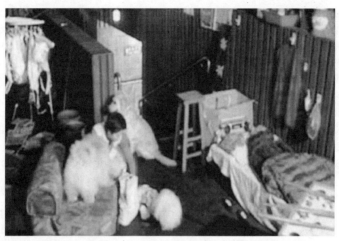

Zero makes her home in an abandoned theatre, in *Ho Yuk: Let's
Love Hong Kong* (Yau Ching, 2002)

the most "feel" (a Cantonese use of English that means "atmosphere"). Yet,
there is also a massive gap between the privileged and the disenfranchised.
The foreign-educated young professional Nicole lives in a beautiful and spacious home, exactly the kind that Zero and Chan Kwok-Chan desire. Yet,
Nicole abuses her living environment (at least in the eyes of the sleazy *feng
shui* master) by enclosing a corner of her house in artificial obscurity, where
she loses herself in cyberporn every night. She escapes into the same extended living space where many of Zero's fellow squatters seek pleasure.
Thus, even though Nicole already occupies the commodifed living space
that Chan Kwok-Chan and Zero long for, she needs habitat of a different
kind. Cyberspace becomes another sort of real estate where exchange relations determine how and which bodies occupy what space.

Ironically, despite everyone's fervent longing for space, intimacy between
people seems possible only when space is *closed up*. Nicole enjoys Chan
Kwok-Chan's body every night across the distance of cyberspace. Chan Kwok-
Chan would not allow herself to sleep with her favourite prostitute "for
free" because she needs to be able to "own" her, and ownership is not possible without an exchange relation and an emotional distance. Time and
again, Zero and Chan Kwok-Chan find themselves looking at each other
across a distance, never connecting. Intimacy seems to demand a closing of
physical space, such as the time when Zero slides across the seat on the
MTR to get close to Chan Kwok-Chan, or when Chan Kwok-Chan climbs
down the bunk bed and crowds into the tiny lower bed to sleep closely next
to her mother. The film thus projects a complicated and at times contradictory relationship between the longing for commodifed space and the need

Chan Kwok-Chan rolling up her turleneck, in *Ho Yuk: Let's Love Hong Kong* (Yau Ching, 2002)

for sexual and emotional intimacy. The footage of the giraffes, which always cross-cuts with scenes of suspended desire circulating between the three women, marks a mock-utopian place that transcends such contradictions. When the first giraffe sequence appears, the voiceover jokingly explains: "Do you know why giraffes reach up so high for food? It's because the less evolved low-lives cannot reach up there to compete with them!" There is an interesting combination of self-mocking pathos and utopian longing in this simultaneously silly and romantic use of the images of the giraffes. They seem to imply that the problems of post-1997 Hong Kong have turned its inhabitants into less evolved low-lives who are unable or unwilling to reach high for a different kind of space and a different kind of human relation. In an attempt to make a connection with Chan Kwok-Chan, Zero flirtatiously compliments her on her exquisite long neck, which reminds Zero of a giraffe. Yet, at the end of the film, Chan Kwok-Chan rolls up the collar of her turtleneck sweater to cover her neck in front of Zero, still refusing to close up the distance between them. The longed-for but ultimately unfulfilled union between the two women may be explained by the allegorical significance of their names. "Kwok-Chan" *(guochan)* literally denotes "national product," a name burdened with the demands and responsibilities of nationalist belonging and filiation. By contrast, the minimalist "Zero" signifies a kind of freedom in which relations may be imagined without prior restraints. Through its exploration of the social consequence of overdevelopment, *Ho Yuk* crystallizes the need for an alternative kind of living space that is not primarily defined by consumption, that facilitates rather than obstructs emotional and erotic connections. The imperative of its subtitle – "Let's

Love Hong Kong!" – also suggests with some urgency that the survival of the city may well depend on it.

On These Streets

> To love a city, one must begin by loving a street.
>
> –Lu Wei-Luan, "Scenes on the Boulevard"

> Hong Kong becomes one type of
> heartburn on a map
> called home
>
> –Yau Ching, "New Year Resolution"

> Queer feelings may embrace a sense of discomfort, a lack of ease
> with the available scripts for living and loving, along with an
> excitement in the face of the uncertainty of where the discomfort
> may take us.
>
> –Sara Ahmed, *The Cultural Politics of Emotions*

The word "patriotic" in Chinese literally means "loving the country" *(ai guo)*. Facilitated by this linguistic convenience, the discourse of love is ubiquitous in Chinese nationalism. In Hong Kong the "pro-establishment" politicians *(baohuang dang)* like to self-identify as "ones who love the country and love Hong Kong" *(aiguo aigang renshi)*, and they brand dissident views as statements against such love. As Sara Ahmed has shown in *The Cultural Politics of Emotions*, an appeal to collectivity "in the name of love" – whether in the right-wing fascist rhetoric of hate-groups or in the apparently more benevolent politics of multiculturalism – inevitably involves the positing of an ideal that requires some (those who do not live up to the ideal) to fail while masking its own interested stake in reproducing the script of this idealization.[55] The litmus test of national love, as scripted in the patriotic discourse in Hong Kong, is whether the city as an object of love matches the ideal image of its harmonious place in the nation. Claiming to love a *different* Hong Kong, one that would appear dissonant and out of place in this script, is a sentiment not recognized as love. When read against this nationalist discourse, Lu Wei-Luan's admonishment to love a city by first loving a *street* provides us with a means to rescript emotions abstracted for an immutable ideal (the country) into an attachment to the fragmentary and ever-changing particulars (the streets). The quotation is taken from a series of essays entitled "Walking on the Streets," in which Lu, from the perspective of a thoughtful pedestrian, details traces of the city that she finds to be changing day by day. Referring to a group of artists' efforts in Taipei to document minute changes of three of the city's main streets over an extended period of time, Lu describes the project as an expression of love for Taipei. She characterizes this love as a willingness to "read each street carefully and with feelings."[56] The project is not about recording things as they are but about perceiving and feeling everyday locales as they mutate. For Lu, love for the city involves not only an attachment to these familiar and fragile streets but also the capacity to apprehend their ever-changing contour and texture. In a similar way, the films I analyze in this chapter pay loving attention to the haunting, layered, and not immediately perceptible details of Hong Kong's locales. Through the twists and turns of lives on these streets, the films map ways of living in the city that honour intense feelings of attachment while heeding the gut-wrenching discomfort – the "heartburn" in Yau Ching's poem – that often accompanies such feelings. This entangled sense of intensity and discomfort, manifest in the films through queer lives, may be thought in relation to what Sara Ahmed calls "queer feelings."[57] Heteronormativity, Ahmed suggests, functions as "a form of public comfort by allowing bodies to extend into spaces that have already taken their shape."[58] While queer lives resist the reproduction of this shape, they do not suspend the feelings and attachments that are crucial to the reproduction. Rather, queer lives continually work to fit into spaces that do not comfortably reproduce their contours.[59] At the same time, the efforts involved in the "fitting" put pressure on the shape of normativity itself, bringing about a transformational possibility that is cause for excitement.[60] The films discussed in this chapter show how queer relationality strains to (mis)fit the cityscape and, in so doing, reveals the city's secret nooks and crannies, its margins and borders, its unreality and its possibilities. Only on *these* streets could one locate the postcolonial city's clamorously queer place in the national order and experience feelings for Hong Kong that are as intense as love – and as uncomfortable as heartburn.

2
Between Girls

Schooled In Passion: The Queer Time of Girlhood

> Inside the school, there was a sea of white tunics. Aside from a
> carpenter and two science teachers, there were no other men. A
> single-coloured image. A single melody of sounds. Years later, when·
> I recall my time at the school, I still feel as though I was in a dream,
> as though this was a whole other plane of existence. Curiously,
> although there was only one sex in this existence, it made up a
> unique and complete world of its own.
>
> —Ng Kit-Fen, "A Pure World"

Thus begins one of the most affecting stories – the only one about female
desire penned by an author from Hong Kong – collected in *His-His Her-Her
Stories,* an anthology of fiction on same-sex desire by Hong Kong, Taiwan,
and Mainland Chinese authors. Narrated from the point of view of "a
seventeen-year-old girl who came from an outside world where gender difference exists,"[1] the story's apparently sexually innocent setting – an elite
all-girls high school – is gradually revealed to this outsider's eyes to be an
alternative universe, with a unique code of relations between girls that is
fraught with desire and jealousy, intensity and excess. In the story's afterword,
the author attributes her inspiration to an incident from her own high school
years: "A girl slit her wrist in the bathroom after losing her girlfriend to a
rival. Blood splattered onto the high, moss-grown wall. She even wrote her
girlfriend's name on the door, and then ran around the building while still
dripping with blood."[2] This melodramatic event, which finds its way into
the story's conclusion, reminds me of a tragic news story from my own high
school years in Hong Kong during the 1980s: two teenage girls from St.
Stephen's Girls' College jumped to their deaths together from a high-rise
building. I recall a detail that was neither confirmed nor denied in reports

but spread like wildfire among students claiming to be "in the know": the dead girls' hands were apparently bound together by a red ribbon. The detail signalled a special bond between the girls that was immediately understood among those of us in the same age group who were attending similar institutions. Yet, such an intimation would never be explicitly acknowledged in the adult world of parents, principals, and teachers. The intense and erotically charged relations between girls in these strict and solemn halls of education was ironically both invisible and commonplace – willfully unacknowledged by the adult world but freely let be as long as they did not disrupt the day-to-day business of our education.

This erotic culture among school girls exists beyond one short story and my anecdotal recollection. In fact, it has a long and distinguished literary lineage. In her introduction to *Red Is Not the Only Color,* a collection of stories on same-sex love between women in China, Patricia Sieber discusses the significance of the "new style, single-sex education" that was launched in China in the 1910s and 1920s. The establishment of missionary, private, and public girls' schools located in large cities and provincial capitals provided opportunities for girls to be educated away from home and to form "passionate and enduring" relations with nonkin women.[3] Sieber finds numerous examples of prominent Republican-era women writers who portray "same-sex intimacies with homoerotic overtones" flourishing in these new social spaces.[4] Seiber goes on to show, however, that the Communist victory in 1949 brought about a break in this thematic tradition in Mainland China.[5] The Communist state's emphasis on the reproductive nuclear family as the foundation of socialist revolution was accompanied by the systematic degendering of social life, including dress codes, terms of address, and the organization of workplace and educational units. Under these conditions, the specific erotic culture (and its literary expressions) that arose from single-sexed settings like girls' schools inevitably declined, although scattered expressions of same-sex eroticism recurred throughout the Maoist era in other, less obvious contexts, such as workers committees and collective farms.[6] Meanwhile, under vastly different historical conditions, the setting of schools as an erotic site between girls has not diminished but thrived in various forms of cultural expression in Taiwan and Hong Kong. In the essay "Alternative Classics," written as an introduction to *Selections of Tongzhi Fiction from Taiwan,* Chu Wei-cheng discusses the prevalence of the genre of "campus fiction" in Taiwanese literature:

> There are obvious reasons for, as well as a long tradition of, using schools as a setting for stories about same-sex desire between girls. This is particularly prevalent in Chinese-language/Taiwanese literature. During the Republican era in China, virtually all the works that have anything at all to do with same-sex desire between women were written in this genre of "campus

fiction" [*xiaoyuan xiaoshuo*] ... The same is true of the much-celebrated Taiwanese fiction that came after, such as Cao Lijun's "The Maiden's Dance" ["Tongnu zhi wu"] in this collection. Last year, the publication of a story written by Eileen Chang during the late 1970s, about female friendship in Shanghai's missionary schools during the 1930s and 1940s, has delightfully enriched the depth of this classic lineage.[7]

Chu's objective in the article is to offer a history of the development of *tongzhi* fiction in Taiwan. His account of the vicissitude of the "campus fiction" genre in this history illustrates the impact of social movements on cultural expressions. Chu characterizes the early depictions of female intimacies in "school fiction" as "unintentional" *(wuxin)* lesbian writing. Chu notes, however, that since "such innocence could not continue forever," many authors who previously wrote implicitly about homoerotic friendship between girls began to write explicitly on homosexuality from the late 1980s on.[8] This development is in part a result of Taiwan's democratization and the attendant rise of social movements on the island after the end of martial law in 1987.[9] Ambivalent depictions of same-sex intimacy and desire *without* an attendant narrative of sexual identity became almost unimaginable in an era when the *tongzhi* movement had already gained significant visibility in the social and political spheres. The concomitant rise of "queer" *(ku'er)* as a critical and aesthetic category in intellectual and artistic circles also means that lesbian and/or queer female subject positions are not only intelligible but also virtually inevitable in the aesthetic expression or critical understanding of any narrative of same-sex desire between women.

While there is no comparable literary development in Hong Kong that matches Taiwanese literature's richness in queer expressions, the cultural medium that has seen an explosion in queer representations is of course the cinema. Yet, with regard to representations of intimacies between women, the trajectory in Hong Kong cinema has not parallelled the one that Chu maps out for Taiwanese fiction. In her survey of lesbian representations in Hong Kong cinema during the past two decades, Yau Ching lists the following five major trends: the "bent becoming straight" genre, in which queer women inevitably "become" heterosexual by the end of the film; period drama, in which lesbian desire is imaginable or possible only in the distant past; the violent-gangster genre, in which queer women (usually butch) are "objects of fear, contempt, or pity"; soft-porn films, in which lesbian sexuality provides a titillating spectacle for a straight male audience; and the "temporary transvestite" film, in which cross-dressing plots temporarily facilitate moments of lesbian desire but heterosexuality is "restored" when the disguise is abandoned.[10] It is evident from Yau's analysis that the recent history of Hong Kong cinema illustrates a *failure* in lesbian subject formations. In contrast to the trend that Chu observes in Taiwanese fiction, where a long lineage of implicit references to intimacies between girls gives way to explicit representations of self-conscious lesbian desire and self-identified lesbian subjects, Hong Kong cinema has continued to sustain highly ambivalent narratives on this theme. Does this trend reflect only a relatively inhospitable climate for lesbian representations? What other concerns may be illuminated by these films? In this chapter, I examine a body of films that show thematic continuity with the tradition of "campus fiction" in their exploration of the complex and erotically charged relations among adolescent girls and young women. While only one of these films project adult lesbian identity as the *telos* of such relations, all of them reveal ambivalence about adult heterosexuality as an inevitable and desirable "outcome" of girlhood. Why is there such a persistent return to the scene of girlhood intimacies? What kind of tension do such returns reveal about adult (hetero)sexuality? And even if these films fail to project a trajectory of lesbian subject formations, do they not *also* cast doubt on the inevitability of heterosexual subject formations?

One way to approach these questions is through a consideration of identity and temporality. In her study of girls' friendship and self-identity in Hong Kong, Ng Ka Man observes that a salient means of self-identification among girls is ironically their *disidentification* with the category of "woman."[11] Ng's analysis draws on the study of Tuula Gordon and Elina Lahelma, which tracks the myriad ways that girls in Finland try to "protract their transitions and remain girls," a process that the researchers colourfully dub "the art of not becoming women."[12] Adult womanhood is typically scripted as a temporal progress, to which girlhood is simply a precursor, a stage to be outgrown. To approach girlhood as a form of disidentification – indeed, as "an art of not becoming women" – means to understand it not as a stage in a temporal progress but as an identity located in a different *kind* of temporality that defies the gendered expectations and responsibilities arising from the normative narrative of maturity. Judith Halberstam characterizes normative time in this way:

> The time of reproduction is ruled by a biological clock for women and by strict bourgeois rules of respectability and scheduling for married couples. Obviously, not all people who have children keep or even are able to keep reproductive time, but many and possibly most people believe that the scheduling of repro-time is natural and desirable. Family time refers to the normative scheduling of daily life (early to bed, early to rise) that accompanies the practice of child rearing. The time of inheritance refers to an overview of generational time within which values, wealth, goods, and morals are passed through family ties from one generation to the next. It also connects the family to the historical past of the nation, and glances ahead to connect the family to the future of both familial and national stability.[13]

Halberstam goes on to study queer subculture as a modality of "queer time": a way of living a "stretched out adolescence" in defiance of the temporal logic of bourgeois reproduction.[14] Living such an extended adolescence does not signify a reluctance to grow up. More radically, it rejects the linear narrative of adulthood that equates maturity and responsibility with the heterosexual prerogative of marriage and childrearing. In what follows, I approach the recurrent cinematic returns to girlhood sexuality as flashes of queer time – figures of alternative life-paths whose values and goals are not mappable within the temporal framework of adult heterosexuality.

Snap/Shot: A Time to Kill

> I will never love boys, ever. Not in this life.
>
> –Jiney to Jas, *Ab-Normal Beauty*

> Photography is the medium in which we unconsciously
> encounter the dead.
>
> –Jay Prosser, *Light in the Dark Room*

The spectre of male betrayal, whether experienced as abuse, infidelity, or deception, is one of the most frequently expressed anxieties over heterosexual womanhood. A recent trend in Hong Kong cinema dramatizes this anxiety with an intriguing twist: the endurance of intimate bonds (eroticized to varying degrees) between women is pitched against the inevitability of male betrayal as a reverse mirror of contrast. Examples from a variety of genres, including the melodrama *The Intimates* (Jacob Cheung, 1997), the suspense drama *Midnight Fly* (Jacob Cheung, 2001), the black comedy *Beyond Our Ken* (Pang Ho-Cheung, 2004), and the horror thriller *Koma* (Law Chi-Leung, 2004), all exemplify a version of this trend. *Ab-Normal Beauty* (Oxide Pang, 2004) offers a psychologically complex variation on this theme and pushes its implications for queer female subject formation further than most of its predecessors. Directed by Oxide Pang and co-produced by his brother Danny, the film continues the Pang brothers' penchant for exploring horror from a female protagonist's perspective, *literally*. Their two previous films, the hugely popular *The Eye* (Danny Pang and Oxide Pang, 2002) and *The Eye 2* (Danny Pang and Oxide Pang, 2004), deal with women's capacity to *see* ghosts. More provocatively, *Ab-Normal Beauty* dramatizes the role of young women in the creative production of visual horror. More so than the English title, the Chinese title of the film, *Siwang xiezheng* (literally "death photography"), draws attention to the relation between visual media and the production of horror. Photography, video, and painting play roles in the film that are as significant as those of the principal characters.

The plot revolves around Jiney and Jas, two students in their late teens who share a love for photography. After witnessing a fatal car accident, Jiney becomes fascinated with images of death. She obsessively turns her camera on dead and dying animals, while reading voraciously about photographers who attempt to capture death on film. After an unsettling evening when she turns her camera on her secret admirer, Anson (who has been secretly stalking and filming her with his video camera), and nearly harms him in the process, Jiney fears she is heading toward a nervous breakdown. She confesses to Jas about being sexually abused by a cousin when she was a child and later witnessing the cousin falling to his death on a flight of stairs. She promises Jas, who has earlier revealed her love for her, that because of the abuse, she will "never love boys." Together they destroy Jiney's photographs of dead animals and victims of accidents and suicides. Just as the girls' lives seem to settle down into domestic happiness, Jiney receives a copy of what appears to be a snuff film. After a failed attempt to identify the sender, Jiney receives a similar tape and, to her horror, sees Jas being violently beaten on video. Shortly afterward, Jiney herself is kidnapped and brought to the set, restrained in chains, and surrounded by flashing cameras. Through cunning manipulation, Jas convinces the killer (who turns out to be a bookstore salesman who notices Jiney's obsession with photography books on death) that she both identifies with and desires him. Having lured him into a vulnerable position, she manages to kill him and escape. At the end of the film, we see Jiney painting an image of a woman in a pastel-coloured drawing. On the voiceover, she confesses that it was she who pushed her abusive cousin to his death many years ago.

Influenced by Laura Mulvey's seminal work in the 1970s, early feminist studies on the horror genre are primarily concerned with the lack of women's identification both within the film text and among spectators. Linda Williams likens the female protagonist to the female spectator, both of whom are punished when adopting an active gaze.[15] Barbara Creed's well-known formulation of the "monstrous-feminine" associates the abject monster with femininity and suggests that viewing pleasure is derived from an expulsion and renunciation of the feminine.[16] This gendered paradigm is subsequently complicated as critical focus shifts either to the perspective of the female viewer who experiences pleasure (as Williams does in a revision of her earlier study)[17] or to the possibility of a cross-gendered spectatorial identification (as exemplified by Carol Clover's famous study of slasher films).[18] In *Ab-Normal Beauty* the gendered structure of the gaze is complicated by several additional elements: the capacity of women to be the creative *producer* of horror through visual media; the egalitarian potential of a relationship between girls; and the gender dynamics involved in different forms of visual production.

In the film Jiney initially appears to be a stock victim figure, vulnerable to a predatory male gaze. The opening sequence cuts from a photography exhibition in which Jiney has received the top prize to a drawing class in which Jiney and her classmates are painting a nude. The editing shows a seemingly predictable relay: Jiney looking at the female model, while a male classmate, Anson, gazes at her, showing sexual interest. However, immediately after this sequence, the film signals a twist in the expected development of a boy-girl relationship. When Anson asks Jiney out on a date after class, Jiney refuses and points into the camera, which immediately cuts to a shot of Jas. A rapid shot/reverse shot sequence shows a close-up of Anson's quizzical look, Jas flipping him the bird, Anson's still-confused look, and finally a long shot of the two girls' backs as they nonchalantly walk away from the camera (and Anson's gaze). Already in the opening sequence, Jiney is established as a creative visual artist (a photographer and a painter) who will not be easily captured by the heterosexual male gaze. The boy-meets-girl set-up is also interrupted by the framing of two young women as a couple, something that is not assimilated by the male gaze with pleasure (as signalled by Anson's humiliated and confused expression). Later, when Jiney discovers Anson stalking and videotaping her at her house, she reverses the gendered hierarchy of looks by pretending to seduce him and then over-powering and immobilizing him on the floor. Afterward, she simulates a scene of death by splashing him with red paint and turns him into the monstrous object of *her* camera.

The film also contrasts Jiney's photography with the killer's penchant for snuff films. In *Light in the Dark Room,* a meditative study of the photographic reflections of four major writers on the medium, Jay Prosser characterizes photography as a realization of loss and a reminder of death:

> Photographs contain a realization of loss in the fundamental sense that every photograph represents a past real moment that actually happened but is no longer. It is a myth that photographs bring back memories. Photographs show not the presence of the past but the pastness of the present. They show the irreversible passing of time ... For [our most lyrical writers on photography], photography is a melancholic object. Not an aide-mémoire, a form for preserving memory, it is a memento mori.[19]

Jiney's obsession with photographing death can be understood as a *literalization* of the essential function of photography. If every photograph (whatever its content) is a reminder of death, a mark of what is no more, then literally photographing death is a means to lay bare this very function. Like a *mise-en-abyme,* Jiney's photographs of death become photographs of photography itself. It is, however, not this contemplative dimension of Jiney's project that attracts the killer's attention. Rather, it is the aggressive – what Susan Sontag in *On Photography* famously and rather plaintively calls the "imperial" and "acquisitive" – nature of the photographic act that the killer identifies with and attempts to reproduce in his snuff movies.[20] When Jiney and Jas watch the first tape of violence together, Jas questions its veracity: "Look at the editing and the soundtrack ... Isn't this just some experimental film?" Jas is drawing attention to the video's reliance on narrative and sound to generate meaning, in contrast to the silent stillness of the photographic image. Photography captures death by evoking a sense of loss, what Prosser calls "the pastness of the present," thus representing death precisely by what *cannot be made visible* in photography: the "life" behind the image. By contrast, the killer's snuff movies aspire to the *opposite:* the violent and forced visualization of death. In Linda Williams's study of "snuff" films – both the original film *Snuff* as well as the entire genre subsequently named after it, denoting films where actual acts of killing are supposed to take place on screen – she analyzes violent horror by distinguishing it categorically from sadomasochist pornography through the former's concern with visibility.[21] For Williams, the violence in putative snuff films aspires to a new order of the "frenzy of the visible": it reflects a desire to view the visible pain of death as "a perverse substitute for the invisible involuntary spasm of orgasm that is so hard to see in the body of a woman."[22] In Williams's formulation, the violent horror exemplified by the snuff genre is primarily concerned not with the representation of death (there is, after all, no real evidence to date of actual snuff films existing) but with the visual fetishization of an otherwise visually elusive (in sexual terms) female body. Furthermore, this obsession with sexual visibility relies on a *staged* narrative of death. Mikita Brottman's study of *Snuff* shows that spectatorial fascination with the film stems far more from moral panic than from any claim that it may make about the verisimilitude of its representation of death, which was in fact quite obviously and clumsily simulated.[23] In the same way, just as Jas has observed, the killer's videos, regardless of whether he captures an actual act of killing on screen, relies on the *staging* of death to violently fetishize a female body. Not at all concerned with the contemplation of death-as-absence, the videos bear only a false and facile resemblance to Jiney's project.

Another dimension of Jiney's photography is the therapeutic relief it provides for her childhood sexual trauma. Prosser draws our attention to Freud's comparison between trauma and photography: "Freud himself compared the unconscious to a camera, at the beginnings of psychoanalysis and not far along in the history of photography ... Freud later described trauma as a photograph. The child receives impressions like 'a photographic exposure which can be developed after any interval of time and transformed into a picture.'"[24] In the film, Jiney is unable to talk about, or even to properly remember, her sexual abuse until her photography triggers these traumatic memories. Scenes of her abuse are inserted into the film as rapid flashbacks that are not edited together as a coherent narrative. We never see the actual sequence of events, nor are we shown the motives and reactions of the people involved. Rather, we see rapid shots of disjointed black-and-white images flash like a series of still photographs. Jiney's pleasure in photography thus serves a function unbeknown to her: it provides her with a way to cope with her trauma not by "remembering" it as a verbal narrative but by *repeating* it in its essential form – like a photograph.

Jiney also copes with her sexual trauma through another avenue, one that the film implies may be a more fulfilling alternative to her photographic obsession: by "never loving boys." From this perspective, sexual trauma at the hand of her abusive cousin has become the foundation of Jiney's queer subjectivity. While many queer activists and theorists are wary of linkage between queer identities and sexual abuse, Ann Cvetkovich makes a provocative and convincing case for just such linkage in *Archives of Feelings*. Cvetkovich argues that delinking sexual abuse categorically from the formation of queer identification may not be the best response to the injurious history whereby sexual abuse is used as a means to stigmatize queer identities. Instead, she wonders why the narrative cannot be turned on its head to *affirm* queerness instead:

> But why can't saying that "sexual abuse causes homosexuality" just as easily be based on the assumption that there's something right, rather than something wrong, with being lesbian or gay? As someone who would go so far as to claim lesbianism as one of the *welcome* effects of sexual abuse, I am happy to contemplate the therapeutic process by which sexual abuse turns girls queer. I introduce the word *queer* to suggest the unpredictable connections between sexual abuse and its effects, to name a connection while refusing determination or causality.[25]

Cvetkovich's suggestion refuses two untenable either-or options: either attribute sexual abuse as a cause of homosexuality and something to "get over" *or* dissociate homosexuality categorically from *any* form of sexual abuse. By acknowledging a connection between sexual trauma and queer identities, without presuming the former to be necessarily a *cause* of the latter, Cvetkovich is carving out a new space in which queer subject formations and sexual trauma can be understood in complex relation to, and without stigmatizing, one another.

Jiney's intimate relationship with Jas is portrayed in the film as a potential site of recovery from her history of abuse. While there is a long tradition in the cinema, and in the horror genre in particular, of associating queerness with menace and montrosity – what Henry Benshoff theorizes as the "monster queer"[26] – the relationship between Jiney and Jas veers away from this tradition to represent everything that is *not* monstrous in the film. Their relationship *reverses* the cinematic trope that Anneke Smelik dubs "murderous girls in love."[27] In contrast to films like *Heavenly Creatures* and *Butterfly Kiss,* where the intense excess of queer bonds between girls inevitably turn murderous, Jiney is *saved* from her potentially murderous excess by her relationship with Jas. In a film that is predominantly lit in muted, grey colours to create a menacing and claustrophobic atmosphere, one scene stands out as a dramatic exception. After a choppily edited and visually disorienting sequence during which Jiney and Jas spend a long night after Jiney's breakdown getting rid of the remnants of Jiney's lurid project, the camera settles into a still shot of a spacious kitchen bathed in morning light. It then cuts to a smiling Jiney cooking breakfast for Jas. The scene is brightly lit, showing a spacious room suffused with the morning sun. The image of the girls laughing and enjoying breakfast together provides a relief from the kinetic frenzy of the night before, signalling a turning point at which the nightmare seems to be momentarily lifted. In this scene, the loving, domestic relationship between the girls is emotionally and visually located *apart from* the film's scenes of horror. It signals a space of safety where Jiney can recover from her traumatized past and self-destructive tendencies. Jiney does not have to "get over" her sexual trauma to be reintegrated into heterosexual adulthood. Here, her queer girlhood is the cure, *not* the symptom. Furthermore, the girls' relationship as fellow photographers frees them from a gendered hierarchy of looks: as creative equals, neither is the object of the other's gaze, in contrast to Anson and the killer, both of whom want to turn Jiney into their visual object.

This scene of domestic happiness between girls, however, does not last: in the end, neither creative photography nor a lesbian relationship is allowed to provide the theraputic closure to Jiney's trauma. The young queer photographer is punished by the killer, who not only harms Jas but also attempts to turn Jiney back into the female victim and thus into an object of his camera rather than his creative equal. Even though Jiney successfully fights back, her potential future with Jas has already been destroyed. The concluding scene of the film also signals Jiney's abandonment of photography as her creative medium. Her return to painting seems to concede that Jiney's photography indeed comes *too close* to the horrific medium of snuff film because the killer (or even Jiney herself) cannot tell the difference between the two. Jiney's confession on the voiceover that she too was a killer in the past implies that her trauma is rooted not only in her abuse by the cousin but also in her violent response to it. It is unclear whom Jiney is painting: Is it Jas, Jiney herself, or an idealized image of a "happy ending" that Jiney is unable to attain? This unnamed female figure stands in for what the film seems unable to resolve, thus remaining elusive, abstract, and resistant to photographic (and filmic) representation.

Girl, Interrupted: Time without Future

> In the future, we'll show them.
>
> —Jo Jo to Mimi, *Hu-Du-Men*

> I used to tell a story about the colour blue. It felt really good. Every time I told my friends about it, they would ask me, "And then what?" I would say, "And then nothing!" And the story would be over.
>
> —Xiao Jie, *20-30-40*

> Future? What future?
>
> —Cookie, *Spacked Out*

It has frequently been noted in both film history and critical studies of queer cinema that sexual minorities suffer from virtual invisibility. In the few instances when queer characters are on screen, they largely occupy marginal roles – as neighbour, best friend, victim, or killer – and (until quite recently) are rarely the protagonists. In a historical study of queer images in American cinema, Henry Benshoff and Sean Griffin have documented the scores of by turns silly and villaneous minor characters that have appeared in Hollywood films throughout the decades.[28] Not surprisingly, there is a similar history in Hong Kong cinema, especially during the late 1980s and into the 1990s, when minor queer roles recur as ridiculous, loathsome, or confused characters.[29] In the past few years, however, queer characters in supporting roles have been portrayed in a far more interesting light: they are no longer one-dimensional villains or figures of comic relief but complex characters in their own right whose impact on the main plot is significant. In this section, I examine films with subplots that portray girls in intimate relations with each other: they are daughters, neighbours, or best friends of the main characters. While their sexual intimacy often remains underdeveloped or unresolved, their very presence significantly troubles the main plots, especially in relation to adult heterosexuality.

A Different Kind of Mother: *Hu-Du-Men*

Set just prior to the handover in the late transitional period, during which many middle-class families that had not yet secured foreign citizenship were preparing for emigration out of Hong Kong, *Hu-Du-Men* (Shu Kei, 1996) gives a comic portrayal of the trials and tribulations of one family getting ready for its impending move to Australia. Lang Kim-Sum, a charismatic

Cantonese opera performer who specializes in male roles, finds herself in a whirlwind of chaos on the eve of her retirement: she has to take English classes in preparation for immigration, mediate a conflict within her opera troupe when a Chinese American director attempts to introduce reforms, and confront the sudden appearance of her son, whom she has long ago given up for adoption in order to pursue her stage career. Furthermore, Kim-Sum's teenage stepdaughter, Mimi, is rousing suspicion in her father as her intimacy with a classmate, Jo Jo, seems to go far beyond mere friendship. Frustrated with his wife's nonchalance toward the situation, Kim-Sum's husband accuses her of treating her stepdaughter not as a mother should but "with loyalty, like a friend" *(gou yiqi, gou pengyou)*. The word he uses for "loyalty" is *yiqi*, the highest form of masculine ideal in the classical tradition, a trait that most of Kim-Sum's opera roles personify.[30] The film's title, *Hu-Du-Men (hudumen)*, refers to the imaginary "threshold" through which a Cantonese opera performer crosses to "become" a character. Kim-Sum's putative failure to "be a proper mother" (implicit in her husband's accusation) thus stems from her inability – or refusal – to maintain this threshold between the stage and her real life. Yet, it is precisely this "confusion" that allows Kim-Sum an unusual insight not only into her stepdaughter's relationship but also into the queer complexity of gender identification and sexual attraction *in her own life*. The intricate process by which Kim-Sum comes to her self-understanding unfolds, to perfect comedic timing, in the scene where Kim-Sum confronts Jo Jo in a bar. Kim-Sum enters the establishment, clearly feeling out of place but curious enough to pause and observe the other patrons, especially a couple of young women kissing. As Kim-Sum accepts a joint from a friendly customer at the bar, Jo Jo appears:

Jo Jo: (approaching Kim-Sum) Hi, Uncle ... I mean, Auntie.

Kim-Sum: (inhaling) Wow, this stuff is strong ... Do you come here often?

Jo Jo: Often enough. My sister owns the bar.

Kim-Sum: Have you ever tried wearing a skirt? You would look good in a skirt, with your long legs ...

Jo Jo: Auntie, why don't you just say what's on your mind.

Kim-Sum: All right. Are you in love with Mimi?

Jo Jo: (shrugs) I enjoy the feeling when we're together. Mimi feels that too.

Kim-Sum: But you're both girls ...

Jo Jo: There's no rule that says a girl can't chase after another girl.

Kim-Sum: Then why are you always dressed like a boy?

Jo Jo: Well, you dress like a man too.

Kim-Sum: No, I only play a man on stage. Off stage, I am all woman. One hundred percent woman. Lots of men chase after me.

Jo Jo: How do you know those men are not gay?

> *Kim-Sum:* (surprised) Gay? Gay men would find me attractive ...?
>
> *Jo Jo:*   To be honest, Auntie, you are so much more cool on stage than you are right now.

Despite Kim-Sum's evident curiosity about, even enjoyment of, the bohemian environment of the bar, she immediately tries to "normalize" Jo Jo by questioning her butch gender presentation ("Why don't you try wearing skirts?") and her sexual choice ("But you're both girls!"). However, Jo Jo unexpectedly rebuffs Kim-Sum by suggesting that the older woman *shares* these queer traits, an observation that makes an immediate impact on Kim-Sum. Following the bar scene, Kim-Sum has lunch with her best male friend from the opera troupe, whom she suspects has had a crush on her for years. Awkwardly dressed in hyper-feminine clothes, Kim-Sum asks her friend whether he likes her because he is gay. While the scene exploits Kim-Sum's insecurity for comedic effect, it also denaturalizes both her gender presentation and sexual attractiveness, precisely in accordance with Jo Jo's observations. Kim-Sum's hilarious efforts to dress feminine only accentuate how much "more cool" she *does* look as a man on stage, evidenced by her legions of devoted female fans. In a deliberate play for ambiguity, Kim-Sum's friend neither affirms nor denies her question about whether he is gay. He merely looks bemused, as though pondering the myriad implications of the question. It is through this strangely convoluted and indirect avenue of identification (with both a masculine embodiment and a homoerotic attraction) that Kim-Sum finds an empathetic connection with the girls. Instead of adopting the "proper maternal role" as her husband wishes, Kim-Sum accepts Jo Jo's self-image as well as the image that Jo Jo attributes to *her*. Toward the end of the bar scene, it is Jo Jo's turn to be surprised:

> *Jo Jo:*   (defiantly) Auntie, if you try to separate us, you will fail.
>
> *Kim-Sum:* All right, then, I'll let you take care of Mimi. (Takes paperwork out of her bag.) Fill in these application forms and if you get into the university, you can join Mimi in Australia.
>
> *Jo Jo:*   (shocked) ... But I'll never get in ...
>
> *Kim-Sum:* You must work hard and try. Silly boy ... silly child, you have to prove your love to Mimi.

Throughout the evening, both Jo Jo and Kim-Sum address each other in masculine terms before correcting themselves ("Uncle ... I mean, Auntie"; "Silly boy ... silly child"). Instinctively, they are already addressing each other as masculine figures but hesitate, as such an address would completely transform their respective roles within the familial setting. Eventually, however, Kim-Sum realizes that it is precisely by stepping out of her prescribed role as a concerned mother (a role she has been accused of not inhabiting properly) that she will be able to handle the situation at hand. Reprising the roles that she is so used to playing on stage, Kim Sum and Jo Jo speak as masculine equals, admonishing one another to protect their beloved. It is unclear in the end whether Jo Jo will actually make it to Australia or whether the girls will sustain their relationship: we hear only their vows to each other that they will "show them" (the adults) in the future. What may be ironic is that they have *already* "shown them." The girls' relationship begins, for the adults, as a pesky problem but ends up showing Kim-Sum that her own experience of gender and sexuality may have been a little queer all along. Even the father seems to have softened his attitude near the end of the film, when he unquestioningly includes Jo Jo in a family photograph. Through Kim-Sum's improvised role as a not-quite-mother who treats the girls with masculine "loyalty," the film has presented an unusually optimistic portrayal both of a nonviolent parental response to love between school girls and of the possibility that "improper" roles and relations can harmoniously function within the familial unit.

Innocence and Innuendo: *20-30-40*

With their focus on emotional intensity, external threats, or family obstacles, the love stories between girls that I have examined so far have shied away from one obvious question: how do girls come into sexual awareness of each other? *20-30-40* (Sylvia Chang, 2004) sheds some light on this theme in a subplot where two teenage girls half-knowingly seduce each other but without any sexual outcomes. Director Sylvia Chang seems particularly fond of inserting minor queer roles into her films. In her previous film, *Tempting Heart* (Sylvia Chang, 1999), a conventional love story is complicated by the lovers' go-between, a young woman who turns out to have been in love with the female protagonist – her best friend in school – all along. However, her story is not given much exposition, as she dies rather abruptly in the middle of the film. Perhaps as a way of revisiting this theme, Chang inserts another subplot involving girls' attraction for each other into *20-30-40*, this time developed in greater depth. Set in Taipei, *20-30-40* consists of three loosely linked vignettes, penned by three different female screenwriters from Taiwan and Hong Kong. Two of the three stories deal with adult women's relationship problems: a middle-aged florist copes with her recent divorce as she discovers a new sex life, while a thirty-something airline stewardess with a predilection for married men struggles with her fear of commitment. The third story concerns a trio of outsiders: two girls in their late teens, Xiao Jie from Malaysia and A Tong from Hong Kong, have come to Taipei to record with Brother Shi, a down-and-out record producer who is also originally from Hong Kong. The girls never even come close to making a record but have a good time nonetheless: they are depicted in most of their initial scenes as giddy, fun-loving girlfriends playing, joking, shopping, and exploring the city together. The tone of their intimacy starts to shift when sexual innuendo seeps into their jovial conversations. In a sequence that starts with a close-up of Xiao Jie putting makeup on A Tong – a shot that visually frames the girls in a breathless intimacy – their conversation takes a suggestive turn:

Xiao Jie: Have you ever kissed a girl?
A Tong: No, have you?
Xiao Jie: No ... But in my school, lots of girls like other girls.
A Tong: In my school too! (Naughtily) And do all Malaysian girls sleep with their bra on?

A fight ensues in which they playfully try to tear their bras off each other. The camera stays still, as the mock-fight moves hysterically within the frame, until suddenly the girls stop and fall into a hug in front of a mirror. The film then cuts to the reflection: an image of the girls framed as a *couple*. We see them look at themselves for a few seconds, then playfully begin to dance together. No words have been exchanged, but the brief look of sexual recognition in the girls' self-reflection will, from this point onward, punctuate all of their jovial interactions. Just as their sexual awareness stays unspoken, their physical intimacy also remains one step removed from full consummation. In the scene following the dance in front of the mirror, we see another tightly framed close-up of the girls lying in bed together. While Xiao Jie softly sings while drifting off to sleep, A Tong stealthily puts a small sound recorder close to Xiao Jie's shoulder. The next shot shows the girls sleeping peacefully in each other's arms, with the sound recorder in the foreground of the shot, lodged between their bodies. The recording device, used so tenderly here in a gesture of intimacy, becomes exemplary of the girls' mode of sexual communication, which is always conveyed by acts or expressions of seeming sexual innocence but is rife with innuendo that neither girl seems able to acknowledge or ignore. For instance, during a playful conversation in which they expose the most daring things they have done, A Tong suddenly asks Xiao Jie whether she dares to sleep with her. Without waiting for an answer, A Tong runs into a washroom and begins to inspect each toilet stall, giving each a rating for cleanliness while a nervous Xiao Jie looks on, laughing uncontrollably. There is a relay of close-ups of each girl's expression: A Tong's changes from expectation to displeasure (perhaps interpreting the laughter as a sign of rejection), while Xiao Jie's, with her eyes closed for a second (perhaps waiting to be kissed), clouds with mounting disappointment when she opens her eyes to find A Tong already gone.

This tantalizingly unacknowledged desire between the girls is eventually exteriorized through a third term – a boy – and with him the "threat" of heterosexuality. After the washroom scene, A Tong starts to hang out with a school boy, plunging Xiao Jie into such jealousy and despair that she begins to break her silence and vocalize her anger to A Tong. A heteronormative narrative (like, for instance, that of *Tempting Heart*) usually begins with the sexually innocent intimacy of two girls, which then becomes interrupted when sexual awareness brings into the picture a boy who will eventually supplant one of the girls in the pair. By contrast, the boy in *20-30-40* serves to intensify, rather than displace, the intimacy of the girls. He becomes the vehicle through which the girls gradually come to grips with their budding sexuality and desire for each other. At the very end of the film, when both girls have run out of money and are forced to return home, a scene in the airport finally lifts the thin veil of suggestion to expose real passion underneath, although only for a brief moment. As A Tong gives Xiao Jie a video recording of their first day together in Taipei, Xiao Jie suddenly pulls her close and kisses her passionately on the lips. Then, as A Tong speechlessly looks on, Xiao Jie turns and walks away with a smile. The scene concludes the vignette, leaving the future development of the girls' relationship open. Xiao Jie's enigmatic voiceover preceding this scene summarizes the dynamics of the girls' tentative dance of seduction: it "felt really good," but before one can ask "and then?" the story is already over. Yet, despite this maddening reticence, the vignette has illuminated, in subtle emotional details, the difficulty, tension, and hesitation, as well as the incredible excitement, that girls experience as they become sexually aware of each other.

Furthermore, the girls' story is structured in a provocative and ambivalent relation to the other two vignettes. The film highlights the spatial and temporal simultaneity of the three otherwise unconnected stories. Characters from different subplots often occupy the same space but remain unaware of each other, such as when Brother Shi and the divorced florist sit next to each other at a noodle bar, or when Xiao Jie, in her jealous despondency, stops at the florist's shop to stare at the flowers. The three vignettes occur within the same time span (during the weeks following an earthquake in Taipei), but the title, *20-30-40*, also suggests three transitional stages in women's lives: from adolescence to adulthood, on the cusp of middle age, and in mid-life. The situations in all three stories skew the narrative of "repro-time," as they represent glitches, struggles, or detours in the timeline of marriage and reproduction: the forty-year-old is rediscovering an active sex life after her divorce, the thirty-something stewardess is struggling with her pattern of noncommital relationships outside the stricture of marriage, while the almost-twenty-year-olds are falling in love with each other. The temporal relation between the three stories can be read in different ways: as literally occurring at the same time (denoting distinctly different life-paths for women) or as symbolic points on a linear narrative (denoting three stages succeeding one another in a woman's life). The latter can also be read backward or forward (the girls' stories as an early "phase" to be eventually outgrown in the adult women's situations or as a *new* generational possibility that eluded the older women in their pasts). However we choose to read the relation between the three vignettes, the inclusion of Xiao Jie and A Tong's story in the film has one important implication: sexual attraction between girls is here rendered as a life experience that is as significant and common as the trauma of divorce or the sexual dilemma of single women.

Friends Forever: *Spacked Out*

In the films examined so far, sexual intrigue has occurred only between girls from middle-class families and elite schools. By contrast, *Spacked Out* (Lawrence Lau, 2000) portrays a youth subculture, with various forms of sexual and emotional attachment between girls, that sets itself completely outside of middle-class society. Set in Tuen Mun, an old coastal market town in the north-western part of New Territories that has now become one of the most developed "new towns" on the city's outskirts, the film gives a slice-of-life view of four girls in their early teens – Cookie, Bananna, Sissy, and Bean Curd – whose daily routines involve drug trafficking, casual on- and offline sex, gang fights, stealing, and the occasional abortion. The Chinese title, *Wuren jiashi,* meaning "auto-pilot" (literally "without driver"), signals the directionless but perpetual motion of the girls' impetuous lives. Tuen Mun's geographical isolation from the city centre is visually accentuated in the film. The opening sequence consists of a slow tracking shot from a moving car in a tunnel – a blurred vision that only slowly and gradually emerges into focus and into a view of Tuen Mun. Later on, a sequence showing the girls on a long bus trip into Mongkok (a bustling commercial area in the centre of Kowloon) lasts well over two minutes, intercutting images of the bus's interior with wide shots of the endlessly sprawling highway and the spectacular new bridges that connect the city centre with its outlying areas. When Cookie visits her lover in Mongkok, he mocks her by asking what "special occasion" brings her "all the way out here." It is arguably this physical distance from the urban centres that gives rise to Tuen Mun's distinct character and to the dynamics of its youth subcultures. Tuen Mun and its sprawling public-housing estates are portrayed in the film as a relatively comfortable and livable communal space, removed from the extreme population density, haphazard overdevelopment, and haunted histories of the older urban areas. Daytime location shots uniformly depict a brightly lit environment, with a library, playground, and swimming pool where the girls like to hang out. Most indoor shots are of shopping malls, karaoke suites, and game parlours, where the girls make (legal and illegal) transactions, spar with rivals, and have fun with friends. The neighbourhood provides the girls with a sense of belonging and evident ease of mobility. In stark contrast to this environment is, ironically, the girls' homes, which are depicted over and over again as sites of isolation, neglect, and abuse. Cookie is frequently left on her own because her mother has left and her father is never home. Bananna's parents are divorced, and her father is living an affluent life elsewhere with his new wife and son. The closest he ever gets to his daughter is handing her money through the window of his car. Bean Curd's mother works in a bank but is too ashamed to even acknowledge Bean Curd as her daughter at her workplace. A drug-induced flashback gives a brief glimpse of a younger Bean Curd enduring sexual abuse at her own home. The girls' listless dissatisfaction and loneliness thus result from the dysfunction of their families, supposedly the bourgeois haven of safety and protection. Instead, the girls are (emotionally and financially) exiled from this home space and abandoned to fend for themselves and for each other.

The failure of familial bonds paradoxically creates the conditions for the formation of an alternative social universe, with its own code of loyalty and camaraderie. In her study of Fruit Chan's films, which are famous for their depictions of Hong Kong's public-housing estates, Esther Cheung notes this paradoxical deformation and counter-formation of communal relationships:

> The term "community" often connotes stability, regularity, and security; it also signifies the desire to have a sense of shared space, orderly and re-spectful of personal space. The sense of "community" has to a great extent broken down in public housing estates. Neighbourhoods are paradoxical spaces where proximity does not reciprocate intimacy but at the same time the biggest irony is that when familial relationships are shattered, hence new alliances and solidarities, for example those among gangsters, are established.[31]

Unlike the predominantly heterosexual youth-gangster culture depicted in the films Cheung discusses, the girls' alliance in *Spacked Out* often blurs the boundaries between sexual intimacy and friendship. Bean Curd, a self-identified lesbian, is a tough-talking butch with a jealous streak, while Sissy plays up the role of a sassy femme who constantly tries to push Bean Curd's buttons by flirting with men but remains primarily attached to Bean Curd. Bananna habitually uses her sexuality to get what she can out of any man who falls for it but stays fiercely loyal to her girlfriends. Cookie, the film's narrator and its most finely drawn character, seems to embody the complex sexual and emotional dynamics of the other three characters. Having been thoroughly disappointed with heterosexual relationships (upon discover-ing that Cookie is pregnant, her lover's only response is: "Go abort the damn thing!"), Cookie acknowledges that her emotional centre has al-ways been her best girlfriend, Mosquito, who unfortunately has been sent away to reform school for misconduct. Later, Cookie is befriended by an older girl, Fengyi, whose uncynical enthusiasm and sincerity provide Cookie with a glimpse into another way to live. The sexual and emotional connections between the girls are thus not easily disentangled, although what is common to them all is a knowing rejection of societal expectations of propriety and the path toward familial responsibility. In a drug-addled conversation, one of Bananna's friends laments: "We're all going down the same road: you move in with a man, you get married, you have kids." Bean Curd and Sissy immediately reply, "No way! *We* won't!" At the friend's protest, they gesture at themselves and say proudly, "How would *we* ever have kids?" Notwithstandng the possibility of lesbian motherhood, what is important here is that the "inability" to replicate repro-time is flaunted by the girls as a triumphant trophy, *not* as an inadequacy or loss. As the girls' own home life and experience of heterosexual love have shown, the "respectable" path to love and marriage seldom provides fulfilment. When Cookie wonders on the voiceover about what the "future" holds for her, the question also signals an anxiety about the future outcome of the girls' universe, which above all else (certainly above their families and their relationships with boys) has provided them with a degree of security and happiness. By the end of the film, however, Bean Curd and Sissy have broken up, while Mosquito, since going away to reform school, seems to have abandoned Cookie. The closing scene in the film deliberately foregrounds a disjuncture between soundtrack and image. On the voiceover, Cookie cautiously notes that Fengyi has gone off to Japan but hopes that she will not turn out to be the "third person to betray" her. The film's closing image, however, shows Fengyi, Cookie, and Bananna laughing and playing around in the swimming pool. The disconnection between sound and image here also signals the disconnection between the present and its potential future. The friendship, intimacy, and solidarity between the girls, as well as the independent universe that they sustain, are precarious and vulnerable to change. The queer time of girlhood has no sanctioned counterpart in the adult world: its "future" remains merely an improbable possibility, hardly ever a certainty.

Becoming a Butterfly: A Time to Love

She said, if you can't fly, then you're not a butterfly.

–Chen Xue, *Mark of a Butterfly*

Adapted from a novella by Taiwanese author Chen Xue, *Butterfly* (Yan Yan Mak, 2004) is, in one respect, unlike all the other portrayals of girls in love discussed in this chapter: the queer time of girlhood is allowed to develop into a narrative of adult lesbian identity. It is, however, a complex narrative that is haunted by histories of violence and trauma as well as framed within a very specific and localized interpretation of sexual identity. Thus, while *Butterfly* overtly delineates a lesbian "coming out" narrative, it does so without exactly reproducing the "global gay" formation. In other words, *Butterfly* is a "lesbian" narrative with a highly local twist.

A plot summary does not do *Butterfly* justice because its simplicity belies the film's visual exuberance and daring editing, which are elements that give the simple story its emotional complexity. Flavia, a teacher in an all-girls high school, leads a seemingly uncomplicated and contented life with her husband, Ming, and their infant daughter. The picture-perfect bourgeois life falters when Flavia encounters Xiao Ye, a vagabond singer from Wuhan, in a supermarket. Flavia cannot get Xiao Ye out of her mind, and fragments of her past begin to haunt her. In her youth she was involved in an intense sexual relationship with a high school classmate, Jin. Their relationship continued into their university years but started to show strain when Jin became actively involved in student activism, while Flavia had to deal with family problems as well as parental disapproval of her same-sex relationship. The girls eventually broke up, and Flavia finds out many years later that Jin has become a Buddhist nun and now works in an old people's home in Macau. As Flavia becomes more and more emotionally and sexually involved with Xiao Ye, she realizes that she has never come to terms with her past. Several subplots complicate the central story: the divorce of Flavia's parents, the tragic fate of two of Flavia's female students, who are broken up by their unsympathetic families, and Ming's conflicted response to Flavia's infidelity. At the end of the film Flavia chooses Xiao Ye over her marriage despite the risk that she may lose custody of her baby daughter.

Chen Xue is a major figure on Taiwan's queer literary scene, and her fiction is known for its frank portrayal of sexuality and its daring evocation of queer, often incestuous, relationality.[32] Chen's early fiction has sometimes been criticized for its hermetically sealed universe and seeming divorce from social reality.[33] Fellow queer author and critic Chi Ta-wei has defended Chen's wilful departure from social realism as an alternative form of idealism, a way to imagine a "wishful landscape."[34] The film respects the integrity of this "wishful landscape" while subtly framing (but not subsuming) it within the historically and culturally specific context of Hong Kong during postcolonial transition. The novella's minimal references to external social events are "filled in" with oblique references to Hong Kong's history of radical activism during the 1990s, an extraordinary period in which many students and artists became politicized by the incomprehensible tragedy of the 1989 massacre in Beijing. For instance, whereas the novella describes Zheng Zheng (Jin in the film) simply as "a student involved in labour activism," the film gives a much more extensive documentation of Jin's activist work with the Hong Kong Federation of Students (Xuelian) during 1989, culminating in the scene during the early hours of 4 June, when Jin returns home after days of continuous protests and tearfully watches the crackdown on television. Years later, in the scene when Flavia finally comes out to her

Flavia and her husband talking while the television broadcasts a protest, in *Butterfly* (Yan Yan Mak, 2004)

husband, a wide shot of the sitting room in which the couple's painful conversation takes place gives equal screen space to the couple talking on the right and to a television on the left broadcasting a news segment about a protest while an activist explains how their work now is not dissimilar to what they were doing in 1989. The sound is edited to make sure the broadcast is audible above the conversation. This shot deliberately splits our attention and, in so doing, forges an unspoken connection between Flavia's personal struggle to come to terms with her sexuality and a larger, continuous struggle for social justice.

Unlike the novella, which narrates the past in the voice of A Die (Flavia in the film), the film slides events back and forth between different temporalities without establishing any one of them as the time of narration. The most distant temporal past consists only of one sequence: Flavia as a little girl with her mother on the beach. It looks as though the mother may want to commit suicide with the girl but changes her mind in the end. The second temporality depicts the time when Flavia and Jin are teenagers: scenes portraying their high school life, the blossoming of their sexual relationship, their university life, and the slow disintegration of their relationship. The third temporality denotes the time when the adult Flavia encounters and falls in love with Xiao Ye. When the narrational time shifts, there is no voiceover or a shot of one character in the act of remembering to establish the temporal shift as a flashback. Furthermore, as different actors play the child, teenage, and adult Flavia, the narrative relation between the three time frames is further weakened. The film refrains from anchoring a narrating agency in any one of the loosely connected time frames: the temporal fragments are thus "cut loose" from each other and do not add up to óne linear overall event. One particularly effective stylistic manoeuvre to this end is the insertion of footage shot in 8 mm, which shows a discontinuity in colour, texture, and lighting from footage shot in 35 mm. At first, the 8 mm footage predominates in sequences of the "past," seemingly producing a nostalgic visual cliché. As the film goes on, however, the 8 mm footage also appears in the "present" diegesis, often at points of emotional or erotic intensity. For instance, during the first dinner date between Flavia and Xiao Ye, when Flavia sees Xiao Ye after missing her for many days, a close-up of Xiao Ye from the perspective of Flavia suddenly cuts to exactly the same image shot in 8 mm. The 8 mm footage is also implicitly associated with Jin, who is frequently shooting with an 8 mm camera during her university years. One scene shows Flavia watching old 8 mm movies, presumably made by Jin. The 8 mm footage can thus be seen as an intrusion of a "past" perspective that recurrently haunts the "present," its affect not moored in a particular time frame but rather recurring across temporalities. As we will see later, this visual emphasis of affective recurrence also finds thematic echo in the girls' own interpretation of their lives.

A linear retelling of Flavia's life, made up of a past in which she denies her love for Jin and a present in which she embraces her sexual identity, would reproduce what Biddy Martin has critiqued in discourses on lesbian autobiography as the standard "coming out" narrative. For Martin, the oversimplified movement from a repressive past into a liberated identity has become a generic convention not only in the writing but also in the reading framework of lesbian lives.[35] The film's visual deformation of the story's narrative linearity, which already undermines such generic conventions, is further reinforced by a thematic interruption of the "coming out" narrative. The first mention of Flavia's lesbian identification occurs in the scene when, after months of tension, she finally admits to her husband that she loves a woman:

Flavia: I have fallen in love with a woman.
Ming: I know, she was your high school classmate ... I know something happened in your past, but you have recovered now. It's not a problem anymore. Right?
Flavia: I did not "recover." I am a *lesbian*. I have never changed.

Flavia does not use *tongzhi* or other local slang terms but says "lesbian" in English, as though only this globally intelligible term is weighty enough to convince her husband of who she is. However, when Flavia talks to her lovers, past or present, a somewhat different understanding of their sexuality emerges. When young Flavia and Jin escape to Macao for some privacy, the young lovers refer to a haunting feeling they have about their lives:

Young Flavia and Jin in Macau talking about their lives, in 35 mm and 8 mm, in *Butterfly* (Yan Yan Mak, 2004)

> *Jin:* Sometimes I feel as though I am not me, as though everything has been confused and mismatched ... I feel as though I have seen this image before. In fact, it's like everything has already happened ... everything's been scripted.
>
> *Flavia:* Scripted?
>
> *Jin:* Some people are always trying to change themselves ... But no matter what, their lives have been scripted already. Their choices and the outcomes ... We should call all this ... premeditation.

Later on, after a love scene, the girls resume this theme in their conversation:

> *Jin:* How long will you love me?
>
> *Flavia:* (laughs)
>
> *Jin:* What are you laughing at?
>
> *Flavia:* I thought it's all been scripted!
>
> *Jin:* Right! Aren't we smart ... at least we know it's all a conspiracy *(yinmou)*.
>
> *Flavia:* Conspiracy? You mean premeditation *(yumou)*!
>
> *Jin:* (laughs) Yes, premeditation!

It is common among students in colonial Hong Kong, who are formally educated in English but communicate in Chinese in their everyday lives, to be orally fluent in Cantonese but to lack conceptual and intellectual vocabulary, which they tend to acquire in English. In these scenes the girls struggle to articulate philosophical notions of predestination and causality in relation to their life experiences. Lacking knowledge of the formal terms, they comically borrow words familiar to them from TV crime drama: "premeditation" and "conspiracy," struggling even to distinguish between these terms! These funny and moving conversations between the girls, so evocative of an adolescent experience that is singularly specific to a time-space in

Hong Kong, are not found in the original novella. However, they may be read as a dramatization of the novella's opening line: "I knew right from the beginning, that what must happen *will* happen."[36]

When framed within this notion of "scriptedness" or inevitability, Flavia's story appears not as a unique, one-off life experience but as a recurrently run script that has been happening over and over again. In one subplot in the film, two of Flavia's students, Murial and Sammi, who share an intense love relationship, are forcibly and violently separated by Murial's parents. *Their* story in the film is yet another reenactment of the same script. Yet, the questions remain: *What* is the script? How is it *supposed* to run? Are the tragic outcomes of these forced separations inevitable? The film offers a different reading through an enigmatic statement that Xiao Ye makes to Flavia, which also appears in the novella: "If you can't fly, then you are not a butterfly." If the script is the butterfly's becoming, then stopping the butterfly from flying – from realizing its truest self – is the disruption, rather than the outcome, of "what must happen." Even when what is already scripted appears to outsider eyes as aberrant, wilful, unnatural (like the school girls' love for each other or Flavia's pursuit of Xiao Ye at the expense of her roles as wife and mother), it will nonetheless recur, no matter what obstacles are thrown in its way. Thus it is the violent interruption of the script, not the script itself, that is aberrant, wilful, and unnatural. Framed in these terms, *Butterfly*'s understanding of sexual identity is remarkably different in spirit from that of the "coming out" genre. It does not pitch individual sexual freedom against social conformity but rather tries to resolve the two through a local, bastardized (thus thoroughly Hong Kong) understanding of the precepts of predestination. In the film the intense love developed during queer girlhood is the inevitable, recurrent script that must be enabled. Violent suppression and interruption do not halt its (always already scripted) recurrence but instead breed endless cycles of trauma. Flavia's choice at the end of the film is thus represented not as a form of liberation but, strangely, as a queer sort of conformity to what *must* happen, despite her attempts at denial. She has not so much come out as come *back* to herself.

Let the Moon Quiver: Story Time

> And if they told me they had forgotten everything, I would say,
> Make it up, girls. Give yourself a story that you need – even if it's
> confounding, contradictory. Imagine a love so fierce it brings
> thunder to its knees. I would tell them life is a balance of finding
> who we once were and filling in the gaps with dreams and
> longing and the imagination of a child.
>
> –Anna Camilleri, "Girls Run Circle"

Anna Camilleri's beautiful injunction to girls illustrates the importance of stories as a means to recreate one's past. Storytelling becomes a form of remembering when it deals with a past that has repeatedly been written out, suspended, or denied. In this chapter I have tried to uncover threads and fragments of queer girlhood sexuality wherever I can find them. These stories, while often truncated and unfinished, are traces of what has been obscured, overshadowed, or bleached out of existence in the inexorable narrative of heterosexual womanhood. In the absence of systemic studies or official history, stockpiling these traces – however confounding and contradictory they may appear – can provide points of identification, flashes of fantasy, or echoes of memories that provisionally fill in the gaps of what we cannot yet remember.

Recently, in the wake of successful oral-history projects that aim explicitly to challenge the dominance of official history with "small stories" from the margin,[37] there have also been efforts to recreate and recover stories of queer girlhood. In 2000 Lucetta Kam issued a call for stories on first love between girls, which resulted two years later in the self-published anthology *Lunar Desires: Her Same-Sex Love, In Her Own Words*.[38] The Chinese title, literally *The Quiver of the Moon,* refers to the frisson, anxiety, and turmoil that these audacious stories – about a love and an eroticism so rarely acknowledged – may rouse in their readers. Two years after the publication of *Lunar Desires,* an oral-history project on same-sex desire between women was launched, with one section specifically devoted to the experience of school girls. Both of these projects insist that queer girlhood desire is not unique to lesbian-identified adults. Kam's anthology explicitly cautions readers not to "crudely attribute only one sexual identity to the stories' authors."[39] Day Wong, who documents the making of the oral-history project, also argues that the stories collected do not all constitute a rejection of heterosexuality; some, in fact, are culled from heterosexually identified women.[40] Wong uses the amusing metaphor of "7-11" (the convenience-store chain that is omnipresent in Hong Kong) to describe the equally omnipresent experience of female same-sex desire: "there must be one on every corner."[41] These disclaimers reflect a refusal to dissociate queer girlhood sexuality from *any* form of adult womanhood. These two projects invite (or perhaps dare) us to see the queer traces in everyday life. Indeed, if we look closely enough, we will see that the queer time of girlhood lingers, recurs, and sometimes never ends.

3
Trans Formations

In Search of Trans Formations

When Stanley Kwan received an invitation from the British Film Institute in 1996 to make a film for the commemorative series "The Century of Cinema," he set out to make a well-researched and informative documentary about the general history of Chinese cinema. As he immersed himself in the film archive in Shanghai, however, a queer turn of events steered the project in an entirely different direction. Kwan was struck by two phenomena in Chinese cinema that have wielded enormous influence on his life and career: a strong undercurrent of homoeroticism and a long tradition of non-normative gender expressions. As Kwan became more and more absorbed in these issues, he abandoned his original vision. *Yin ± Yang: Gender in Chinese Cinema* (Stanley Kwan, 1996), a cinematic essay that combines film history with Kwan's personal reflections on gender and sexuality, emerged from these side-tracked efforts. The film has often been characterized as Kwan's first public declaration of his identity as a gay man: the film critic Sek Kei, for instance, calls it a "frank and direct expression of his homosexuality."[1] Yet, this narrative of gay desire is also complicated at every turn by continual – if not always coherent – musings on issues of gender variance. The Chinese title, *Nansheng nuxiang*, literally "boy with a girl's face," refers to a type of "face" within the ancient "face reading" tradition *(xiangxue)* that portends prosperity. Indeed, this "face" of the girl-boy – the transgender face – leaves an indelible imprint on the winding narrative of the film, which meanders from Kwan's ambivalent relation with his father, his early obsession with the hyper-masculinized figures of action stars Bruce Lee and Wang Yu, and his later penchant for making "women's films" to the various forms of cross-dressing and cross-gender embodiments that he traces in Chinese cinema. The film ends in a conversation Kwan has with his own mother, in which he asks her three strategically ordered questions: how she feels about a son who makes "women's films"; what she thinks of the relationship between cross-dressing opera performer Yam Kim-Fai and her on- and (rumoured) off-stage lover, Bak Suet-Sin; and finally, whether she accepts her son's relationship with his lover, William. The links Kwan leads his mother to forge between these three questions are by no means straightforward. Earlier in the film, Kwan has wondered aloud whether his penchant for making films about women means that "he identifies with women at some level." Kwan's reference to Yam and Bak invites his mother to make sense of his relationship through her admiration for the iconic duo. But is he asking his mother to understand Yam and Bak's relation as same-sex love, or is he comparing his own identification with women to Yam's masculine embodiment throughout her career? In short, is Kwan drawing a parallel between himself and Yam as transgender, rather than gay, subjects? At the same time, does he necessarily have to be articulating a clear distinction between the two?

I draw out these entangled threads from *Yin ± Yang* to show that, despite the globalization of lesbian, gay, bisexual, and transgender (LGBT) identities and the increased need to categorically distinguish between the histories, experiences, and practices of these identities, there remain many narratives – whether autobiographical, fictional, or cinematic – that resist such distinctions. These narratives may be understood, in Peter A. Jackson's very useful formulation, as "pre-gay, post-queer."[2] By "pre-gay," Jackson means ways of understanding gender and sexual practices in many Asian societies that predate the advent of gay and lesbian politics in the West and that remain irreducible to its terms and trajectories. These notions are also "post-queer" in the sense that they exceed, escape, or at the very least confound Anglo-American understanding of sexual identity, sexual orientation, and gender difference. Jackson's formulation is particularly useful for interrupting the linear temporality of gay politics: "pre-gay" subjectivities and embodiments are not necessarily "backward," for they will not necessarily "become" gay if only they could; rather, many "pre-gay" formations are *already* "post-queer" in the sense that they can illuminate *other* possible trajectories that are not accounted for in LGBT or even queer frameworks of understanding.

The recent emergence of transgender theory and politics in the West has provided both possibilities and challenges for approaching "pre-gay, post-queer" formations. In her introduction to the *Transgender Studies Reader,* Susan Stryker sketches in detail the confluence of historical conditions, intellectual currents, and political dynamics that gave rise to the currency of the term "transgender" and to the consolidation of the field of transgender studies.[3] One development, to which transgender studies is a particularly salient response, is the "homonormative" tendency within gay and lesbian analysis, what Stryker describes as "a privileging of homosexual ways of differing from heterosocial norms, and an antipathy (or at least an unthinking blindness) towards other modes of queer difference."[4] Transgender discourse thus provides a set of analytical tools to approach relations between desire, gender embodiment, and identity that resist being understood only as gay. At the same time, there is a danger of "transgender" itself reifying into a normative trajectory. Stryker cautions us to acknowledge the history of colonial fascination with the "gender erotics" of non-Western cultures and the attendant ethnographic impulse to categorize "third genders" under the terms of Eurocentric knowledge:

> The conflation of many types of gender variance into the single shorthand term "transgender" particularly when this collapse into a single genre of personhood crosses the boundaries that divide the West from the rest of the world, holds both peril and promise. It is far too easy to assimilate non-Western configurations of personhood into Western constructs of sexuality and gender, in a manner that recapitulates the power structures of colonialism ... Recently, however, various non-European, colonized and diasporic communities whose members configure gender in ways that are marginalized within Eurocentric contexts, have begun to produce entirely new genres of analysis. Such encounters mark the geo-spatial, discursive, and cultural boundaries of transgender studies ... but also point toward the field's untapped potential.[5]

This simultaneous "peril and promise" of transgender discourse is carefully explored in a recent issue of *Inter-Asia Cultural Studies* devoted to the emergence of transgender studies in Asia. Editors Fran Martin and Josephine Ho characterize the development of the field in this way: "While the subject matter of the new wave of transgender studies in Asia is not new – although the concrete forms taken by Asian transgender cultures are continuously shifting along with historical transformations in the social field – what *is* new is the range of ways of thinking and writing about these cultures in the present."[6] Transgender discourse thus provides new ways to articulate experiences and expressions of gender variance that long predate its theoretical emergence. Martin and Ho are careful to insist on the "specificity of place in shaping and giving meaning to transgender cultures as they are lived in local contexts" without "presuming the trans-cultural universality of transgender experience."[7] There should thus be a *mutual constitution* between theory and its object rather than the application of the former to the latter. Furthermore, "local specificity" should not merely signal local variations on a global theme but also reflect elements that *resist* (and thus have the potential to transform) the theoretical premises of transgender discourse.

Compared to the burgeoning diversity of works on transgender in Taiwan, Japan, Thailand, and the Philippines, the engagement with transgender issues in Hong Kong has so far been somewhat limited to an exclusive focus on legal issues, along with scattered studies of media misrepresentations and mainstream societal perceptions.[8] Subcultural expressions remain the best source for understanding trans issues in Hong Kong: for instance, the Internet radio show "What the Hell Kind of *Tongzhi* Movement" features a monthly segment on transgender in which different guests are invited to tell personal stories and to discuss a variety of issues related to trans lives.[9] As yet, there have not been any systematic efforts to archive such subcultural works, and they run the danger of being forgotten or ignored. Whereas Viviane Namaste has critiqued the field of transgender studies in the West for its predominantly theoretical focus, relative lack of empirical studies, and increasing distance from activist struggle,[10] the opposite is true in Hong Kong. The lack of theoretical engagement has left some foundational questions unexamined, consequently limiting the scope of empirical research as well as activist projects. For instance, the most frequently invoked research has been the inquiry into the legal right to change gender status on birth certificates in Hong Kong, a subject on which legal scholar Robyn Emerton has published several journal articles.[11] One recurrent question posed by Emerton is why, unlike in other Asian societies, "Hong Kong's transgender community has not yet fought for the right to legal recognition of their gender identity."[12] Emerton concedes that unlike the identity card (the gender status of which *can* be changed), the birth certificate is not a form of identification used in everyday situations, nor is it the document required in applications for driver's licences or passports; thus the need to change its gender status may not be the most urgently practical issue. Nonetheless, she concludes her article in this way: "Hong Kong's transgender community has found its courage, and found its voice. In time, I hope that someone within the community will find the personal bravery to fight for legal recognition, to claim the privacy, respect and dignity which are owed to all transgender people in Hong Kong, and which are long overdue."[13] The lack of enthusiasm for this particular legal battle is thus interpreted as a lack of "personal bravery" on the part of the "transgender community." The assumption is that "in time" some transgender people will "find" the bravery required for this struggle. I am not discounting the importance of this form of legal activism, but I am troubled by the lack of interest in fully understanding why *this* may not be the most needed work and *what else* may be deserving of attention. Emerton has very frankly disclosed the limits of her study, most significantly that it was conducted in English about a legal initiative that was spearheaded by TEAM (Transgender Equality and Acceptance Movement), an organization perceived to be "orientated towards English-speakers, and/or expatriates" with only thirty-two members at the end of 2005.[14] Furthermore, Emerton has pointed out the difficulty of identifying Hong Kong's actual "transgender population" because the only data are obtained through the public health service and include exclusively those who have used the services of the "sex clinic" (and only those identified *by the clinic* to be transgender).[15] Emerton also suggests that "transgender visibility" is very low in Hong Kong because of the lack of "transgender-specific professions" like those in Thailand and the Philippines.[16] It thus seems to me premature and somewhat misleading for her to conclude that "Hong Kong's transgender community has ... found its voice." Not only is it unclear *whose* voice has been "found," but it seems to me that there is in fact no "community" to speak of and no coherent subject formation around transgender identities. For a "community" to want to fight for legal "recognition," a *recognizable* subject must first exist as such. Subjects, however, are not formed within the predetermined parameters of activist efforts. In Taiwan, for instance, one of the earliest anthologies of trans studies includes discussion of *T/po* (roughly analogous to butch/femme) in lesbian communities, sissies among gay men, and transvestites and drag performers, thus showing an awareness that transgender subject formations are diverse and not easily defined.[17] Not only would some of these groups *not* be concerned with the legal change on birth certificates, but they may not self-identify as "transgender" per se, especially not in English! It is thus important to insist, as Josephine Ho consistently does in her work, on paying detailed attention to the efforts of transgender subjects' "self-fashioning" and to the ways such efforts are entangled in the materiality of everyday life and social interactions.[18] By contrast, identity terms used in the publicity material put out by TEAM – *huanxing ren* (literally, "a person who exchanges their sex") for "transsexual" and *kuaxing ren* (literally, "a person who traverses between sexes") for "transgender" – are completely new terms that did not evolve from community usage but were invented and adopted by activists for specific purposes.[19] The adoption of these terms is a well-intentioned gesture to replace medicalized and/or stigmatized categories. Yet, can newly minted "translated" identity categories immediately give rise to subject formations? Moreover, while these categories derive from the way gender variance is differently experienced by transgender subjects in the West (some will say, even more specifically, Anglo-America), how will they account for experiences that traverse, overlap, or altogether escape them? Filipino scholar Jose Neil Cabañero Garcia has written about the problematic application of imported categories of gender variance, and in his work he insists on deploying indigenous terms in Tagalog – not so much as terms of authenticity but as means to critically locate and interrogate the limits of imported categories.[20] What is thus needed in Hong Kong is cultural work that traces local formations of gender variance – however incoherent, fragmented, or contradictory they may be – that sometimes coincide with and sometimes resist (and are always potentially transformative of) the parameters of transgender studies.

After all, the critical importance of the term "transgender" lies far beyond its articulation of a form of gender identity. "Transgender," and the even more expansive term "trans," signifies not a single type of identification or embodiment but any "bodily effects" that trouble the putatively "natural" coincidence between what Kate Bornstein has conceptualized as the four constituents of gender: assignment (the M or F on the birth certificate), role (masculine and feminine ideals), attribution (how others "read" one's gender), and identification (how one identifies).[21] Susan Stryker also highlights the "epistemological concerns" at the heart of transgender critique: transgender phenomena are not simply to be "known" but should point to critical understanding of the ways of knowing – that is, "how bodies mean, how representation works, and what counts as legitimate knowledge."[22] Judith Halberstam further suggests that "transgender" may be thought of as a "term of relationality," as "a relation between people, within a community, or within intimate bonds."[23] Drawing from these theoretical insights, I will explore what transgender theory enables (and at times disables) in the reading of gender variance in Hong Kong culture. Following Josephine Ho's emphasis on "self-fashioning," I trace narratives of transgender self-fashioning through realigning the relation between embodiment, desire, and identity in ways that are untenable in hetero- and homonormative readings. In conclusion, I will argue for the importance of theoretical and cultural work that engages with trans issues in Hong Kong, particularly their capacity to illuminate the specificities of everyday experience.

Transsexual Emergence

In Sam Winter's "Country Report" on transgender issues in Hong Kong, he uses the example of the film *Swordsman 2* (Ching Siu-Tung, 1992) to illustrate what he views as "overwhelmingly negative views" of cross-gender expressions:

> One of the films made by [sic] Lin Qing Xia [Brigitte Lin] called *Xiao Ao Jiang Hu [Swordsman 2]* illustrates the gender complexities involved in this film genre. The actress plays a male, Dong Fang Bu Bai, who cross-dresses [sic] as a female in order to sexually attract the female [sic] character, Ling Hu C[h]ong. Contrary to most depictions of MtF TG in classical Chinese art, Dong Fang Bu [Bai] is portrayed unsympathetically. In this the film was possibly echoing overwhelmingly negative views of cross-gender that had by that time been imported from the West. However, perhaps the most interesting aspect of this film was that it was an actress that played a man cross-dressing as a woman. No *dan* actors here.[24]

It is clear from the sloppy and quite inaccurate description[25] of the film that Winter has not taken much time to examine it with any care, yet he arrives at the quick conclusion that the film portrays negative views of cross-gender expressions. Analyses of this nature signal that theoretical and, in particular, cultural work is not taken all that seriously by current research-ers on transgender issues in Hong Kong. What would a serious and careful reading of the film reveal about transgender subjectivity?

Swordsman 2 is the second instalment in a series of films loosely adapted from Jin Yong's 1963 novel *Xiao'ao jianghu (The Smiling, Proud Wanderer)*.[26] The film features one of the most memorable villains in Jin Yong's oeuvre: Dongfang Bubai, an ambitious swordsman who has castrated himself in order to acquire an awesome form of martial art. There is a dramatic differ-ence between the novel's and the film's treatments of this remarkable char-acter. In the space of this difference it is possible to locate the emergence of a transsexual subjectivity and, in so doing, to expose a profound contradic-tion in the martial arts genre's central conception of masculinity.

In the afterword to the 1980 edition of *The Smiling, Proud Wanderer,* Jin Yong recalls the anxious political climate under which he wrote the serial-ized novel. The intense power struggle between warring factions in China, which at the time was teetering on the brink of the Cultural Revolution, inspired some of the major themes in the novel. The character Dongfang Bubai, whose name literally means "undefeated in the east," is a cunning parody of Mao Zedong's self-appellation as the "red sun in the east" and a pointed allusion to his megalomaniacal appetite for power. The critical force of Jin Yong's allusion, however, derives from a transphobic understanding of the gendered body. In the novel the extremity of Dongfang Bubai's thirst for power is marked by his willingness to castrate himself. This trope of castration as a desire for power recalls a historiographic cliché: the conten-tion that many of the political disasters in imperial China can be attributed to the usurpation of power by eunuchs.[27] Jin Yong stretches this symbolic equation even further. The monstrosity of power corruption is symbolized not only in the fact of castration but also in the very process of bodily transition from male to female. When Dongfang Bubai appears in the novel for the first time, her enemies are confounded. They remember *him* as "an awe-inspiring and fearsome fighter" who has "usurped the leadership of the Sun-Moon Holy Sect and reigned supreme in the martial world for twenty years." *She* now appears in front of them, "beardless, rouged, and wearing lurid clothes that appear to be neither masculine nor feminine."[28] She sits embroidering in a perfumed chamber, "having lost all previous appetite for women" and having become completely devoted to a man and obsessed with becoming a woman.[29] Dongfang Bubai has become, in the words of the novel's heroine Yingying, "not a human, but a monster."[30] The novel dis-poses of Dongfang Bubai within one chapter, but its anxiety over the "mon-strosity" of sex change continues. One of the most important narrative developments hinges on the secret of an elder swordsman and his son-in-law, both of whom have self-righteously persecuted the novel's hero, Linghu Chong, who is being wrongfully blamed for a series of crimes. The novel subsequently reveals the two men to be the real criminals. Hungry for power, they have been practising the same dark art that has transformed Dongfang Bubai. The physical changes in the elder swordsman are described through his wife's observations. She chillingly starts to notice the change in the pitch of her husband's voice, the shedding of his beard, and the loss of his (hetero)sexual appetite.[31] These are not, of course, medically accurate symptoms of castration nor literal descriptions of transsexual transitions. Rather, the horror of power corruption is projected, through the wife's terrified observations, onto a sex-changed body. The novel allegorizes transsexuality, likening the somatic transition from male to female to a process of moral degeneration. Such transphobic understanding of ultimate villainy as a form of literal emasculation reveals the novel's own anxiety about the free-spirited and hermetic masculinity that it celebrates in its hero Linghu Chong.[32] In the afterword Jin Yong suggests that Linghu Chong never achieves the true freedom that he desires *not* because of worldly political struggles that have entangled him throughout the novel but because of his committed love first for Yue Lingshan and later for Yingying. According to Jin Yong, Linghu Chong is "imprisoned" when he returns a woman's love and most free in "Yilin's unrequited love for him."[33] Apparently, a man is free in a relationship with a woman only if he does not return her love and thus escapes the "prison" of her influences! Jin Yong's remarks betray an acute anxiety about feminine sexuality and its constricting effects on the masculine freedom he envisions for Linghu Chong. Jin Yong's anxiety becomes *literalized* on the villainous male bodies: Dongfang Bubai and the other corrupted swordsmen are portrayed as literally and monstrously bounded by their feminizing bodies. Ironically, it is exactly at the moment that these swordsmen are becoming feminized that they lose their sexual desire for women, thus escaping from the very influence that Jin Yong identifies as constraining for masculine freedom. In this light, the novel's transphobia actually reveals an underlying crisis in the genre's conception of masculinity and freedom. On the one hand, an idealized masculinity is perceived to be vulnerable to the constraints of heterosexual desire. On the other hand, the ultimate freedom from heterosexual desire is inevitably coded in metaphors of castration (which, in this novel, is further imagined as a form of sex change) and, by implication, as the *loss* of masculinity. This contradiction may explain why Jin Yong, even as he laments Yingying's constraining influences, does not end the novel differently, with Linghu Chong wandering free and unfettered by heterosexual desire. To do so would, I suspect, bring Linghu Chong too monstrously close to Dongfang Bubai, who in fact represents what is both most abhorred and most desired in the novel's conception of masculinity and freedom.

If such a critique of the novel simply reveals the ideological limits of its times, then the dramatic transformation of Dongfang Bubai on the screen in 1992 owes something to the first stirrings of *tongzhi* politics in Hong Kong. The debates over the decriminalization of homosexuality throughout the 1980s resulted not only in the emergence of gay and lesbian identities and organized activism around these identities but also in a new discursive space where issues of sexual and gender transgressions can be openly voiced.[34] *Swordsman 2* was made at this time, feeding the public's newfound fascination with queer subject matter while reinvigorating a gender-bending tradition that, as Kwan so convincingly shows in *Yin ± Yang,* has arguably always existed in Chinese cinema and has certainly been prefigured in Chinese theatre.[35] One of the film's most glaring departures from the novel's treatment of Dongfang Bubai is the centrality it accords to the novel's villain. While Dongfang Bubai dies within a chapter in the four-volume novel, she occupies the most prominent role in the film, usurping even the limelight of Linghu Chong, not unlike the way she has usurped the leadership of the Sun-Moon sect in the novel. The film also invents an erotic relationship between Linghu Chong and Dongfang Bubai, further blurring the line between hero and villain. Most unexpectedly, Brigitte Lin was cast in the role of Dongfang Bubai. The box office success of the film would later revitalize Lin's sagging career and instigate a trend of gender-bending roles that distinguish the careers of actors like Leslie Cheung, Anita Yuen, Anita Mui, and most prominently, Lin herself. The casting of Lin, an actress famous for her immense beauty, is significant. No longer represented as a castrated half-man, Dongfang Bubai remerges on screen as a *woman.* The film's inclusion in the Netherlands Transgender Film Festival in 2001, almost ten years after its initial release, completes Dongfang Bubai's remarkable transformation.[36] Conceived as a symbol of masculinity under threat by a transphobic imagination during the 1960s, Dongfang Bubai is emerging in the new millennium as a transsexual icon. However, the film has not always enjoyed such enthusiastic critical reception. In fact, it was routinely criticized in the first wave of queer critical writing to emerge from Hong Kong in the 1990s. This critical gap in the film's reception reveals an interesting contradiction between queer theorizing and transsexual subjectivity. In his introduction to *Second Skins,* Jay Prosser calls our attention to queer theory's foundational reliance on the figure of transgender. As a body of knowledge that takes as its point of departure the "queering" – that is, the destabilization and displacement – of established categories of gender and sexuality, it is no surprise that queer theory finds the trope of crossing and traversing genders immensely valuable to its theoretical enterprise. Prosser suggests, however, that the queer appropriation of transgender privileges only a particular segment of the conceptual umbrella represented by the term "transgender": "Crucial to the idealization of transgender as a queer transgressive force in this work is the consistent decoding of 'trans' as incessant destabilizing movement between sexual and gender identities."[37] Prosser argues that the formulation "transgender = gender performativity = queer = subversive" results in a conceptual split between queer and *transsexual*. The transsexual subject position, as Prosser shows, does not necessarily value fluidity, movement, and performativity but rather "seek[s] quite pointedly to be non-performative, to be constative, quite simply to *be*."[38] Prosser's subsequent articulation of a theory of transsexual embodiment delineates a specifically transsexual experience of the body that is not easily reconciled with the queer imperative. While queer theory celebrates disruption and instability as transgressive forces, the transsexual subject in Prosser's formulation is invested in gender transitivity not in and of itself but as a process that eventually *arrives* at a more stable form of gendered embodiment. It is not surprising, then, that critics who turn to *Swordsman 2* for a queer reading are often disappointed. In one of the earliest pieces of queer criticism on Hong Kong cinema, Chou Wah-Shan offers a scathing critique of the film. He takes issue in particular with the casting of Brigitte Lin: "Dongfang Bubai and Linghu Chong are clearly homosexual lovers. Casting the beautiful actress Brigitte Lin in the role completely takes away the shock and anxiety a male actor would inspire in playing that role."[39] Chou is especially irked by one scene: Dongfang Bubai asks her concubine, Sisi, to substitute for herself while making love to Linghu Chong in the dark. Chou interprets this scene as the film's final reinscription of heterosexuality: the only sexual scene in the film occurs unambiguously between a man and a woman. In a much more complex and nuanced reading, Yau Ching shifts the interpretive focus and locates queer pleasure in the spectatorial gaze. Yau argues that the film in fact offers its spectators "layered and diverse paths to project their desire" and that the character Dongfang Bubai "allows us to refuse identification through sexual difference."[40] For Yau, the spectator's simultaneous recognition of the actress's female body and the character's male body means that identification with the character demands a (temporary) suspension of seamlessly gendered identification. Thus, as the gender discrepancy between actress and character becomes less intelligible – that is, as Dongfang Bubai's transition progresses – the queer pleasure of the film also diminishes: "When Dongfang Bubai becomes more and more like a woman, the spectatorial pleasure of the female audience also becomes less radical and more conservative, until they finally only see the reflection of their own gender identification."[41] Both critics, in their very different readings, view Dongfang Bubai as a subversive character only in so far as s/he remains a symbol of gender instability. Chou prefers to see Dongfang Bubai played by a male actor, thus displaying a feminized male body and serving as an object of homosexual desire for Linghu Chong. Yau relishes the casting of Brigitte Lin as long as a queer discrepancy is maintained between Lin's (meta-textual) female body and Dongfang Bubai's (textual) male body. Both critics become disappointed when they are confronted with what is arguably

Dongfang Bubai's subjective emergence – that is, as a transsexual woman who challenges Linghu Chong's (and our) demand to *tell the difference* of transsexuality. In this light, the scene that has appeared so *un*queer to critics can be reread as an inscription *not* primarily of heterosexuality but of transsexual agency.

Prior to the seduction scene, Dongfang Bubai has just told her concubine, Sisi, about her somatic changes, citing them as the reasons for their recent lack of physical intimacy. At this moment, Linghu Chong enters the compound and asks Dongfang Bubai, known to him only as a beautiful stranger, to run away with him from the turmoil of worldly affairs. Dongfang Bubai extinguishes the lights and asks Sisi to substitute for her. She then pushes Sisi into Linghu Chong's arms, and the two make love in the dark. Later on in the film Linghu Chong discovers the true identity of Dongfang Bubai and fights alongside his allies against her. Yet, when she is about to die, he tries to save her life, repeatedly asking whether it was really *her* with whom he has spent that memorable night. In fact, he begs her to confirm that it was indeed her. Dongfang Bubai neither confirms nor denies this, telling him that he "will never know, and will always regret this moment" (presumably the moment of her death). She then lets herself fall to the bottom of the cliffs, leaving Linghu Chong none the wiser.

Why does Dongfang Bubai offer Sisi to Linghu Chong? And what is her motive for "deceiving" Linghu Chong to the very end? Chou, who insists on reading Dongfang Bubai as "rightfully" a gay man, argues that it is the film's way of "avoiding an explicit male-male sex scene." Yet, Chou has already critiqued the casting of Brigitte Lin as a heterosexualization of the relationship between Dongfang Bubai and Linghu Chong. Why would her recognizably female body be in danger of suggesting a homosexual scene? The substitution in fact makes sense only as part of a transsexual narrative. In his discussion of transsexual embodiment, Jay Prosser theorizes the transsexual subject's relation to his or her transitioning body through Didier Anzieu's notion of the "skin ego." Anzieu's reworking of psychoanalytic theories departs from the emphasis Lacan and his followers place on language as the defining structure of ego formation. Instead, Anzieu returns to Freud and the importance he attributes to the body, especially its surface, in the formation of the ego.[42] It is from this *tactile* origin of the psyche that Prosser derives his theory of transsexuality: "Writing against the grain of most poststructuralist theories of the body informed by psychoanalysis, Didier Anzieu suggests the body's surface as that which matters most about the self. His concept of the "skin ego" takes the body's physical skin as the primary organ underlying the formation of the ego, its handling, its touching, its holding – our experience of its feel – individualizing our psychic functioning, quite crucially making us who we are."[43] Prosser goes on to explain the untouchability, or "stoneness," of the pretransition body – a recurrent motif in transsexual narratives – as a feeling of the noncoincidence between "the contours of body image" and the material body, a "description simply of the refusal of body ego to own referential body."[44] Dongfang Bubai's refusal of sexual intimacy, both with Sisi and with Linghu Chong, can be explained in Prosser's scheme as precisely this wilful nonrecognition of the (transitioning) body that is not (yet fully) her own. Furthermore, as Prosser suggests, it is this "dis-ownership of sex ... [that] maintains the integrity of the alternatively gendered imaginary."[45] In other words, Dongfang Bubai's refusal to be sexualized during physical intimacy as either "not quite man" (by Sisi) or "not quite woman" (by Linghu Chong) is her means of maintaining her subjectively gendered imaginary of being a woman. However, she does not simply stop there but literalizes this alternative gendered imaginary, through Linghu Chong's desire for her, *on* Sisi's body. Prosser deploys Oliver Sacks's work on neurology to draw a parallel between the way amputees feel and animate their prosthetic limbs through a phatasmatic memory of their real limbs and the way transsexuals experience their postsurgical bodies. In place of actual memory, Prosser suggests that transsexuals experience their surgically transformed bodies through *nostalgia* for an idealized body that *should* have existed: "The body of transsexual becoming is born out of a yearning for a perfect past – that is, not memory but nostalgia: the desire for the purified version of what was, not for the return to home per se *(nostos)* but to the romanticized ideal of home."[46] Sisi's body represents for Dongfang Bubai the idealized gendered body that she longs to become/return to. In substituting for Dongfang Bubai, unbeknown to Linghu Chong, Sisi is serving as a phatasmatic extension of Dongfang Bubai's body. By denying Linghu Chong the power to tell the difference, Dongfang Bubai has in effect closed the gap between her subjectively embodied gender and Linghu Chong's actual experience of her body. The price of Dongfang Bubai's subjective emergence in this erotic encounter, of course, is the erasure of Sisi. In this scene, she is disowned from her own body, which has become a phantom limb possessed by both Dongfang Bubai (through identification) and Linghu Chong (through desire). It is thus fitting that the figure of the concubine returns with a vengeance in the film's sequel, *The East Is Red* (Ching Siu-Tong, 1993). In the latter film one of Dongfang Bubai's former concubines, Xue Qianxun, refuses to be abandoned like Sisi. In a scheme to lure Dongfang Bubai (not dead after all) out of hiding, she impersonates her former lover and embarks on a killing spree, thus sending the entire martial world on a search for the real Dongfang Bubai. Xue's scheme is similar to Dongfang Bubai's deception of Linghu Chong in one important way: successfully disguised as a transsexual woman, Xue challenges the world to "tell the difference" of transsexuality, with the confidence that they, like Linghu Chong (and the audience), will be unable to do so.

Dongfang Bubai may never qualify as a "positive image" of transsexual femininity: after all, she is a brutal, cunning, and power-driven villain. Yet, what is different about her representation in the film, in contrast to the character's treatment in the novel, is the intelligibility of Dongfang Bubai as a *woman* that is actualized through a narrative of transsexual self-fashioning. Her power, although awesome and terrifying, is worthy of her enemies' respect. Most of all, she is no longer a symbol of damaged masculinity, to be conquered by Linghu Chong's free-spirited heroism. Instead, she has fully emerged into her self-chosen subject position as a woman. Unlike the novel, the film is not primarily about masculinity under siege. Rather, it offers a spectacular display of transsexual femininity that has successfully eclipsed the centrality of masculine heroism in the genre.

Transgendering Homoeroticism

The transsexual narrative that I trace, through Jay Prosser's theory of transsexual embodiment, in *Swordsman 2* is by no means the only possible articulation of transgender subjectivity. While the transsexual trajectory tends to be marginalized within queer theory, it is by contrast the *dominant* expression of transgender identity within the medical discourse of gender dysphoria, which views transgender people pathologically as patients in need of treatment. The "treatment" offered is a rigid process of sex reassignment that follows strict medical protocols, prescribed and monitored by medical and mental health professionals. A "cure" is understood to be the patient's successful reassignment from one sex to another. Until very recently, narratives of transgender embodiment that do not conform to, or that consciously *reject,* this grammar of binary gender transitions have been viewed with suspicion and hostility by the medical community. Since the 1990s the medical establishment has relinquished some of its exclusive claim to expertise on transgender lives. With increasing input and participation of activists, academics, and cultural producers who are themselves the consumers of transgender care, a much more complex and diverse picture of the experiences and needs of transgender people is starting to emerge, both in the medical community and in mainstream culture. Leslie Feinberg's 1992 novel *Stone Butch Blues,* for instance, has brought a new visibility to transgender narratives that explicitly depart from the transsexual trajectory. The protagonist, Jess, who has first lived as a butch lesbian, then taken hormones and undergone surgery and lived as a man, finally realizes that neither of these identities fully encompasses who s/he is. Toward the end of the novel, Jess asks this poignant question: "I felt my whole life coming full circle. Growing up so different, coming out as a butch, passing as a man, and then back to the same questions that had shaped my life: woman or man?"[47] The novel deliberately refrains from answering the question. In the end Jess stops passing and resolves to live as s/he is: neither man nor woman but "transgender" in "hir" (Feinberg's preferred pronoun) own way. All of Feinberg's subsequent writing, as well as the works of authors like Kate Bornstein and Riki Wilchins, are committed to a sustained critique of the binary conception of gender at the same time that they demonstrate the diversity of transgender lives. In my reading of *Portland Street Blues* (Raymond Yip, 1998), I would like to trace, in the protagonist, Sister Thirteen, a form of transgender subjectivity that does not conform to the transsexual trajectory. Previously overlooked by critics, the possibility of reading Thirteen as a transgender character also has critical implications for the debates on homoeroticism in the gangster genre and for the discourse of sexual orientation in general.

Portland Street Blues is the fourth instalment of the *Young and Dangerous* series of films, which are blockbusters adapted from a comic book series about young Triad gangsters. The film documents how Sister Thirteen, leader of the Portland Street branch of the Hung Hing Triad, rises to power. From her first appearance in the opening scene, where she is dressed in a classy black suit, with her hair slicked back and a cigarette between her lips, Thirteen perfectly embodies the heroic masculinity made famous by Chow Yun-Fat's characters in John Woo's films from the 1980s. In the *Young and Dangerous* series this tradition of heroic masculinity is modulated and reinvented through the youthful characters played by Ekin Cheng and Jordan Chan. What is Thirteen's subjective relation to his/her masculinity? The first flashback sequence in the film is initiated by a scene of mourning. While Thirteen burns incense in front of a portrait of her late father, she explains to her Triad brother: "I've always thought of myself as a man. Do you know why?" A dissolving shot cuts from the late father's portrait to the past, where the father is playing mah-jong with Triad bosses who use him as a pawn in the game. The narrative of Thirteen's transgender identification is thus visually linked to her father, a man who has never been able to live up to the heroic masculinity glorified in the genre. As a result, he is harassed and bullied and eventually dies in brutal humiliation. Thirteen's masculine identification thus also signals her identification with Triad power. However, the desire for Triad power alone does not explain Thirteen's transgender identification, only the *type* of masculinity she embraces. Her masculinity is not simply "functional": it is not just a means to gain Triad power. Subsequent flashback sequences show that long before her Triad ambitions, Thirteen was already a tomboy in her youth. Scenes of Thirteen and her girlhood companion A Yun playing, smoking, joking, and cuddling in bed together consciously echo what would be recognized in the Hong Kong lesbian lexicon as a TB/TBG (literally "tomboy/tomboy girl" and signifying butch/femme) relationship, even in the absence of any explicit sexual relations between the two. Thirteen may be understood as what Judith

Halberstam would call a "transgender butch." Halberstam first formulated this category in order to challenge the overlapping, often blurry, but frequently contested "borders" between butch and FTM (female-to-male transsexual) identities:

> There are real and physical differences between genetic females who specifically identify as transsexual and genetic females who feel comfortable with female masculinity. There are real and physical differences between female-born men who take hormones, have surgery, and live as men and female-born butches who live some version of gender ambiguity. But there are also many situations in which those differences are less clear than one might expect, and there are many butches who pass as men and many transsexuals who present as gender ambiguous and many bodies that cannot be classified by the options transsexual and butch.[48]

The category of "transgender butch," which emphasizes a cross-gender identification (transgender) while retaining a reference to a masculine form of femaleness (butch) that is distinct from either "man" or "woman," provides a more flexible category for those who inhabit the borderland between butch and FTM. I describe Thirteen as a transgender butch to signify her masculine identification and masculine presentation as well as to underscore that she does not seek to pass as a man or transition physically. This specificity is important to my reinterpretation of the film's sexual dynamics.

The romantic plot of *Portland Street Blues* is full of twists and turns and offers an especially interesting example of the way transgender theory complicates the discourse of sexual orientation. Throughout the film Thirteen suspects that A Yun is in love with Coke, a hit man from the rival Dong Sing Triad. To Thirteen's surprise, A Yun admits toward the end of the film that the true object of her love has always been Thirteen. Her apparent desire for Coke is, like her many scheming acts of seduction earlier on in the film, simply a weapon of manipulation. In retrospect, it becomes clear that she seduces Coke in order to keep him away from Thirteen, who, in a further twist of the romantic plot, greatly admires Coke and later betrays her intense affection for the man. Thirteen also runs a prostitute ring, cruises young women, and is widely known to be a lesbian. Yet, the only emotionally charged and intimate encounter she has in the film is with Coke. As a result, many reviewers are puzzled by the film's sexual dynamics. The veteran film critic Sek Kei, for instance, ends his review of the film with this question: "moreover, is [Sister Thirteen] actually homosexual or heterosexual? This was never made very clear."[49] Sek Kei wants to know, once and for all, whether Thirteen is "actually" lesbian or straight. What Sek Kei, or any other critic for that matter, fails to take into account is Thirteen's transgender identification and its implication for our understanding of her sexuality. If we read Thirteen not simply as a woman but more specifically as a transgender butch – that is, as a *masculine* figure – then her desire for Coke is neither lesbian nor straight but *gay*. Admittedly, my use of the term "gay" here is tongue-in-cheek, as the word inevitably invokes a discourse of sexual orientation that categorizes desire according to the sex of the desiring bodies, regardless of their gender presentation. Yet, if we take transgender identifications seriously, sexual orientation may be much more complex than what the binary scheme of heterosexuality and homosexuality can describe. Is Thirteen's desire for Coke still heterosexual if she does not identify as feminine? In fact, since she is attracted to Coke as a self-identified *masculine* woman, would it not be more accurate to describe this attraction as *homoerotic?* This latter suggestion makes particular sense in the scene where Thirteen and Coke show immense tenderness for each other. The two are reunited for the first time after many years. They reminisce and make sexual jokes in ways that are typical of male-male camaraderie. Then, all of a sudden, the mood shifts and Thirteen awkwardly asks Coke for a hug, and he obliges, tentatively but tenderly. The film critic Shelly Kraicer has observed that during the exchange, the editing consistently violates the 180-degree rules, which means that from our perspective, the two characters keep switching position from left to right, continually replacing one another in placements.[50] The editing of the sequence recalls John Woo's famous manoeuvre in *The Killer* (John Woo, 1989). In a formal analysis of the film, David Bordwell describes the ways that Woo "cuts across the axis of action" to make the two heroes, John and Li, "pictorially parallel":

> Thereafter John and Li are compared by every stylistic means Woo can find: crosscutting, echoing lines of dialogue, and visual parallels ... He intercuts tracking shots in John's apartment to make Li literally replace John, and he will have them face off again and again, in a dizzying series of variant framings, while telling the blind Jenny they're childhood friends. Woo violates Hollywood's 180-degree cutting rule in order to underscore graphic similarities between the two men.[51]

In the scene from *Portland Street Blues* the "quotation" of Woo is significant in two ways: it anchors Thirteen's transgender identification in the mirror of Coke's masculinity at the same time that it represents an intense intimacy between two masculine figures. In a later scene when Thirteen arrives at the place where Coke has been shot dead, she grieves for him in a highly masculinized gesture: she picks up three burning cigarettes, lays them down on the ground together like three burning sticks of incense, and then kneels down to pay respect to Coke. Furthermore, in another implicit romantic subplot between Thirteen and her Triad partner Han Bin, who awkwardly tries to give her a ring to express his affection, the relationship is also coded in generic images of male-male camaraderie rather than heterosexual romance. The bonding scenes between the two show them getting drunk together while heading out to cruise women, expressing mutual respect for each other's abilities, and loyally watching each other's back amid Triad power intrigue. All of these scenes typically occur between male characters in the genre. Thus Thirteen never once steps out of her role as masculine hero, even – in fact, especially – in her romantic relations with men. What, then, is the significance of Thirteen's appropriation of this hitherto exclusively male homoeroticism (now understood as eroticism between two masculine-identified figures, regardless of their assigned birth sex)? To answer this question it is necessary to turn, for a moment, to the debates on homoeroticism in Hong Kong action cinema.

In Jillian Sandel's analysis of John Woo's pre-Hollywood films, she suggests that the implicit homoeroticism in Woo's films signifies a repudiation of femininity, heterosexual desire, and the burden of family, all of which threaten the hero's ideal of individualism and freedom. However, this homoerotic tension is never allowed explicit expression in the films and is instead resolved in an aestheticized excess of violence inflicted on the male bodies. For Sandel, the homoerotic relationships in Woo's films are impossible to sustain because they articulate a form of freedom that the films associate with capitalism, which, for Sandel, is an economic system that permits only competitive relations between individuals.[52] Sandel's analysis is quite compelling, but it is premised on an overly hasty identification of femininity and the family with Chinese tradition. Violently masochistic masculinity, by contrast, is linked to capitalism, with the unresolved homoerotic relations between men as its (impossible) fantasy of freedom. In another reading of the films' masculinity, Mikel J. Koven reverses Sandel's argument in an equally problematic move. Koven contends that the discussion of homoeroticism in gangster films is a Western "misreading" of "traditional Chinese masculinity," which he characterizes as more openly expressive of emotions. For Koven, the intense affective investment in honour, duty, and loyalty commonly experienced by Chinese men is misrecognized as eroticism by Western critics.[53] Both Sandel and Koven, in their rush to set up a Chinese vs. Western dichotomy, are unable to see the interconnections, rather than oppositions, between homoeroticism, masculine freedom, and "traditional Chinese masculinity." While Sandel insightfully links the homoeroticism in Woo's films with the repudiation of femininity and family, she overlooks the possibility that the masculine freedom idealized in these homoerotic relationships is not necessarily an embrace of capitalist individualism and a repudiation of Chinese tradition. Rather, it is a nostalgic reconstruction of traditional masculinity, precisely in response to the competitive individualism of capitalism, which eclipses such relations. Kovel, by contrast, recognizes the action genre's investment in traditional masculinity but is unable, or unwilling, to understand it as anything but categorically heterosexual. Contrary to Kovel's assumption, homoeroticism abounds in premodern Chinese culture and is far from incompatible with "traditional Chinese masculinity."[54] As I argued earlier, there is a crisis in the conceptualization of masculinity in the martial arts genre. While heterosexual desire is perceived, on the one hand, to be a constraint on masculine freedom, the repudiation of heterosexuality, on the other hand, seems to lead dangerously to feminization and homosexuality. While Jin Yong alleviates this crisis with an expression of transphobia, Woo represses it by offering a homoerotic subtext that is forever deferred by outbursts of violence and thus never in danger of developing into homosexuality.

Just as *Swordsman 2* provides an intriguing variation on the theme of masculinity in Jin Yong's novel, so *Portland Street Blues* provocatively modulates the homoeroticism in Woo's genre films. The film attempts to imagine a male-female relationship that departs from the generic portrayal of heterosexuality. The "homoerotic" relationship between Thirteen and Coke (or Han Bin) is unfettered by the burden of family and free from feminine influences. It is built on loyalty and mutual respect. Yet, for such relationships to be intelligible within the gender dynamics of the genre, the film must fully articulate Thirteen's transgender identification as a masculine subject. This portrayal, which in effect concedes that masculinity is not the exclusive property of male bodies, is simply too threatening to be accommodated fully in a genre film. In a discussion of the cross-dressing opera performer Yam Kim-Fai, Natalia Chan argues that Chinese culture seems to have more tolerance for women who cross-dress as men than vice versa because a cross-dressing female performer like Yam Kim-Fai, who embodies a "tragic" version of feminized *(yinrou)* masculinity, does not pose a real threat to the tradition of tough, strong *(yanggang)* masculinity.[55] Thirteen's decidedly *un*feminine masculinity in *Portland Street Blues* certainly departs from this tradition of feminized masculinity exemplified by Yam. More important, unlike Yam, the role of Thirteen is not a cross-dressed performance. Sandra Ng is not playing a male character as Yam was in Cantonese operas. Rather, Thirteen *is* a masculine character who has announced her transgender identification and who embodies a masculinity that rivals that of any other male character in the film. She even forges a homoerotic relation with another hero. As a result, she represents a far greater threat to the gendered structure of power than the examples of cross-dressed masculinity in Chan's analysis. The film's concluding scene exposes the anxiety of the genre toward this threat, which ironically is the fruit of its own production. After Thirteen has avenged the death of Coke, a mass of young gangsters led by Ho-Nam, the hero of all the early *Young and Dangerous* films, congregates around her. This show of mass collectivity is a signature scene in all the films in the series. As Thirteen grieves Coke's death, Ho-Nam remarks coolly, "She is a woman after all." Here, Ho-Nam speaks in the anxious conservative voice of the genre in this sudden attempt to tame the transgender butch, who has until this moment been its shining star. However, his remark sounds oddly disingenuous, as the sight of a masculine hero grieving for another man is a commonplace in gangster films. A Ho grieving (far more emotionally than Thirteen) for Brother Mark's death at the end of *A Better Tomorrow* (John Woo, 1986), for instance, would not have shown him to be "a woman after all." Ho-Nam's insistence on Thirteen's "difference" is the film's anxious last-minute disavowal of her transgender identification, and the remark ends up undermining the film's own innovative reworking of generic masculinity.

Trans Formations in Everyday Life

Swordsman 2 and *Portland Street Blues* are interesting because they illuminate, through their central characters, tactics of transgender self-fashioning. Dongfang Bubai's and Sister Thirteen's experiences of gender variance are actualized, through their own agency, into specific forms of self-understanding, self-presentation, and affective and sexual bonds with others. Neither character self-identifies as transgender, nor, as critical histories show, are they readily recognizable as such. Signifying transgender through these characters does not mean to bestow new identities on them. Rather, it is a reading tactic that traces, in narratives of gendered self-fashioning, ways to know bodies, desires, and relationality that are not fully intelligible in hetero- or homonormative understanding.

Such tactics of reading are relevant not only as a theoretical exercise but also, more broadly, as a politics of representation that may address some of the current limits of research on transgender issues in Hong Kong. Aside from efforts at legal reform discussed earlier in the chapter, another area of research has focused on public perception of transgender people. Mark King has conducted a study among secondary school teachers based on a questionnaire that asks respondents to give various opinions on trans women and their sexual partners. The word King uses on the questionnaire for trans women is *renyao,* a largely derogatory term that was originally used to describe transgender performers in South East Asia. It comes as no surprise that the result shows "a significant level of discriminatory perceptions and attitudes towards transgendered females and their sexual partners."[56] There is in fact a kind of self-fulfilling prophecy at work in this type of study. The terms of the questionnaire are constructed through an abstracted (and prejudicial) conceptualization of an imaginary group. How else could the respondents react but with prejudice? Their responses are then used as "proof" of their discriminatory perceptions. King explains that he uses the derogatory term in the questionnaire because there is a lack of alternative vocabulary. Yet, instead of perceiving this lack as an obstacle, is it possible to approach it as a potential opening for a different kind of investigation? What the lack of vocabulary indicates is that "transgender" denotes ways of being that are not fully thinkable to the respondents. Are there more creative ways to approach this immensely interesting site of the as-yet-unthinkable than containing it within the abstracted, and already prejudicial, category of *renyao* (which almost *ensures* the predictable result)? What if a questionnaire proceeds along the lines of Stanley Kwan's questions to his mother in *Yin ± Yang?* Kwan does not ask his mother whether she accepts transgender identification and homosexuality. Instead, Kwan takes her through lived experiences in which she has encountered both without necessarily understanding them as such: for instance, her feelings toward her son's penchant for making "women's films," her admiration for a female cultural icon who perfectly embodies masculinity, and her reactions toward the iconic opera couple. Kwan's mother's answers may not equate with "her perception of transgenderism and homosexuality." Yet, they reveal a complex and not readily perceptible relation that Kwan's mother has to gender variance and queer desire, something that would never have emerged from questions bound by available categories and divorced from her everyday experience. Trans formations that lurk in films like *Swordsman 2* and *Portland Street Blues,* or that are ambivalently embodied in icons like Yam Kim-Fai, abound in everyday culture, only they are not necessarily understood or experienced *as* trans formations. Paying attention to these cultural fragments in all their unruly details, rather than ignoring them in the interest of preserving categorical coherence, would pave the way for a much more complex engagement with transgender issues in Hong Kong.

4
In Queer Memory

Leslie Cheung (1956-2003)

Death of an Icon

"2003 was a damn tough year to swallow!" This widely shared sentiment finds dramatic expression in *Golden Chicken 2* (Samson Chiu, 2003), the runaway box office hit that portrays events in that year through the eyes of a quirky and resilient sex worker. Indeed, for a population still reeling from years of economic downturn and living under an inept postcolonial administration that was nonetheless "reelected" in 2002 through an undemocratic political system, 2003 must have felt like an insult added to injury. The unexpected onslaught of SARS had ravaged the city in both health and economic terms, while the government was planning to write into law a highly unpopular piece of anti-sedition legislation – the controversial Article 23 – despite widespread popular dissent. Boiling discontent erupted on the sixth anniversary of the handover when a half-million people took to the streets to protest the proposed legislation and, by implication, life under the (then) current administration.[1] It was during such a tumultuous year and on the most absurdist of dates – 1 April – that actor and singer Leslie Cheung took his own life by jumping from the twenty-fourth floor of the Mandarin Oriental Hotel in Central, Hong Kong's downtown core, against the backdrop of a magnificent sunset over Victoria Harbour. Only forty-six at the time of his death, Cheung was an eclectic and long-established artist at the height of his professional powers, with more than forty best-selling albums and fifty-six films – many internationally acclaimed – to his credit. The suicide was attributed to severe clinical depression, but the public responded with an overwhelming wave of shock and grief, as though channelling the pent-up frustrations and unhappiness from their own lives. Even in the drizzling spring rain and under the grim threat of SARS, thousands came out to mourn Cheung's passing. For weeks the site of his death was awash in a sea of flowers and mementos. Through both print and digital media, eulogies poured in. Cheung's death was repeatedly mourned as the passage of an era. Sociologist Ng Chun-Hung declared that "a generation has officially ended."[2]

Music scholar Joanna Lee called Cheung's twenty-six-year career "a testament to Hong Kong's transformation" and a marker of the city's "years of glory."[3] Writer and artist Mathias Woo described Cheung's passing as "a traumatic blow to a city already so bereaved" and "a death-toll to an era."[4] Almost as frequently, Cheung was also praised for his sexual courage. An editorial in the *Economic Daily* characterized Cheung's sexual openness as "a challenge to the normative social value of masculinity."[5] Film critic Lam Pui-Li stated that he regards many of Cheung's film roles as "a gay person's brave coming out journey."[6] Reporter Wat Wing-Yin lambasted those who expressed contempt for Cheung's homosexuality and voiced her admiration for Cheung's eighteen-year relationship with his male lover.[7]

It was certainly unprecedented in Hong Kong for a public figure's death to prompt such an outpouring of affection while at the same time eliciting so much positive commentary on his sexuality. Perhaps as a response to this unusually affirmative media attention, *tongzhi* organizations also began to publicly acknowledge Cheung as one of their own. The popular website Gay Station floated a banner with Cheung's picture accompanied by the words "Our Pride," while members of its bulletin board spontaneously launched a campaign that called on its members to post pictures of orchids (Cheung's favourite flower) on a thread that recorded over 20,000 hits and, to this day, remains one of the top ten most viewed topics of all time.[8] Prominent *tongzhi* organizations such as Horizon, Queer Sisters, Rainbow Hong Kong, and Chi Hang Foundation published tributes in major newspapers and followed up with numerous memorial activities. At his death, Cheung had become both a Hong Kong icon and a queer icon. In 2005 cultural critic Natalia Chan published an impassioned article in which she dubbed Cheung an "icon of transgression."[9] The term Chan uses for "icon" in Chinese is literally "sacred figure" *(shengxiang)*, a word choice that nudges the posthumous discourse on Cheung toward a hagiography. While Cheung is without a doubt one of the most iconic figures for the generation in Hong Kong that came of age in the 1980s, a careful look back at his career as well as *tongzhi* communities' response to his public persona reveals that he has not always been considered a figure of "transgression" or the "pride" of the *tongzhi* community. Nor by any stretch of the imagination could his film roles be understood as documentation of "a gay person's brave coming out." Ironically, the well-intentioned rush to memorialize Cheung's life, art, and relation to Hong Kong's *tongzhi* communities in a positive light has instead buried the complexity and ambivalence that in my view contributed *most* to Cheung's iconicity.

It is no accident that so many of those who were moved to write eulogies view Cheung as a symbol of their generation. His life and career reflect the trajectory of a unique historical time-space. From his difficult beginnings in the 1970s to his gradual, eventual rise to mainstream stardom in the 1980s, his abrupt retirement and immigration to Vancouver in late 1989, and his eventual return to Hong Kong in the mid-1990s, Cheung's career follows the vicissitude experienced by many people who belong to the first generation born and bred in Hong Kong and whose identities, unlike those of their refugee parents, are not tied to the Mainland but to Hong Kong. The economic take-off during the 1970s and the historically unique role of Hong Kong as the (then) only gateway into China, created the "golden era" that many mentioned. Cheung's two stunning "exits" also paralleled the city's significant transitional moments. Cheung's sudden and unexpected retirement at the peak of his career in 1989 mirrored the panic experienced by many after the crackdown in Tiananmen in 1989. It was commonplace then to leave successful careers to migrate to countries like Canada and Australia, despite the knowledge that many would not be able to continue the same careers abroad. Cheung's eventual return was also typical of many immigrants, who, after the requisite years of residency to obtain foreign citizenship, promptly returned to Hong Kong, especially during the ecnomic boom after 1992. Finally, Cheung's very public, very tragic death during the darkest hour of the city uncannily completed the parallel. It was as though Cheung's life had encapsulated the culmination and then termination of all the historical factors that had nurtured and made Hong Kong a success.

If it is easy to see why Cheung was so frequently hailed as a Hong Kong icon, it is a more complicated matter to understand his *queer* iconicity. The many eulogies celebrating Cheung's sexual courage seem to give the impression that he was the first openly gay Chinese superstar. Yet, in actuality, Cheung had never publicly identified as gay or acknowledged his lover except as his "very good friend." He declared his bisexuality *once,* and as I will discuss in some detail later, the gesture caused considerable controversy among *tongzhi* audiences at the time. For years, Cheung stipulated that he would never answer questions about his personal life in interviews, often flaring into a temper when asked.[10] Even when speaking with a trusted interviewer, such as during a famous interview with former girlfriend Teresa Mo in 2001, he would cleverly exploit the ungendered pronoun in Cantonese and always speak of his lover in gender-neutral terms. Yet, at the same time, since reappearing from his retirement in the 1990s, he tackled both implicit and explicit gay and transgender roles in high-profile projects and consistently deployed a recognizably queer visual aesthetic on stage and in music videos. Furthermore, as long as the discussion did not veer toward his personal life, Cheung was perfectly willing to discuss queer issues in relation to cinema and music, often in provocative and very intelligent ways. Unlike out gay celebrities in the West like Ellen Degeneres or Rufus Wainwright, who have publicly declared their sexual identities and often ally themselves with gay-related activism and charities, Cheung opted to oscillate between secrecy and openness while maintaining distance from a public gay identity and *tongzhi* causes. In this respect, Cheung more closely resembles a figure like the late Freddie Mercury. In an article written for *AfterElton,* a site that monitors queer visibility in the popular media, Robert Urban looks back at Mercury's life and offers a characterization that would have worked just as well for Cheung: "Mercury did not ally himself to political 'outness,' or to public GLBT causes ... John Marshall of *Gay Times* wrote in January 1992: 'He was a "scene-queen," not afraid to publicly express his gayness but unwilling to analyze or justify his lifestyle ... It was as if Freddie Mercury was saying to the world, "I am what I am. So what?" And that in itself was a statement.'"[11] Coincidentally, Cheung was so fond of the phrase "I am what I am," a line he heard in the film *La Cage Aux Folles,* that he commissioned lyricist Lin Xi to write a song using the phrase as a title. And just as Mercury in his time had incurred the criticism of gay activists, Cheung's deliberate ambivalence has likewise caused rifts within *tongzhi* communities and, as I will show later, provoked both anger and admiration.

By exploring these aspects of his legacy, I want to suggest that Cheung is a queer icon *because* – not in spite – of his ambivalence. Because he was never open or especially proud about gay identity or politics, because of his reluctance to be written into a "coming out" narrative, because of the sustained contradiction between this off-stage reluctance and on-stage/on-screen provocations, Cheung's life and work tell a story that is much less about pride and courage, as the eulogies emphasized, than about negotiation and foreclosure. Thus it is a story that is much more poignantly parallel to the way many queer lives are lived in a cultural space like Hong Kong. More important, it is a story that uncomfortably exposes the limits of the rhetoric of "courage" and "transgression" while challenging the certitude of identity politics. I believe that remembering, rather than forgetting, these contradictions will garner the late, great Leslie Cheung a more enduring and intimate place in our queer memory.

The Uses of Gossip

In "Queering Body and Sexuality: Leslie Cheung's Gender Representation in Hong Kong Popular Music," Natalia Chan proposes to examine "the power and violence of Hong Kong's media" through "Leslie Cheung's lone battle of gender insubordination."[12] Chan charges the media with two forms of attack: their negative coverage of Cheung's suicide and their long-held obsession with exposing Cheung's sexual identity.[13] It is certainly true that for over a decade the tabloid press had maliciously tried to bait and out Cheung, who, in turn, often expressed his impatience and outrage at such efforts. However, there are some problematic implications of the stark opposition that Chan sets up between Cheung's queer transgression and the hostile and powerful media. Chan's account overlooks the contradictory nature of Hong Kong's cultural space, which can be simultaneously hostile to and accepting of sexually adventurous expressions. Furthermore, it gives too much power to the media while eliding both the complex ways Cheung negotiated with the media through the arena of gossip and the form of queer agency that such gossip can unwittingly facilitate.

As I suggest in the book's introduction, the inhospitable climate in Hong Kong for queer activism ironically co-exists with a relatively flexible tolerance, at times even overt public acceptance, of queer cultural expressions. Chan's characterization of the hostile media reveals exactly *half* the picture. For every accusatory article on suicide and every homophobic reference to Cheung's sexuality, there is also a respectful eulogy or an overwhelmingly positive tribute. The numerous articles that I quoted earlier represent only the tip of the iceberg of an enormous volume of published expressions of praise and respect for Cheung.[14] These admiring voices belong as much to Hong Kong culture as the negative references that Chan cites, and it is the co-existence of these apparently opposed voices that lends a distinct character to this contradictory cultural space. Furthermore, Chan's account over-emphasizes Cheung's "uniqueness": "The endless varieties of cross-gender performances Cheung pioneered on stage are unprecedented in Hong Kong's performing arts and popular music. While these performances are legendary, they have also broken a major social taboo."[15] I am in complete agreement with Chan's assessment of Cheung's innovations and especially appreciate her detailed analysis of Cheung's visual aesthetics both in this article and elsewhere. However, I am less convinced by her portrayal of Cheung as a "lone" performer engaged an "unprecedented" battle against gender conventions. Cheung's brilliance had in fact been nurtured through a far more widespread cultural tradition of gender experimentation that has both historical precedence and contemporary manifestations. In her book *City on the Edge of Time*, Chan herself links Cheung's cross-gender performance to that of Catonese opera diva Yam Kim-Fai,[16] whom Cheung openly claimed as an idol and influence.[17] Yam's cross-gender embodiment was completely accepted in the mainstream, as evidenced by her thirty-year reign as the most popular Cantonese opera performer in Hong Kong and abroad.[18] Nor was Yam a lone exception. One of Yam's most famous disciples, Chan Bo-Chu, who did not pursue opera but instead a glittering screen career with legions of female fans, had also cross-dressed on screen to great acclaim.[19] These are arguably not isolated instances but examples of a long-held cultural fascination with cross-gender performances, which Stanley Kwan provocatively claims and documents in his film *Yin ± Yang: Gender in Chinese Cinema*.[20] There are also influences from abroad. Throughout the 1970s and 1980s androgynous rock icons like Britain's David Bowie, Freddie Mercury, and Boy George, as well as Japan's Kenji Sawada, were extrememly popular in Hong Kong, thus mainstreaming another form of gender-bending performance that is different from the tradition found in Cantonese opera and Chinese cinema. Furthermore, several of Cheung's musical contemporaries in the Canto-pop scene have experimented with queer aesthetics to great acclaim. Most notably, Roman Tam introduced a visibly camp and highly sexualized aesthetic in the late 1970s and early 1980s, effectively paving the way for Cheung's later elaborations. Cheung's close friend and sometime musical and screen partner Anita Mui was also celebrated for her gender versatility both in cinematic roles and in her stage performances.[21] Having arrived on the music scene slightly later than Cheung, Anthony Wong is known for his audacious stage performances and an impressive volume of sexually provocative lyrics, both in his work with the group Tat Ming Pair and in his later solo career.[22] Fittingly, Wong collaborated with Cheung on what would be the last album to come out during Cheung's lifetime, released with an advertising campaign that blatantly played with a homoerotic undertone and an album cover that payed homage to the gender experimentation underlying both artists' careers.[23] Obviously, Cheung brought his own originality to his performances, but far from waging a "lone battle," his "gender insubordination" was part of a local/global trend whereby artists' gender experimentation on stage could be widely accepted in the mainstream, while their sexual preference off stage remained ambivalent. In fact, many of the figures I mentioned above negotiated their relation to queer identities through a "glass closet" – that is, as open secrets. Yam's relationship with her on- and off-screen partner, Bak Suet-Sin, remains unacknowledged to this day, but the couple has inspired a big queer following.[24] Chan Bo-Chu, likewise, has provoked rumours that circulate about an "intimate female friend" but has nervously dismissed them as "gossip."[25] The late Roman Tam responded to rumours about his homosexuality by never affirming nor denying them.[26] Anthony Wong, who is still frequently baited by the media, insists that he "has no problems with homosexuality" but maintains that he will never answer direct questions about his sexual identity.[27]

Even though many LGBT activists would prefer these public figures to be "out and proud," and although some may even regard public outness to be a moral obligation, there are also others who view such celebrity closets more positively. In her analysis of lesbian representations in Hollywood, Clare Whatling suggests that stars' "coming out" may in fact ruin something for queer spectators: "What we lose by the imperative to revelation [of sexual identity] is the sense of the shared secret, the 'in' joke, of having access to a cultural knowledge that most straight-identified subjects are blind to, a function of the closet which I would argue is a condition both of our oppression and of our 'liberation.'"[28] For Whatling, the conduit through which such shared knowledge may be transmitted is the overlooked and devalued site of gossip, which she theorizes as a form of "subcultural communication."[29] John Champagne and Elayne Tobin also suggest that gossip is useful as a communal form of knowledge: "Gossip can function to bind a group around particular moral values, ethics, sites of affective intensity. Gossip binds even those whom it might seem to exclude, since some form of intimacy (not to say love) must be intact in order to make gossip valuable in the first place; we don't gossip about strangers or intimately relay anecdotes that have no ethical, moral, or aesthetic function."[30] Champagne and Tobin trace the political usefulness of gossip in rendering visible the process of commodification around institutionalized identities in the academy. They understand gossip as a community-based form of self-criticism that may be mobilized for a queer contestation of identity politics. Gavin Butt's study of the post-Second World War New York art world shows that gossip operates as a mode of communication through which queer meanings are disseminated and should thus be treated as a legitimate form of art history.[31] Unlike in the academy or in the art world, gossip is not as habitually masked or dismissed in mass culture. Rather, it is so blatantly present that it does not always solicit serious attention. I am interested in the way gossip can function through the mass media as a site for self-*making,* both for the celebrity whom the media is bent on "outing" and for the queer spectators "in the know," who must read between the lines to wrest queer meanings out of ambivalence.

One of the most interesting ways that Cheung used gossip was through public discussion of his film roles as a response to gossip about his private life. The previously quoted characterization of Cheung's roles as a "documentation of a gay person's coming out" is a gross simplification of this process of negotiation. Cheung's roles were by no means simple reflections of his "real" sexual identity. Rather, they provided a vehicle through which Cheung could freely discourse on queerness without ever outing himself. Such a tactic does not actually quell gossip; in fact, it intensifies and sustains it in a way that definitively coming out would not. At the same time, the proliferation of gossip can open up complex avenues of identification and contestation.

Some of the earliest rumours surrounding Cheung's sexuality circulated in the early 1990s, when he was still based in Vancouver and had taken the role of Beijing Opera diva Cheng Dieyi in *Farewell My Concubine* (Chen Kaige, 1993). A male-born performer specializing in female roles, whose feminine identification is sustained off-stage and whose primary emotional and sexual attachment is to another man, the character of Cheng Dieyi can be interpreted as gay or transgender in current queer vocabularies without exactly fitting the narratives of either. When Cheung was asked by an interviewer (in a veiled attempt to link the role to Cheung's own life) how he was able to perform the role with such "authenticity," Cheung responded in this way:

I did a lot of research of course. At first I thought a cross-dressing *dan* performer only cross-dresses on stage, and is no different from us off-stage. But when I was in Beijing, I encountered many *dan* performers and I talked to them many times. I discovered that they already regard themselves as real women, whether mentally, or in the details of everyday life. They believe themselves to be women one hundred percent, so on stage, they can be so authentic, like reincarnated goddesses! After I did exhaustive research, I also realized they were not necessarily born to identify with, or even truly believe they were women. Many of them joined the troupes as children and after many years of extremely disciplined training, they acquired incredible stage skills, and their mentality had become feminine.[32]

Cheung thus deflected the question away from himself and focused squarely on what he had learned from "research" as well as from real-life interactions. He left his response to the question of whether these performers' transgender identification is born or bred somewhat open but nevertheless expressed admiration for them (they are "reincarnated goddesses!"). Cheung would later claim Cheng Dieyi as his favourite role but would also highlight his disappointment that the queer relationship is treated in the film as merely a subtext.[33] Cheung also took issue with his co-star Zhang Fengyi, whose quoted reaction to Cheung's femininity betrays a homophobic unease: "Horrible! He's playing a *dan,* and acts just like a woman. At first I was not accustomed to him touching me, which made my skin crawl ... I prefer Leslie in real life, when he's wearing men's clothes!"[34] In the press coverage not a single word appeared about either Cheung's own sexual identity or the personal dynamics between actors on set. Yet, Cheung's detailed, almost scholarly, discussion of his role serves as a dignified rebuff to both the press's prurient interest and his co-star's unease. Furthermore, instead of *denying* the rumours that linked his role to his own life (which many actors portraying queer roles often choose to do), he insistently showed (and implicitly demanded) respect for the queer artist that he was portraying. While Cheung chose not to answer the underlying question "Are you, or are you not ...," he manipulated the site of gossip for an articulation of queer respect. Henceforth, Cheung would become increasingly sophisticated and provocative in his handling of such subtexts.

Made in the same year as *Farewell My Concubine*, Clifton Ko's *All's Well That Ends Well* (Clifton Ko, 1992) has remained one of Cheung's least discussed films, most likely because it is perceived as a mainstream comedy made to capitalize on the holiday market of the Chinese New Year and thus as a film without the artistic merit of most of the other films in Cheung's oeuvre. Yet, for queer audiences, the comedy has significant implications that are once again borne out by Cheung's clever discussion of his role. *All's Well That Ends Well* tells the story of a family with three sons, each of whom has an idiosyncratic personality. Cheung plays the youngest son, a bitchy and effeminate man whose rival is his aunt, a cheerful and butch woman roughly the same age as her nephew, played to great comedic effect by Teresa Mo. Eventually, the two rivals become romantically involved, and through a freak accident both become "transformed" into their "opposite" (i.e., socially normative) gender role. Even though the ending "restores" Cheung's and Mo's characters to their putatively "proper" gender roles, they perform these gendered traits with such comedic exaggeration that they appear no more "natural" (in fact, quite a lot more grotesque) than their initial cross-gender embodiments. In this way, the film denaturalizes gender roles more critically than did any other Hong Kong films at the time. Cheung's character in the film embodies a male femininity that is not uncommon among queer men. In interviews, Cheung drew attention to this dimension of his character:

> When I took the role, I knew I had to play a sissy. I was not concerned with my image, because after all this is only acting. Chow Yun-Fat's performance [of a sissy] in *The Eighth Happiness [Baxing baoxi]* is more staged and exaggerated, and the director initially asked me to perform in that way. But I feel that in real life sissy men don't act like this, and I know lots of them! They should convey their femininity in an unconscious way and the director accepted my interpretation. Even though this is a comedy, I tried to make this role very human.[35]

The cinematic tradition of ridiculing effeminate men has been well documented both in Hollywood and in Chinese cinema.[36] Dennis Lin has also written eloquently about anti-sissy ideologies in Taiwan's gay male culture and about the virtual reclaiming of gay sissiness, in response, online.[37] From the above interview, it is clear that Cheung realized he was *expected* to play his character in this shallow, exaggerated, and derogatory fashion. He contrasted this image with his own experiential knowledge of sissy men: he knew "lots of them," which was also an acknowledgment of his ties to the queer community without directly implicating himself. In the film, Cheung performs his role as a by turns bitchy, charming, funny, and very likable effeminate man, one whom the straight audience had rarely seen on screen but whom a queer audience would have had no trouble recognizing in themselves, their lovers, or their friends.

Cheung's role in *He's a Woman She's a Man* (Peter Chan, 1994) exemplifies his most complex negotiation to that point with the media. He plays, of all things, a homophobic straight man who fears that he may be in love with an effeminate man (who "safely" turns out, in the end, to be a woman). By this time, the gossip surrounding Cheung's sexual identity had become very intense. Headlines such as "Cheung in Relationship with Mystery Person"[38] and "Is Cheung's Companion a He or a She?"[39] appeared frequently, at the same time that the tabloid press was feverishly trying to "expose" Cheung's partner. Playing this role amid such rumours was like playing with fire: a paradoxical gesture to stay in the closet while flaunting it. Cheung coyly exploited the explosive contradiction of the situation. When asked in an interview at the time whether he accepted homosexuality, Cheung answered: "Absolutely. I have lots of gay friends. (Laughs.)"[40] When it comes to the film, Cheung is again cleverly provocative. Cheung's character has a colleague nicknamed Auntie, played by Eric Tsang as a stereotypically effeminate gay man. Asked about the film, Cheung responded in this way: "I don't really agree with the ending of the film. I feel that the treatment of gay roles in Hong Kong cinema is too comedic, too hideous. I don't feel it has to be this way. Even though Eric did a great job in the film, he is not suited to the role ... The best thing would be for *me* to play both characters, as identical twins who go to two extremes, with one becoming the shadow of the other."[41] Cheung's suggestion would indeed have given the film the critical edge that it lacks. It would also have turned the twin roles into a self-parody of Cheung's own ambivalent response to the frenzied media rumours by presenting Cheung as both the out gay man and the questioning homophobe fighting to stay in the closet.

By the time Cheung made *Happy Together* (Wong Kar-Wai, 1997), the first Hong Kong film to include an explicit and extended sex scene between men, he had reached the status of queer icon without ever having come out. In Audrey Yue's critique of the film, where she faults its containment of gay excess, she nonetheless identifies Cheung as the film's "queer interface."[42] For Yue, what is queer about the film lies less in its content (which she argues is constrained by a "straight morality") than in the extra-diegetic spaces in which Cheung performs a "self-parody" and thus a critical reinvention of the film's ultimately heteronormative narrative. Cheung made very few extended commentaries on *Happy Together,* as compared to his earlier films, partly because he was on a concert tour and did not participate actively in the film's promotion. However, his relative silence (and nonintervention into *others'* comments) also enabled the proliferation of gossip. The primary source that Yue uses to illustrate Cheung's self-parodic performance is the unauthorized journal published by Christopher Doyle, the film's director of photography. Doyle's journal includes photographs of Cheung crossing-dressing as a "weekend transvestite," an example Yue cites as a "hyperbole" that mocks the "sad young gay man" stereotype perpetuated in the film.[43] Furthermore, in tabloid-gossip style, Doyle describes Cheung's bitchy reaction to fellow actor Tony Leung's anxiety over filming the sex scene[44] and jokingly claims that a gay-inclined member of the crew offered to help Cheung undo his fly when the actor's hand was immobilized by a cast he had to wear on set.[45] Ironically, like Cheung's comments on his other films, his *silence* regarding Doyle's gossip about *Happy Together* also enabled a subtext to run parallel to the film text, one that, as Yue shows, has become far queerer than the film itself.

Bisexuality and the Art of Cultural Repudiation

Notwithstanding his provocative uses of gossip and wilful maintenance of the closet, Cheung explicitly discussed his sexual identity on record *once*, in an article by Richard Corliss that appeared in the English-language publication *Time Asia:* "[Cheung] also knows that it leads audiences to the suspicion or compliment that he is gay, though he has not publicly declared his sexual orientation. 'It's more appropriate to say I'm bisexual,' Cheung notes. 'I've had girlfriends. When I was 22 or so, I asked my girlfriend Teresa Mo (his frequent co-star in TVB serials of the time) to marry me.' As a guest on Mo's cable TV show last month, Cheung bantered; 'If you'd agreed to marry me then, my life might have changed totally.'"[46] Not surprisingly, the article caused quite a stir within *tongzhi* circles. Right after this issue of the magazine came out, *Gay Station* conducted an Internet poll that asked participants to select one out of four set responses to Cheung's disclosure. The overwhelming response chosen was: "When has Leslie ever liked women?" The poll has long gone offline, but the derisive resentment implicit in this response can still be glimpsed in the exchanges that took place between 8 and 13 May 2000 on *Tongzhi2000*, a listserve for discussion of *tongzhi* issues in Hong Kong, to which many prominent local activists are subscribers.[47] The discussion begins when a member posts the quotation above on the listserve, with snide annotated comments that indicate surprise at what the poster reads as Cheung's simultaneous frankness and reticence (#1175). The post elicits an immediate response from another member, who cynically objects to Cheung's attempt "to use the [bi] identity as an advantage" and as a way to placate his straight fan base. The author of the post feels this phenomenon is "all too common" in show business (#1181). Another member claims not to believe that Cheung is bisexual (#1183). This ignites a heated discussion over the meaning of bisexuality and over the parameters of sexual identity in general. One member questions why there is a demand for bisexuality to be "quantified" (#1192), while another wonders why "coming out as gay" is considered a morally superior position (#1198). In response, one member lectures others on the responsibility of public figures, concluding with a bitter accusation that there is now a trend to "not put a label on anything" (#1201). So far, the discussion has been conducted in English, then one member confesses that he or she writes better in Chinese, which prompts others to start writing in Chinese. One post suggests that Cheung's "unexpected" admission can become a way to challenge expectations of the either-or choice of gay versus straight while throwing some light on the often unlivable condition of being bisexual (#1208). Finally, a post expresses appreciation for the turn to Chinese and reflects on the fact that *tongzhi* now seems to mean only gay or lesbian, that the original promise of the term to reach out to other sexual minorities seems to have been ·abandoned, but adds that "there may be discussion in English that I have missed" (#1212). Parts of this online conversation are later documented by the author and bisexual activist Anson Mak in an article she wrote for the *Hong Kong Economic Daily*.[48] Mak quite rightly observes that the discussion in the end is "both about Leslie Cheung, and *not* about Leslie Cheung," for it is a moot point whether Cheung is "*really*" bisexual (the ostensible subject under discussion); instead, the significance of the discussion lies in its reflection of local *tongzhi* communities' complex attitudes toward a range of issues: what constitutes sexual identity, the morality of coming out, the issue of selling out, the limits of *tongzhi* politics based only on gay and lesbian experience, the unlivable conditions of certain identities, and the issue of language (implicitly also an issue of class) in *tongzhi* communities. Cheung's provocative or disappointing (depending on one's view) pronouncement of bisexuality thus revealed far less about Cheung than about the investment that *tongzhi* audiences have in his queer iconicity. In her study of female icons, Anna Camilleri describes the relation between cultural icons and their audiences in this way: "Some say that icons are born, but it is public recognition – a devoted following, an audience, a 'market' – that creates them. Born of our imagination, desires, and fears, they are emblematic of our cultural climate on every front – social, political, spiritual, and economic."[49] Cheung's complex public persona is indeed emblematic of *tongzhi* audiences' many layers of imaginations, desires, and fears. As some of the initial hostile posts imply, Cheung appeared to be not so much declaring a bisexual identity as repudiating a gay identity (while remaining reluctant to repudiate heterosexuality altogether).

What is the relation between sexual identity and repudiation? In Claire Hemmings's reflections on bisexuality, particularly the subject position of the bisexual femme, she distinguishes between two kinds of repudiation – sexual and cultural – that, in her view, are constitutive of gay and lesbian identities. For Hemmings, gay and lesbian identities are predicated on a repudiation of opposite-sex object choice as well as of heterosexual culture. Some of the derisive responses to Cheung's bisexual identification – expressed, for instance, in the poll result "when has he ever liked women?" – reveal an unease with Cheung's reluctance to repudiate women as a sexual-object choice, which for many is the precondition of gay subjectivity. The question that Hemmings asks in her study, which is indeed a question that informs much of bisexual theorizing, is whether "non-heterosexuality [can] be read through something other than same-sex desire."[50] In other words, can a cultural repudiation of heterosexuality *not* rely on a sexual repudiation of opposite-sex object choice? Hemmings uses the example of femme desire for transgendered/transsexual masculinity as an example of a cultural repudiation of heterosexuality that does not depend on sexual-object choice. In fact, for Hemmings, the femme/FTM couple illustrates how "the relationship is not heterosexual *even though* it is between a man and a woman, rather than how this relationship is not heterosexual because it is *not* (in terms of sexed object choice) between a man and a woman."[51] For bisexual femme/FTM couples, it is precisely their closeness to, rather than difference from, heterosexuality that constitutes their nonheterosexuality. Hemmings elaborates on this insight in a later piece in which she posits a model of queerness that is not predicated either on its difference or on its parodic similarity to heterosexuality: "Rather than denying the often *highly unparodic* closeness to heterosexuality that all gender and sexual performances reproduce, it would seem more generous and indeed politically productive to pay attention to the ironies such closeness produces within sexual and gendered narratives over time."[52] Indeed, the negative responses to Cheung's not quite "coming out" reveal an anxiety about a queer icon who could not be absolutely distinguished from a heterosexual. What seems threatening to some *tongzhi* audiences (and what Cheung often seemed particularly gleeful about), is precisely his *unparodic closeness* to heterosexuality, as seen in his gender-switching performance in *All's Well That Ends Well*, where he performs normative and queer gender roles equally and indistinguishably well, and in his imaginary scenario for *He's a Woman She's a Man*, in which he would play *both* the visibly gay man and the homophobic straight (or closeted) man, thus showing he could inhabit both roles equally convincingly. Such tactics of sustaining a closeness to, rather than categorical difference from, heterosexual culture are consonant with Cheung's deliberate play of ambivalence throughout his career. It is as though he was saying: "I am, or I am not ... either way you cannot tell." In Hemmings's terms, this too can be understood as a cultural repudiation of heterosexuality, the irony of which provides more, not less, ground for queer negotiation. As evidenced by some of the later, more thoughtful responses to the *Time Asia* article, Cheung's provocations were indeed politically useful in challenging assumptions about how straightness and queerness are understood, the (often arbitrary) criteria on which the demarcation is made, and the seeming stability and certainty of gay and lesbian, as well as heterosexual, identities. Had Cheung actually "come out" in the article as gay, as many seemed to have wished, he would not have provoked any of these debates at all but reinforced the absolute distinction between these two (and *only* these two) sexual categories. In retrospect, it is precisely the maddening ambivalence of Cheung's declaration, and the myriad questions it raised, that rendered the moment queerly iconic.

Kinship Trouble

Besides Cheung's declaration in the *Time Asia* article, there was an earlier, equally iconic moment at the beginning of 1997, when Cheung publicly delivered what I will call a performance of the closet. In retrospect, the moment seems to foreshadow the public mourning rites for Cheung, where accommodation of queer kinship within the family structure exposed the limits of what is relationally thinkable and representable in its terms.

At the end of the "Across 1997" concert series in Hong Kong, which sold out all twenty-four shows to a total audience of over three hundred thousand, Cheung, with an uncharacteristically nervous expression on his face, declared that he would like to dedicate the last song to the two most important people in his life. The first person Cheung mentioned was his mother, whom he affectionately addressed among the audience. "The second person," Cheung continued, still addressing his mother, "is someone who has stood by me for more than ten years, who selflessly supported me when I was down and out, even lent me several months of his salary so I could survive. Of course you know who it is I'm talking about: it's my very good friend, your 'bond-son' *(qizai)* Mr. Tong." There was a split second of stunned silence, as though the audience members had not quite grasped what they had heard. Then the auditorium exploded in an amalgam of screams, cheers, and applause as Cheung launched into an old-standard love song.[53]

This was the first time Cheung mentioned his rumoured lover, Daffy Tong, in public, after close to a decade's speculation in the tabloid press. Yet, Cheung neither proclaimed a sexual identity nor acknowledged a spousal relation with his "very good friend" in this curiously structured statement. Cheung's reference to Tong as "*Mr.* Tong" actually mimicked the gossip columns, which had been referring to Cheung's "mystery lover" as "Mr. Tong," either as a way of signifying scandal (as in the use of "Mr. X" for thinly veiled references to public figures caught in compromising acts) or because the press was not yet able to completely identify Tong at the time. Cheung's faux formality in this term of address had the curious effect of maintaining the closet (denying intimacy) while parodying tabloid innuendo (thus suggesting that "Mr. Tong" was much more intimately linked to him despite the formal address). Furthermore, Cheung declared his relation to Tong through his *mother*, identifying him as her "bond-son." The Cantonese term *qizai* refers to the tradition of forming "bond-relations" whereby nonkin relations are "adopted" into the family as one of its own. Entering into "bond-relations" is a very common practice in contemporary Hong Kong and does not necessarily carry any queer connotations. However, in the particularly charged context of the discursive history surrounding Cheung, it seems unlikely that he would be unaware of the historical association between the institution of "bond-brotherhood" *(qixiongdi)* and homoerotic relations. The prevalence of sexual relations between men (especially in southern Chinese culture) throughout recorded history has been well documented.[54] The institution of "bond-brotherhood" as a means to accommodate homosexual relations within the familial structure in the Fujian areas is particularly well known. The most often quoted account appears in the work of Ming Dynasty author Shen Defu: "The people of Fujian are extremely fond of male beauty. Whether rich or poor, handsome of ugly, they all find a companion of similar status. Between the two, the elder one is called 'bond-elder brother' *(qixiong)* and the younger one 'bond-younger brother' *(qidi)*. When the elder brother goes to the home of the younger, the younger's parents take care of him like a son-in-law."[55] In fact, the term for "bond-younger brother" *(qidi)* is still widely used as a nasty term of insult in macho Triad culture, precisely because of its lingering homosexual connotations. By addressing Tong as his "mother's bond-son," Cheung was indirectly acknowledging the younger Tong as his *qidi*. While tortuously indirect, it was still a rather audacious gesture. Not only had Cheung insistently embedded queer kinship within the familial structure, but he had routed the queer relation through his mother while reclaiming injurious and insulting terms (by ironically adopting the tabloid address of "Mr. Tong" and by implicitly acknowledging Tong as his *qidi*).

What may be the significance of Cheung's rather convoluted way of thanking his lover in public? First, it can be understood as a dramatic deconstruction of the identity politics of "coming out." In one of her many discussions of queer performativity, Eve Sedgwick calls attention to the notion's two, related but distinct, theoretical trajectories: the dramatic and the non-referential.[56] The first, derived from theatrical discourse, refers to what is staged, acted out, performed. The second, from speech-act theory, calls attention to the linguistic function of an utterance that enacts meanings not through referentiality but through the very voicing of the utterance. It is not difficult to conceptualize the notion of "coming out" as a performative utterance in the linguistic sense: there is after all no magical threshold across which one is suddenly and fully disclosed as one truly is. "Coming out" does not refer to an actual state of emerging from secrecy into the fullness of one's identity. Rather, one is *out* the moment one *says* one is.[57] The conundrum of "being out" is that the utterance needs to be reiterated, over and over. No one is "out" once and for all. At the concert, Cheung was theatrically performing the closet through a performative utterance of what amounts to: "I'm in the closet; I'm not out." The statement, however, functioned as a paradox, much like "I am lying" or "this sentence is false": the very utterance of "I am in the closet" would appear to belie its meaning. At the same time, the paradox served the critical function of exposing the artificiality of the opposition between being closeted and being out. Cheung had accomplished the paradoxical feat of coming out *as* a closeted queer. Like his bisexual declaration, Cheung's performance cunningly rendered the inside/outside of the discursive closet utterly indistinguishable.

What is also remarkable about Cheung's statement at the concert is the questions it raised for the two most commonly invoked trajectories for framing queer relations: in the terms of gay marriage and in the terms of an alternative community radically separate from the blood family. While the two trajectories appear to be mutually opposed, they may in fact reflect two sides of the same coin: precisely because queer relationality is thought to be radically separate from the blood family, it becomes imaginable only as an absolutely distinct and parallel structure (of which gay marriage is one version and alternative community another). Cheung's tactic shows ways that queer kinship may be thought of in terms other than that of marriage and spousal relations and may be sustained *through,* rather than forever exiled from, the blood family.

Following the recent legalization of gay marriage in the Netherlands, Belgium, Spain, and Canada, the marriage issue has received intense global attention. The debates have been predominantly framed as either-or positions, assuming an automatic equation between queer interest and support for gay marriage. What has been largely eclipsed in mainstream debates is the complex discussion *within* queer communities, where objections to marriage are rooted in a critique of its normalizing effect and of its nonrecognition of sexual practices and affective alliances that fall outside of the parameters of monogamous spousal relations.[58] Judith Butler characterizes the new sexual hierarchy emerging in the wake of the gay marriage debates in this way: the stable gay couple who would marry if only they could is *"not yet* legitimate," whereas relations irreducible to marriage become "the irrecoverable and irreversible past of legitimacy: *the never will be, the never was.*"[59] For Butler, state regulation of social life rarely coincides with existent social arrangements: "Its regulations do not always seek to order what exists, but to figure social life in certain imaginary ways. The incommensurability between state stipulation and existing social life means that this gap must be covered over for the state to continue to exercise its authority and to exemplify the kind of coherence which it is expected to confer on its subjects."[60] The struggle for gay marriage imposes parameters for figuring queer lives and, as a result, renders what falls outside of these parameters not only illegitimate but also *never* (to be) legitimate. By contrast, Cheung invoked a much older form of relational practice whereby kinship terms within the family are appropriated to accommodate affective and sexual relations not intelligible within the familial and social order. Sociologist Chou Wah-Shan has observed this commonly practised process of familial integration among Hong Kong *tongzhi*s:

Coming home can be explicated as a negotiative process of bringing one's sexuality into the family-kin network, not by singling out same-sex eroticism as a site for conceptual discussion but by constructing a same-sex relationship in terms of family-kin categories. The *tongzhi* would establish such a relationship with his/her parents by mundane practices like shopping or playing mahjong together. Dinner has often been quoted as a crucial cultural marker for breaking the insider-outsider distinction. The *tongzhi* may then use quasi-kin categories like half sisters/brothers to integrate her/his partner into the family.[61]

The "quasi-kin categories" of nonblood "brothers and sisters" bestow a certain fluidity and openness on the familial structure, whereby queer relations may be accommodated from within rather than reinvented from without as a parallel structure (such as gay marriage). Drawing from recent studies in anthropology, Butler proposes an understanding of kinship as "a set of potentially unpredictable and contested practices of self-definition that are not reducible to a primary and culture-founding heterosexuality" but rather constitute "a kind of doing ... an enacted practice," the repetition of which may transform and displace dominant arrangements.[62] Understood in this way, Cheung's manoeuvre in the concert should prompt us to ask *not* how gay marriage could render his putatively "closeted" relations legitimate but how such creative kinship arrangements may facilitate aspects of queer lives that are *not* reducible to marriage and spousal relations.

In what may sadly be thought of as the "sequel" to Cheung's address at the concert, the published statements of mourning for Cheung after his death put out by Tong and Cheung's siblings continue this practice of sustaining queer kinship through the blood family, even as the effort confounds the familial order and exposes what is ultimately unrepresentable within its terms. Following the death of a family member, the usual custom is to first publish a statement of mourning, followed by an announcement of the funeral arrangement, including a full list of family members, each slotted in the proper order according to his or her respective relation to the deceased. Funeral rites, and the announcement in particular, are notoriously difficult to negotiate when it comes to relations that do not occupy a "properly" articulated place within the family, including children born outside of marriage, divorced spouses, and unmarried and same-sex lovers. The film *A Queer Story* (Shu Kei, 1998) dramatizes these difficulties in a funeral scene, where the gay lover of the deceased is barred from the funeral rites because he has no status within the family. Even the florist preparing his floral arrangement for the deceased refuses to write the couplet that he chooses because it is deemed appropriate only for a spouse. There was no such melodrama during the funeral preparations for Cheung. Instead, quiet efforts and care to respect queer kinship within the family were evident. Two statements of mourning were released immediately following Cheung's death, each quoting a famous line from his songs. The first came from Cheung's siblings and the second from Tong, who signed off as the deceased's "truest friend" *(zhiyou).*[63] Later, the funeral announcement was put out by Cheung's eldest sister, in the capacity of the closest relation to the deceased in the absence of spouse, parents, or children. The announcement thus opens with, "My brother Mr. Leslie Cheung passed away on April 1, 2003." However, in the place usually reserved for the closest surviving member, who would also have been the one to put out the announcement (in this case, the sister), is Tong's name, in the capacity of the deceased's "beloved" *(zhiai),* followed by all of Cheung's surviving siblings and their children.[64] "Beloved" is of course not a kinship category. Yet, the quasi-kinship term of *qidi,* which Cheung invoked for Tong at the concert, would have placed him *behind* all of the blood siblings on the announcement, as bond-siblings are considered more distant than blood siblings within the family hierarchy. At the same time, the self-invented fictive "kinship" term of "beloved" contradicts that of "brother," which is the sanctioned status used to *initiate* the announcement. The gap between "brother" and "beloved" thus marks the confounding space within the family where queer kinship cannot become entirely intelligible. It also signals, rather movingly, the *care* that was taken to respect and honour a relation that, although unrepresentable, had clearly been lived and embraced, even when taking such care meant publicly straining the parameters of the familial order to a point of incoherence and contradiction.

In her analysis of the ending of the film *The River* (Tsai Ming-liang, 1997), in which a father and son, unbeknown to each other, meet as strangers in a sauna and end up having sex in the dark, Rey Chow approaches the scene not as an instance of "incest" but, more radically, as a rearrangement of affective alliances that have been fragmented or destroyed in a collapsing traditional kinship system. Chow reads the encounter in anthropological language: the sauna is a "transcultural" space between two worlds: on the one hand, an "extinct" culture where the father-son nomenclatures have been eroded and rendered meaningless and, on the other hand, a sexual economy of anonymous cruising where completely different customs, conventions, and relational categories are in operation. What would have been "incest" in the former world becomes an as-yet-unnameable form of relationality in the latter.[65] A similar, albeit quite a lot less dramatic, metaphor of kinship trouble may be glimpsed in the funeral announcement for Cheung. The "incestuous" conflation between "brother" and "beloved" signals the site where a faltering (although not quite extinct) kinship system is being stretched and strained to accommodate what is not yet thinkable within its terms. At the same time, the very enactment of this accommodation transforms the parameters of the familial order, thereby enabling new, half-formed, and not-yet-coherent relational categories (like beloved/*zhiai*) to flourish.

I Am What I Am

I would like to end this chapter with some thoughts on Cheung's own exit from the stage: his last concert performance during the "Passion" tour in 2000. Barefoot and dressed in a white bathrobe, Cheung came on stage to sing a surprise encore for his rapt audience. After a simple preface ("The most important thing ... is to love oneself"), Cheung launched into the Mandarin version of "I Am What I Am," a song titled after a line from *La Cage Aux Folles,* which Cheung had commissioned lyricist Lin Xi to write.[66] Even though Lin considers this commission a "courageous act of disclosure,"[67] the song as well as Cheung's final performance of it remain consistent with Cheung's habitual staging of ambivalence and paradox:

> I am what I am / I will always love myself this way
> Happiness is / There is more than one way to be happy
> Fortunately / Everyone is the creator's glory
> No need to hide / I live the way I want to live
> No need for makeup / I stand under the brightest light
> I am what I am / A differently coloured light
> Free to become the strongest bubble
> I like what I am / Let roses blossom into a kind of consequence
> Naked and blooming in the lonely desert
> Happiness is / Living in a glass house
> Disclosing to the world / What it means to have nothing to hide[68]

The song is replete with metaphors of disclosure ("no need to hide," "no need for makeup," "under the brightest light," "living in a glass house"), transparency ("bubble," "nakedness"), and open space ("the lonely desert"). At the same time, it refrains from naming *what* is being disclosed in the open. All the metaphors in fact end up disclosing "nothing" – that is, what is being disclosed *is* transparency itself. Nothing is being hidden, and thus *nothing* is disclosed. It is also significant that Cheung performed only the Mandarin version of the song. The lyrics of the Cantonese version are thematically similar but include one metaphor linked explicitly to gay politics: "I am what I am / Out of ten there is only one of me."[69] "One out of ten" echoes the famous Kinsey statistic that one person out of ten is gay, while "Ten Percent" is the name of a prominent *tongzhi* organization in Hong Kong. By choosing to perform the song in Mandarin, Cheung eschewed this obvious metaphor and at the same time blocked linguistic immediacy between himself and the Cantonese-speaking audience in Hong Kong. Why would Cheung, in performing a song about disclosure, take such care to *foreclose* what the song seems to advocate?

To understand Cheung's performance, it is useful to turn to Fran Martin's discussion of a prominent trope in Taiwan's *tongzhi* politics: the mask. Originating from the homophobic discourse that characterizes *tongzhi* lives as duplicitous, the trope of the mask was appropriated by Taiwanese *tongzhi* activists in 1997, when a large contingent of *tongzhis* all put on masks and collectively marched in public. Martin's analysis of the effect of the mask is very similar to my interpretation of many of Cheung's tactics: "The voluntary donning of masks by Taiwan's gay men and lesbians in public seems more than anything else ... to dramatize the very workings of *tongzhi* mask, electrifying the boundary between showing and not showing the secret of the individual's *tongzhi* identity, because the mask, as the sign used to disclose that identity, is at the same time the paradigmatic sign of its continuing concealment."[70] The ambivalence of such a paradoxical gesture is not, however, without detractors. One of the debates ignited by this tactic revolves around reticence *(hanxu)*. In their critique of Chou Wah-Shan's work, which regards the creative but unspoken accommodation of alternative sexual practices within the familial order as a form of "silent tolerance" and an alternative to "coming out," Liu Jenpeng and Ding Naifei align these painstakingly convoluted tactics with the aesthetic-ethical values of an elite classical tradition whereby the "virtue" of reticence produces discipline through shame.[71] Martin's own analysis refrains from siding exclusively with either interpretation; she understands the mask to represent not *merely* an expression of reticence but also a complex and creative response: the mask provides a way to articulate new sexual subjectivities without giving in to the demand that these subjectivities be made immediately transparent and consumable. Reformulating a statement that queer critic Chang Hsiao-Hung borrows from Judith Butler, Martin personifies the challenge of the mask in this way: "Before, you did not know whether 'I' am, but now you do not know what that means."[72] Akin to the spirit of the mask, Cheung's various performances of the closet – from the uses of gossip, the bisexual declaration, and the appropriation of kinship terms to his final, staged disclosure of "nothing" – also enacted a refusal to be stripped, consumed, and identified as this or that kind of queer subject. At the same time, in his habitually paradoxical fashion, Cheung performed these acts of reticence loudly, flamboyantly, and publicly – in short, with very little reticence indeed. Further reworking Martin's paraphrase, I understand Cheung's tactic to be saying: I am what I am, but you do not know what that means.

Elaborating on the Foucauldian insight that modern power operates not through repression but through the proliferation of sexual knowledge and the institutional incitement to put such knowledge into discourse, Eve Sedgwick has cautioned against forgoing too readily the category of "ignorance" as something only to be scorned, feared, or fought while appealing to "knowledge" as necessarily a politically redemptive force.[73] Cheung's acts of ambivalence throughout the later part of his life and career incite us to recognize a plethora of ignorances about what we do not or cannot yet know of gender embodiment, sexual identity, queer kinship, and most of all, who and what he was. It thus seems fitting to honour his life's work not with what we think we know of him but precisely with what he so persistently compelled us to *not* know about him. Only in such "ignorance" would Cheung be remembered most fully, most affectionately, and at his queerest.

5
Do It Yourself

Preamble: Speechless

In 2004 the independent film and video organization InD Blue asked seven young filmmakers to each produce a fifteen-minute short on queer themes. The project became *Here Comes the Rainbow.1: 2 of a Kind*, a loosely linked series of shorts that premiered at the 2004 Hong Kong Gay and Lesbian Film and Video Festival. The last video in the series, a very simple but thoroughly engaging piece called *Speechless* (Monica Lee, 2004), features a distracted, irreverent, chaotic, but deeply thoughtful monologue. The entire piece consists of a simple static two-shot with two people positioned back to back in the frame, one (presumably the filmmaker) sitting and silently smoking as the other talks incessantly while leaning against one of the metal railings that are so ubiquitous on Hong Kong's streets. The talker, whose gender presentation appears ambiguous enough to signify (probably) a butch, (maybe) a trans guy, or (possibly) a queer boy, cheerfully mouths off on a series of issues in speedy Cantonese punctuated with English words:

> I do wonder about the kind of floral arrangement I would receive when I die. I mean, we have no status ... In the West, they use the term "long-time companion." What would we be called in Chinese? "The truest friend *(zhiyou)*"[1]?
>
> For me, gender is very intriguing ... You love whom you love, whatever gender. You can't control it. Yet, at some point, people will put a label on you, depending on what haircut you have, what you wear, how you speak ... they label the type, and the gender of the lovers you're supposed to have. I can't differentiate on those grounds. I love whom I love ... it's not up to me to differentiate that way.
>
> What is fidelity? Is it just about remaining faithful sexually? In our circle, it's impossible. It's like living in a soap opera with only ten actors. You will have to date among those ten people! You inevitably become someone's ex- or future lover ... Some people who choose to be monogamous do so to

avoid trouble, to fit into the social structure. A way to get their tax-free credit, their tax refund. A way for your family members to remember the name of your lover ... and not get confused!

What's good about open relationships? Well, I'm not a philosophy student, and I'm not particularly good at theory ... but I think as long as an open relationship has a basis in trust and respect, then it can work. Heterosexuals are funny that way. In Hong Kong a lot of women know their husbands cheat on them, but it's okay as long as they come home at night. They accept it as long as the men are not cheating with just one person! For heterosexuals, it's usually one-sided: basically, it's the man who visits prostitutes or keeps a mistress ... It's a kind of open relationship, only without trust.

I don't think one voice should represent everyone. In some circles, some people want to be called TB, TBG, or Pure Les. In other circles, they are lesbians, or queers, or 10 percent ... No one is representative of all. Sexuality does not work like that. I don't want to talk about theory, I don't have the qualification, but it's my personal understanding ...

I'm not sure how to differentiate between mainstream and minority culture. I feel that my suffering is the same as everyone else's. Every relationship reaches a point where it's about pure endurance. If you endure, you arrive at the great beyond. If not, you separate, due to irreconcilable differences. It's very clichéd really. What's mainstream taste, what's minority taste? The "minority" sexuality of two women can become mainstream taste for straight men ... there goes the difference!

The video ends with a shot of the interior of a moving car and the speaker's best impromptu line: "A roundabout! Do you know what's beautiful about a roundabout? You're never taking a wrong turn – you just end up driving some extra distance. It's life's most sublime state!" S/he enthusiastically repeats this line several times for the filmmaker's benefit ("Now you'll have three takes to choose from!") as the two drive into a roundabout in rollicking laughter.

I am not really able to capture on paper the funny turns of phrase in Cantonese or the hilariously breathless way the rapid-fire monologue proceeds. Nonetheless, just from its content alone, we can see that the disjointed musings manage to touch on a surprisingly wide array of queer concerns: the conundrum of kinship status, the restrictive limits of sexual identity, sanctioned and unsanctioned forms of polyamory, the peril of group identities, and the constructed boundary between mainstream and margin. Although the speaker makes several disclaimers that s/he is not a "theorist," has not studied theory, and does not feel qualified to theorize, the monologue actually fashions quite a few theoretically thoughtful arguments regarding queer lives. I interpret the title, *Speechless*, in a number of ways. The very speechiness of the speaker certainly leaves the (on- and off-screen) audience speechless! More significant, the title may refer to the "speech-less" status of such musings, which tend to be transient, scattered, and frag-mented. Left unarchived, they often disappear into oblivion. The term "speechless" signals to us the importance of heeding, as far as we can, what we scarcely hear: the "speech" which we must strain to catch, often only in disjointed snatches, before it vanishes into speechlessness for good.

In this chapter, I would like to explore the scene – or, more accurately, various shifting scenes – of queer self-writing in Hong Kong. These projects of self-representation provide avenues for queer subjects to articulate their life stories outside of (and at times explicitly against) academic and media representations. As my chapter title suggests, these autobiographical acts embrace the do-it-yourself credo: they are initiated and run by volunteers, driven by community needs, and receptive to audience feedback. They are not finished products but open-ended works-in-progress. Like the mono-logue in *Speechless,* these acts of self-writing are rambling, irreverent, good-humoured, and always thoughtful. They often take you round and round without (yet? ever?) reaching a destination. Still, there is no danger of a wrong turn. At most, we travel some extra distance.

In Theory

Among the many achievements of feminist autobiographical studies in the past decade, the redefinition and expansion of what constitutes "autobiog-raphy" and what comprises the theoretical parameters of its inquiries are particularly productive developments. The critical importance accorded to the narrativity of everyday life – what Sidonie Smith and Julia Watson term "inscriptions of dailiness"[2] – compels a turn away from the generic defini-tion of autobiography as a literary form as well as from the culturally and historically specific notion of autobiography as the solitary writing of an individual life. Theoretical ruminations on subjectivity complicate our under-standing of the "self," which is no longer conceptualized as an integral and interiorized identity awaiting expression but as a subject effect that is dis-cursively constructed and reiterated through autobiographical acts. Studies of self-writing thus extend beyond analyses of recognized autobiographies to include examinations of the discursive process of self-making and self-representation in a great variety of (verbal and nonverbal) texts as well as in the reading practice itself. Leigh Gilmore's influential notion of "autobiog-raphics" marks the location in texts (especially those not recognizable as autobiographical) where elements of self-representation emerge. Gilmore pays particular attention to the multiple and not always legible points at which the *I* is coded in collusion with as well as against available discourses of truth and identity.[3] Jeanne Perreault's theory of "autography" further highlights the ongoing negotiation of the boundary between the "I" and the "we." Perreault's interest in "seeking an alternative both to the suppression of difference that totalization implies and to the dissociations suggested by a fragmented subjectivity" is especially useful for approaching minority forms of self-writing and their frequent oscillation between an investment in "personal, body-specific identity," on the one hand, and adherence to collective solidarity, on the other.[4]

These critical turns in theories of self-writing can productively intersect with recent works on the globalization of queer culture and the emergence of self-identified queer communities in Asia. The phenomenon of what Arnaldo Cruz-Malavé and Martin F. Manalansan term "queer globalizations" offers both promise and peril.[5] On the one hand, the global visibility of queer issues has resulted in an "expandable terrain for the struggle for queer rights," exemplified by efforts of transnational political coalitions – such as the International Lesbian and Gay Association (ILGA) and the International Gay and Lesbian Human Rights Commission (IGLHRC) – to integrate sexual and gender rights into the concept of "universal human rights" and by the global dissemination of diverse forms of queer culture. As a result, there is an unprecedented growth and coalescence of creativity and agency among queer communities, which were, until quite recently, relatively isolated from one another.[6] On the other hand, such global flows in queer traffic also give rise to grave concerns over issues of homogenization, commodification, and depoliticization. For instance, there is a disturbing resurgence of neo-colonial rhetoric in claims about the universality and presumed modernity of gay and lesbian identities.[7] Furthermore, global relations of inequality are often rendered invisible by a queer visibility politics that focuses solely on attaining a globally identifiable queer lifestyle, a trend that Rosemary Hennessy argues reduces radical politics to acts of consumption.[8]

At the same time, the process of "queer globalizations" should not be thought of in unidirectional terms – that is, as a structure imposed by the West on the rest. Nor should it be construed as an either-or battle between wholesale assimilation or absolute resistance. Recent works on queer culture in Asia, for instance, demonstrate that the encounter between local self-understanding and globalized forms of gender and sexual identities is a complex process, one that is increasingly mediated by the use of new media.[9] The proliferation of web-enabled forms of self-narration with varying interactive functionalities means that autobiographical activities are becoming increasingly complex and layered: the lines between public and private, writer and audience, self and other are more blurry than ever before. As the various studies collected in the anthology *Mobile Cultures* demonstrate, local and global self-understanding and self-representation are inextricably entangled and mutually constitutive. For example, there are processes of "glocalization" – that is, local appropriations of global forms that result in hybridized or synchretized formations as well as in an ongoing transformation of the understanding of the "local" facilitated by the post-digital imaginary of space and affiliation. As a result of these dynamic changes, we are also witnessing emergent formations of regional identification (like "queer Asian") that are neither local nor global.[10]

Drawing from the theoretical insights of the critical nexus sketched above, I will explore the following questions in my discussion of various sites of queer self-inscription in Hong Kong: To what extent are queer autobiographical acts facilitated or mediated by the use of new media? How do these sites facilitate self-representations and self-understanding? How are the boundaries between public and private, global and local, and individual and collective negotiated, especially in relation to discourses of globalized sexual/gender identities and categories?

First-Love Stories

Lucetta Kam writes in her preface to *Lunar Desires: Her Same-Sex Love, In Her Own Words* that the idea to collect "first-love stories between women" came to her spontaneously. As the idea took root, she deliberated and reached the conclusion that it would not be difficult to collect enough stories to fill a book. Kam's confidence derives from her faith in the *commonplace* nature of love between women: "Open your eyes, free your heart: where would you *not* find desire between women?"[11] The stories in the collection evoke the "everyday" nature of desire between women by embedding it within the specificity of place. What appears to be illicit desire does not stay within illicit confines. It permeates every corner of the city and becomes emblematic of the taste and texture of life in Hong Kong. In the preface, Kam writes of how she first fantasizes about the anthology: she was walking on the street carrying a book of love stories between women written in English. Suddenly, she began to "see" this love everywhere: "on the bus, on the MTR [Mass Transit Railway], on the ferry." This specificity of place, conjured by Kam through the three most signficant forms of public transport in the city, recurs in different forms throughout the twenty-six stories in the collection. In "Love at Last Site," Trash equates her experience of love to "hanging out, going to movies, eating buffet meals ... necking in the darkness of karaoke suites."[12] In "To Pearl," by M, love is associated with the outlying islands *(lidao)*. These popular hideaways free lovers from the prying eyes of family, while the long ride on the ferries offers a haven for erotic activities: "I remember the first time we held hands while walking across the main street in Cheung Chau.[13] I felt the warmth circulate from the palm of my hand directly to my heart. Do you remember our first kiss on the beach at Discovery Bay?[14] How we could not stop kissing on the return ferry until our necks became sore?"[15] "JN1437," by Noel, locates the author's experience of

first love in the environment of neighbourhood youth centres: "I was working at the reception of the youth centre ... when I became mesmerized by
her eyes ... She came in everyday after school to do her homework ... Then
every morning, we found ourselves monopolizing the basketball court."[16]
The story eroticizes the educational and recreational spaces offered by the
youth centres, which are the most quotidian spaces imaginable for teenagers. Most interestingly, Anson Mak's "1989. It's Love!" conjoins the specificity of place with a historically significant time: the turbulent two months
during May and June 1989, when the city was filled first with hopeful idealism in support of the students' demonstration in Beijing, only to fall later
into the abyss of horror and disillusion when the army opened fire on 4
June. Mak recounts this collective experience through an intimately personal prose poem about her love for a young woman who had gone to
Beijing at the time: "The last few demonstrations / fellow students with

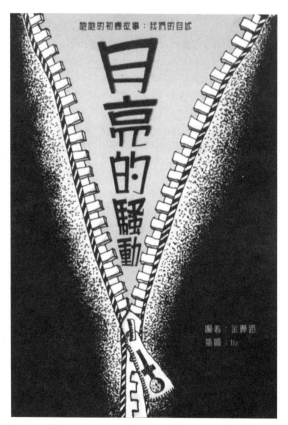

Cover of *Lunar Desires: Her Same-Sex Love, In Her Own
Words*, edited by Lucetta Kam

their radio / marching / listening to news about the army and martial law / advance retreat / even we fall into / chaos / let alone those in the square / those young people / as young as we are / the Beijing residents / blocking the army from entering the city / I think of them / project my hope / and unease / I think of her / between spring and summer / a confounding love."[17] Just as the other stories weave women's desire for each other into the fabric of everyday life in Hong Kong, Mak's narrative entwines her "first love" with a tremendously significant part of the city's collective experience.

Recalling the "campus fiction" that I discussed in Chapter 2, it is no surprise that schools are ubiquitous in the stories, covering experiences in primary school ("Goodbye to Youth"), high school ("We All Loved Like This"), and university ("Life's Irony").[18] The school setting also places many of the stories abroad in boarding schools all over the world ("First-Love Horrors," "Children of the Flower," and "Unsent Letter").[19] These stories extend the emotional space of Hong Kong to include life in the diaspora, which is a common experience among a generation of middle-class youth who were sent abroad during the 1980s and 1990s, usually to acquire foreign citizenship before the handover in 1997.

Finally, there are stories set in cyberspace, especially from younger contributors whose experiences of love are closely tied to the emergence of the Internet as the most preferred meeting venue for queer youth. The stories document different terrain of the cyber landscape. "Writing through Blurry Eyes on a Night without Glasses" equates the Internet to a kind of "first base": the course of courtship between the two young women moves gradually from text messaging to phone calls and finally to meeting in person.[20] "McDull's First Love" identifies a form of tenderness possible only in the "infinitely creative" textual spaces of the chatrooms.[21] "Left 850,000 Km Behind" eroticizes an e-mail address in a story about romantic adventures on an Internet forum.[22]

While the anthology was brought out in the traditional format of print, it was also initiated and enabled by the Internet. Kam describes how she distributed a "call for stories" that was exponentially disseminated through a web of e-mail lists, resulting in rapid and voluminous responses. Kam was moved by the trust that the contributors placed "in the hands of a stranger on the net."[23] The Internet thus allows a certain intimacy to develop within relatively anonymous relations. In this way, the autobiographical elements of the stories also need not be anchored in the actual identities of the individual writers (who all use pennames and supply only their ages). It matters little whether the stories are factually accurate reproductions of the authors' life events. The book's creative expressions generate place-specific experiences rather than body-specific identities, ultimately offering not so much a collection of individual autobiographies as a *city's* autobiography of queer female love.

Making Things Perfectly Ordinary

A similar belief in the quotidian, rather than exceptional, nature of sexual love between women also fuels the project produced in 2004 by the Women's Coalition of Hong Kong entitled "In the Tracks of Their Love: Oral History of Women Who Could Fall in Love with Women in Hong Kong."[24] The somewhat awkward use of the conditional tense in the subtitle is clearly deliberate: it signals that these are not just stories about "women who love women" but also about those who *could* love women – that is, any woman with the potential capacity to experience love and desire for other women. It also indicates an active disidentification with "lesbian" as a unifying category of collectivity and a skepticism toward the progress narrative of "coming out." Instead, the project highlights a more cyclical outlook, which views queer desire as something that circulates throughout women's lives without necessarily "resolving" into any form of identity transformation. I will examine how the project is structured – and at times fractured, although not in unproductive ways – by this self-understanding.

Cover of "In the Tracks of Their Love," booklet for an oral-history project by the Women's Coalition of Hong Kong

In contrast to the relatively integral and solitary format of a book like *Lunar Desires*, the oral-history project "In the Tracks of Their Love" was presented as a series of "events": the centre piece was a multimedia installation around which a series of talks and workshops were scheduled. The installation was also rendered into five "panels" available for download on the Internet, thus extending the project's "afterlife" indefinitely beyond the exhibition events. A booklet documenting segments from the interviews was produced in print with a digital version available for download.[25] The multiple formats of the project – as events, print matter, and digital texts – enlarge its audience base to allow those who are unwilling or unable to physically visit the exhibition to access the project in private. The Internet, which was used to initiate *Lunar Desires,* serves primarily in this project as an ongoing vehicle of dissemination.

"In the Tracks of Their Love" positions itself against two powerful discourses that in effect collude with each other: the problematic "knowledge" about queer female desire produced by academic and media representations and the "ignorance" produced by its erasure in official history and mainstream culture. One section of the exhibition entitled "FAQ" mocks media and academic representations of queer female desire by reproducing questions frequently asked in interviews and surveys conducted on sexual minorities by students, university lecturers, and reporters. Irreverent "comebacks" disguised as answers critically interrogate the questions' blind spots:

Q: When did you discover you are lesbian?

A: One does not wake up and "suddenly discover" one's sexual orientation. From *our* interviews, the process of "discovering" one's desire takes anywhere between a few days or ten years ... Ask me about the *process* and I might have an answer for you.

Q: How do you think most people view homosexuality?

A: I have not talked to "most people," how would I know? Ask the government to conduct a poll.

Q: Is it possible for you to be attracted to men?

A: Sexual desire is unpredictable. I'm not dead yet, and I'm not a prophet, how could I tell you about the future?[26]

The mock question-and-answer format illustrates that autobiographical utterances of sexual minorities are often framed in problematic ways by the restrictive questions of the researchers, whether academic or journalistic. The project's own stories function like the mock answers: they enable the storytellers to "talk back" to the discourses that have attempted to author their lives.

The project's historiographic impulse is highlighted in the preface to the booklet produced for the exhibition: "We hope our individual histories can become building blocks of a collective history, one that illuminates differences between individuals."[27] There is a tension – one that permeates the entire project – in the statement between the need for a collective history and the concern that this history does not subsume individual differences. Day Wong's article on the making of the project sheds some light on this ongoing but productive tension. Wong's piece is an interesting document, as it becomes itself an autobiographical act: a self-representation of the group as it launched the oral-history project.[28] Wong argues that the group's objective is to "avoid the exclusionary and normalizing effects associated with identity politics" in order to construct a history "without presupposing the development of a collective consciousness that unites the historical experiences, or a center, some essential quality, that marks the lives of these women."[29] It is, however, apparent from Wong's documentation that this is not an easy balance to achieve. The group, for instance, speaks of the need for "community" but qualifies it as one that is "articulated in a minimal and loose sense," one without "shared norms, shared lifestyles, or shared support."[30] Such cautious wording reflects the group's need for and simultaneous suspicion of collective identity. Wong's conclusion raises a thoughtful possibility that comes surprisingly close to resolving what appears an irresolvable tension. Wong invokes the Buddhist term "ordinary consciousness" *(pingchang xin)* to describe what the group advocates as an approach to the stories: "an attitude of letting go, or being unemotional, nonjudgmental, unprejudiced ... [an attitude Hong Kong people like to stress when] facing divergent views or experiencing ups and downs in their lives."[31] There is certainly much more room to pursue this point at length because an elaboration of "ordinary consciousness" would involve a discussion of detachment not just from emotions or judgments but, more important, also from the notion of "self." What would it mean to engage in an autobiographical act without an attachment to "self"? How might this seeming contradiction intervene in the paradoxical longing for and refusal of collective identity? Wong's invocation of "ordinary consciousness" also echoes Chu Wei-cheng's observation that there is a strong current in Taiwan's *tongzhi* fiction that explores "transcendence and detachment" *(kanpo chaotuo)* as an alternative response to the ceaseless opposition enacted in queer circles between identity and difference, individuality and collectivity, sexual excess and sexual repression.[32] Since the oral-history project looks poised for a series of sequels (there is already a "call for stories" issued in the booklet), this notion of "ordinary consciousness" could be further developed in ways that may transform current debates on identity, collectivity, and difference.

"Fuck the Categories!"

During a session on "Queer Asia" at *Persistent Vision,* a conference held in conjunction with the 2001 San Francisco Lesbian and Gay Film Festival,

Hong Kong-born filmmaker Quentin Lee prefaced the screening of a clip from his early work, an experimental exercise in "autobiography" entitled "Anxiety of Inexpression and the Otherness Machine," with a simple statement that he loudly belted out in front of the microphone: "Fuck the categories!"[33] Lee's irreverent shout was an appropriate introduction to his piece, which is a highly ironic and self-consciously disruptive pastiche that thoroughly rejects categorizations of "Asian" or "gay" or, indeed, "autobiographical." Lee's shout signals an impatience with categories and an indifference to identity labels. Yet, it is never quite clear what "fucking the categories" may actually achieve: it certainly does not result in categories disappearing (nor do we necessarily want them to). There are also different forms of categories in varying and changing hierarchical relation to the norms. In Hong Kong, for instance, *tongzhi* as a category has shifted from its multivalent, irreverent, tongue-in-cheek origin to its currently stable, nonthreatening, virtually normalized status. While *tongzhi* now describes virtually nothing specific about a person, it functions well as a collective identity that is flexible enough to allow ongoing coalition building. One would want *tongzhi*, as a category, to neither rule nor disappear! Even Anson Mak, one of the most vociferous critics of the term *tongzhi*, argues not for its demise but for its continual existence in tandem (and in tension) with other, ever-more-inventive categories.[34] What Mak advocates for may be understood as what Judith Halberstam, after Eve Sedgwick, calls "nonce taxonomies": "classifications of desire, physicality, and subjectivity that attempt to intervene in hegemonic processes of naming and defining."[35] It seems to me that "nonce taxonomies" arise in the aftermath of "fucking the (hegemonic) categories" out of a need to live, express oneself, and interact with others in the ruins of categorical coherence. What intrigues me particularly about the next scene of self-writing that I want to examine is its lively and thoughtful approach to the art of "nonce taxonomies."

The Internet radio program "What the Hell Kind of *Tongzhi* Movement"[36] was launched in 2005 and currently broadcasts weekly on People's Radio Hong Kong.[37] The independent radio station was set up in response to a wave of "white terror" in 2004 when Albert Cheng and Wong Yuk-Man, high-profile radio commentators who had been vocally critical of the government, were forced off the air. Operated on the model of community radio, the station is committed to remaining nonprofit, community-owned, and community-run. Its mandate is to "give voice to the voiceless" and facilitate "true freedom of speech."[38] Hosted by Connie, Ah Lik, Wai Wai, and Siu Chou, all long-time activists in various *tongzhi*-related projects and organizations, the show facilitates weekly discussion of a wide range of issues: sex education, sex work, government-run surveys on sexual minorities, queer gender roles, queer sex, cruising venues, married people exploring queer desire, workplace issues for trans people, the Christian right in Hong Kong, and so on.[39] The show takes an informal and free-wheeling approach to broadcasting, never censoring sexually explicit material (although a good-humoured verbal "warning" is always given), sarcastic asides, unexpected interruptions, or rollicking fits of laughter. While the discussion tends to get distracted, it always manages to veer back on course. The hosts take text messages and phone calls off the air during the show, which enables listeners to ask questions or steer the discussion in specific directions. Every program begins with a segment on recent mainstream news reports related to queer issues, followed by irreverent but insightfully critical comments on the (often problematic) reports. Most important, the show invites a different guest every week to tell stories from his or her own life. The highly informal atmosphere of the show works particularly well for this segment, as the guests are not "interviewed" or "surveyed" with pre-scripted questions but rather invited to chat among queer friends. The guests' stories thus come across as spontaneously expressed fragments of queer lives that are not filtered or shaped for the sake of categorical coherence. The show's monthly focus on transgender topics, for instance, goes a long way toward bridging the many serious gaps in current formal research on transgender lives in Hong Kong.[40]

The program has shown a particular interest in gender/sexual categories that are in vogue (or at least in use) in the local queer scene. The hosts approach the issue from experiential as well as analytical perspectives, often giving insight into how these categories are used but at the same time contested at every turn in everyday life. A good example is the show that aired on 14 December 2005, entitled "'1' '0' 'B' 'G': Let Me Tell You!" The titular sexual/gender categories are roughly equivalent (but not reducible) to top or bottom and butch or femme. They are often perceived to be rather rigidly practised among *tongzhi* in Hong Kong. The show starts off with this premise, as the hosts and guest Jason (a young gay man) define the terms:

–B, short for TB, as in tomboy, those who "imitate" boys.
–G, TB's G, a derivative category: the tomboy's girl, the "little wife"!
–0: like G, the "little wife" among gay men!
–1: the "man" among gay men!

Then two other categories are introduced, described as "more recent inventions":

–Pure, for those who do not differentiate between B or G, otherwise known as Pure Les
–10, can be both 1 or 0

The sarcastic laughter that accompanies this initial round of definitions already signals that these categories are not taken entirely seriously. As the conversation turns to a more detailed discussion of how the categories operate in each speaker's life, the categories' coherence begins to collapse immediately.

First, Jason describes how he never used to identify with either 1 or 0 but has recently felt more and more like 0 because he enjoys feeling dependent in a relationship. When asked whether this equates to feeling feminine, Jason responds with, "Yes, but *not* while I'm at work." For Jason, it seems that 0 is a category that describes an emotional role in a relationship that is only partially linked to sexual preference and gender identification. Most interesting, he seems to be able to compartmentalize his life – not out of conformity but out of a strong preference for his work life to operate independently of his emotional, sexual, and gender dynamics. For Jason, then, 0 is a useful category to express a part of himself, but the category does not describe all areas of his life and personality.

Connie offers a similarly intriguing interpretation of TB when she begins to describe how it operates in her own life. She says that she has been *told* she is B because she "likes girls, and likes to court girls." She is also frequently reminded to "not sit in such feminine ways and be more like a man." Connie concedes that she takes on the gender expectations of B partly as a way to attract the girls that she likes. To her, masculine identification operates as a fashion statement, a way to "look good" to other girls. When asked why she binds her chest, she admits that she does so primarily because it makes her look good in men's clothes! Connie also adds that the "B look" seems to change with fashion trends, causing the other hosts to muse upon the curious fact that "B in the '60s must have sported long hair like hippies at the time"! Connie's experience illustrates that gender identification and sexual attraction sometimes influence or even constitute each other. Connie's masculine identification appears to be the *effect* rather than the cause of her attraction to feminine girls. Her understanding of masculinity in relation to fashion trends also prompts others to reflect on the historicity of queer and countercultural masculinity.

As the show goes on, the conversation takes increasingly complex turns. When the speakers' own personal experience seems limited, they begin to tell stories about people they know who pose problems for the categories: for example, they talk about Gs they know who are bossy and fierce and who love to "pretend to be B" or about Bs who have long hair, wear lipstick, and like skirts but still strongly identify as B. When the hosts probe Jason about what would happen in a sexual encounter when the "numbers" are mismatched, a text message comes in from the listeners pointing out that there are many sexual activities between men that do not require preferences for penetrating or being penetrated. There are interesting observations about the category "Pure," which seems to have been invented as a way to circumvent the gendered requirements of B and G. Yet, as the speakers observe, recent usage of "Pure" has taken on its own gendered dimension, and categories like "Pure slanting toward B" or "Pure slanting toward G" are circulating. They also remark on the ambiguity of these categories, as they can mean gender self-identification *or* sexual-object choice *or* both. They observe as well that "Pure" has somehow also come to signify a particular "look" (citing the phrase "You are looking a little 'Pure' today!"), even though the term started off as a rebellion *against* other looks. Finally, as the show concludes, the speakers observe that heterosexual gender categories are just as fuzzy, only they are not discussed in the same ways: What do you call a feminine straight man who likes masculine women? Or a feminine straight woman who likes similarly feminine men? They would all be swept into the category "heterosexual," which turns out to describe very little indeed!

This show is typical of the way the program approaches various issues. The spontaneous, interactive ways that categories are gradually taken apart to be "tested" against the complexity of everyday experience allow a nuanced and complex glimpse into different aspects of queer lives in Hong Kong. At the same time, categories are not dismissed or abandoned. In fact, they are shown to be vital in the (always partial) communication of needs, preferences, and self-understanding.

Work in Progress

In Judith Halberstam's study of subcultural lives, she argues that queer subcultures undo at least two powerful lines of division: between queer theorist and cultural producer and between queer archive and cultural production. Halberstam points to the phenomenon of a new generation of queer theorists who – unlike the previous generation of cultural theorists, who have tended to study groups of which they are not necessarily a part – approach their object of study not from the position of an expert outsider but in the capacity of a collaborator, friend, and fan: "The academic might be the archivist, a coarchivist, a full-fledged participant in the subcultural scene that the scholar writes about. But only rarely does the queer theorist stand wholly apart from the subculture, examining it with an expert's gaze."[41] Furthermore, while there are academic forms of queer archiving, Halberstam reminds us that subcultural works themselves often *already* serve an archival function by constructing genealogies, sustaining memories, and marking mutual influences.[42]

This chapter is meant to reflect the blurring of both these boundaries. When I first came into contact with the projects discussed in this chapter, I did not do so as an academic. I learned of *Lunar Desires* and "In the Tracks of Their Love" in much the same way that the projects' organizers, participants, and readers/audience did: via an e-mail list and through the word of mouth of a friendship network. I have been an avid listener of "What the Hell Kind of *Tongzhi* Movement" since its inception, not as a researcher with an agenda but simply as a fan of the show's funny and irreverent conversations. As I write this chapter, I realize also that my impetus is not only to analyze the significance and impact of these projects but, more important, also to document them – before the last print run, before the Internet links disappear, before volunteers disperse and do something else with their lives – as part of a thriving scene of queer self-writing in Hong Kong. Unlike in other chapters, I have often let the objects of my analysis "overwhelm" my analytical space, thereby juxtaposing their insights with mine rather than subsuming them within my inquiry. As much as any queer theoretical discourse, these scattered, ongoing, and dynamic do-it-yourself projects vitally contribute to the understanding and nurturing of queer lives. Just as these projects strive to recover illegible and ephemeral traces of subcultural lives, so too should their efforts – which so often go under the radar of academic and mainstream attention – be continually marked as an important and integral part of Hong Kong culture.

Notes

Introduction

1 Michele Aaron, *New Queer Cinema: A Critical Reader* (Edinburgh: Edinburgh University Press, 2004), 5.

2 Harry M. Benshoff and Sean Griffin, *Queer Images: A History of Gay and Lesbian Film in America* (Oxford: Roman and Littlefield, 2006), 11.

3 Chi Ta-Wei, "Ku'er lun: Sikao dangdai Taiwan ku'er yu ku'er wenxue" [On ku'er: Thoughts on *ku'er* and *ku'er* literature in contemporary Taiwan], in *Ku'er Kuanghuan Jie* [Queer carnival], ed. Chi Ta-wei (Taipei: Meta Media, 1997), 9-28.

4 Yau Ching, *Xingbie guangying: Xianggang dianying zhong de xing yu xingbie wenhua yanjiu* [Sexing shadows: Genders and sexualities in Hong Kong cinema] (Hong Kong: Hong Kong Film Critics Society, 2005), 124.

5 For ongoing campaigns for legal reforms, see Civil Rights for Sexual Diversities, http://www.cr4sd.org/issues/advocacy1.html; for documentation of past and present activist activities, see Equality For All, http://equality.wchk.org/.

6 Chu Wei-cheng, "Queer(Ing) Taiwan and Its Future: From an Agenda of Mainstream Self-Enlightenment to One of Sexual Citizenship?" Paper presented at Sexualities, Genders, and Rights in Asia: 1st International Conference of Queer Asian Studies, Bangkok, Mahidol University, 7-9 July 2005, 8-12. Also available in Chinese as "Tongzhi · Taiwan: Xonggongmin, guozu jiangou huo gongmin shehui [Queer(ing) Taiwan: Sexual Citizenship, Nation-Building or Civil Society]. *Nuxue xuezhi: Funu yu xingbei yanjiu* [Journal of Women's and Gender Studies] 15 (2003): 115-51.

7 A poignant example of this political tendency can be seen in the widely publicized squabble among the organizers of the annual pro-democracy march on 1 July 2005. As it was customary for community groups with relatively low visibility to lead the march, *tongzhi* organizations were invited to do so that year. There was immediate opposition from many quarters, with some accusing *tongzhi* groups of "kidnapping" the pro-democracy agenda. As the media quickly turned an internal discussion into a public spectacle, virtually none of the pro-democracy members of the Legislative Council spoke up on behalf of the *tongzhi* groups. Most remained silent, while a few pleaded with outraged *tongzhi* representatives to "tone down" their militant stance.

8 *BBC Chinese.com*, "Hu Jintao: Yiguo shi lianzhi de qianti" [Hu Juntao: One country is the precondition of two systems], 1 July 2007, http://news.bbc.co.uk/chinese/trad/hi/newsid_6250000/newsid_6258000/6258048.stm.

9 Leung Ping-Kwan, *Xianggang wenhua* [Hong Kong culture] (Hong Kong: Hong Kong Arts Centre, 1995), 4.

Chapter 1: Sex and the Postcolonial City

1 Lu Wei-Luan, *Xianggang gushi: Geren huiyi yu wenxue sikao* [Hong Kong stories: Personal memories and literary reflections] (Hong Kong: Oxford University Press, 1996), 4.

2 Eileen Chang, *Qingcheng zhi lian* [Love in a fallen city] (Taipei: Crown, 1991), 208.
3 Esther M.K. Cheung and Chu Yiu-wai, "Introduction," in *Between Home and World: A Reader in Hong Kong Cinema,* ed. Esther M.K. Cheung and Chu Yiu-wai (Hong Kong: Oxford University Press, 2004), xvii.
4 Esther Cheung, "Introduction: Cinema and City at a Moment of Danger," in *Between Home and World,* ed. Cheung and Chu, 248.
5 Leung Ping-Kwan, "Urban Cinema and the Cultural Identity of Hong Kong," in *Between Home and World,* ed. Cheung and Chu, 369-98.
6 David Harvey, *The Condition of Postmodernity: An Enquiry into the Origins of Cultural Change* (Oxford: Blackwell, 1991).
7 Ackbar Abbas, *Hong Kong: Culture and the Politics of Disappearance* (Minneapolis: University of Minnesota Press, 1997), 8.
8 Longtin, *Hou jiuqi yu Xianggang dianying* [Post-97 and Hong Kong cinema] (Hong Kong: Hong Kong Film Critics Society, 2003), 30.
9 Ibid., 204, original emphasis.
10 Michelangelo Signorile, *Queers in America: Sex, the Media, and the Closets of Power,* 3rd ed. (Madison: University of Wisconsin Press, 2003).
11 Urvashi Vaid, *Virtual Equality: The Mainstreaming of Gay and Lesbian Liberation* (New York: Anchor, 1996), 381.
12 Claire Hemmings, *Bisexual Spaces: A Geography of Sexuality and Gender* (New York and London: Routledge, 2002).
13 Jay Prosser, *Second Skins: The Body Narratives of Transsexuality* (New York: Columbia University Press, 1998).
14 Chloe Brushwood Rose and Anna Camilleri, eds., *Brazen Femme: Queering Femininity* (Vancouver: Arsenal Pulp Press, 2002).
15 See, for example, Silviano Santiago, "The Wily Homosexual (First – And Necessarily Hasty – Notes)," in *Queer Globalizations: Citizenship and the Afterlife of Colonialism,* ed. Arnaldo Cruz-Malavé and Martin F. Manalansan IV (New York and London: New York University Press, 2002), 13-19; and Joseph Massad, "Re-Orientating Desire: The Gay International and the Arab World," *Public Culture* 14, 2 (2002): 361-85.
16 Judith Butler, *Undoing Gender* (New York and London: Routledge, 2004), 20.
17 Ibid.
18 Gordon Brent Ingram, "Marginality and the Landscapes of Erotic Alien(N)ation," in *Queers in Space: Communities, Public Places, Sites of Resistance,* ed. Gordon Brent Ingram, Anne-Marie Bouthilette, and Yolanda Retter (Seattle: Bay Press, 1997), 32.
19 Judith Halberstam, *In a Queer Time and Place: Transgender Bodies, Subcultural Lives* (New York and London: New York University Press, 2005), 37.
20 Ibid., 39.
21 Huang Tsung-yi, "Hong Kong Blue: Flâneurie with the Camera's Eye in a Phantasmagoric Global City," *JNT: Journal of Narrative Theory* 30, 3 (2000): 388.
22 Ibid., 389.
23 Ackbar Abbas, "Hong Kong: Other Histories, Other Places," in *Between Home and World,* ed. Cheung and Chu, 278.
24 Ibid., 279.
25 Jean-Ulrick Désert, "Queer Space," in *Queers in Space,* ed. Ingram, Bouthilette, and Retter, 17-26.
26 For an evocative look at women's cruising practices, see Dianne Chisholm, "The City of Collective Memory," *GLQ: A Journal of Lesbian and Gay Studies* 7, 2 (2001): 195-243; for debates over the meaning of cruising for women, see Denise Bullock, "Lesbian Cruising: An Examination of the Concept and Methods," *Journal of Homosexuality* 47, 2 (2004): 1-31.
27 Mark Turner, *Backward Glances: Cruising the Queer Streets of New York and London* (London: Reaktion Books, 2003).
28 J.J. Lai, *Qu gongsi shangban: Xin gongyuan de nan tongzhi de qingyu kongjian* [Going to work in the office: Homosexual space in New Park] (Taipei: Nushu Wenhua, 2005).
29 For a detailed discussion of the development of New Park, see Fran Martin, *Situating Sexualities: Queer Representation in Taiwanese Fiction, Film and Public Culture* (Hong Kong: Hong

Kong University Press, 2003); and Wang Zhihong, "Taibei Xin gongyuan de qingyu dituxue: Kongjian zaixian yu tongxinglian réntong" [The erotic geography of New Park: Homosexual identification and spatial emergence], *Taiwan shehuiyanjiu jikan* [Taiwan journal of sociology] 22 (1996): 195-218.

30 Cruising spaces in Beijing are mentioned in Chapter 6 (on "social interactions") of a pioneering study of gay male homosexuality by Li Yinhe and Wang Xiaobo, *Tamen de shijie* [Their world] (Hong Kong: Cosmos Books, 1993). Li later published a much longer ethnographic work, which also includes a chapter on "fish ponds" (gay cruising areas); see his *Tongxinglian ya wenhua* [The homosexual subculture] (Beijing: Jinri Zhonghua Chubanshe, 1998), 302-13.

31 For an analysis of *East Palace, West Palace,* see Chris Berry, "Staging Gay Life in China," *Jump Cut: A Review of Contemporary Media* 42 (1998): 84-89. For an introduction to Cui Zi'en's films, see Chris Berry, "The Sacred, the Profane, and the Domestic in Cui Zi'en's Cinema," *positions: east asia cultures critique* 12, 1 (2004): 195-201.

32 Mathias Woo, *Xianggang fengge* [Hong Kong style] (Hong Kong: TOM Publishing, 2005), 97.

33 Ibid., 94-97.

34 Cao Minwei, *You gannai fengliu: Xianggang bainian qingse shi* [Hong Kong erotic history] (Hong Kong: Lok Man, 2004), 176.

35 Travis Kong, "Queering Masculinity in Hong Kong Movies," in *Masculinities and Hong Kong Cinema,* ed. Laikwan Pang and Day Wong (Hong Kong: Hong Kong University Press, 2005), 77.

36 For a study of the the influence of Japanese popular culture on the film, see Romit Dasgupta, "The Film *Bishonen* and Queer(N)Asia through Japanese Popular Culture," in *Popular Culture, Globalization and Japan,* ed. Matthew and Rumi Sakamoto Allen (New York: Routledge, 2006), 56-74.

37 Turner, *Backward Glances,* 59-61, original emphasis.

38 Maria Pramaggiore, "Epistemologies of the Fence," in Hall and Pramaggiore, *Representing Bisexualities,* 3.

39 Maria Pramaggiore, "Straddling the Screen: Bisexual Spectatorship and Contemporary Narrative Film," in *Representing Bisexualities: Subjects and Cultures of Fluid Desire,* ed. Donald E. Hall and Maria Pramaggiore (New York and London: New York University Press, 1996), 282.

40 Aaron Betsky, *Queer Space: Architecture and Same-Sex Desire* (New York: William Morrow, 1997), 141.

41 Leung Ping-Kwan, "Urban Cinema," 397.

42 Lawrence Pun, "Wei he yao yiben Wang Jiawei zhuanlun?" [Why a critical anthology on Wong Kar-Wai?], in *Wang Jiawei de yinghua shijie* [The cinema of Wong Kar-Wai], ed. Lawrence Pun and Bono Lee (Hong Kong: Joint Publishing, 2004), v.

43 Bono Lee, "Nanyadao de bianyuan shenhua" [Lamma Island's legends of marginality], in *Xianggang 101: Aihen Xianggang le yilingyi ge liyou* [Hong Kong 101: One hundred and one reasons to love and hate Hong Kong], ed. Bono Lee and Fan Tsang (Hong Kong: Crown, 2001), 72.

44 Ibid., 73.

45 Long Yingtai, "Xianggang ni wang nali qu?" [Hong Kong where are you going?], *Ming Pao,* 9 November 2004, A4.

46 Abbas, *Hong Kong,* 4.

47 Aihwa Ong, *Flexible Citizenship: The Cultural Logics of Transnationality* (Durham, NC: Duke University Press, 1998).

48 Ronald Skeldon, "Hong Kong in an International Migration System," in *The Hong Kong Reader: Passage to Chinese Sovereignty,* ed. Ming K. Chan and Gerard A. Postiglione (Armonk, NY: M.E. Sharpe, 1996), 47.

49 William Corlett, *Community without Unity: A Politics of Derridean Extravagance* (Durham, NC: Duke University Press, 1989), 185.

50 Marjorie Garber, *Vice Versa: Bisexuality and the Eroticism of Everyday Life* (New York: Simon and Schuster, 1996), 90.

51 Ann Cvetkovich, *An Archive of Feelings: Trauma, Sexuality, and Lesbian Public Culture* (Durham, NC: Duke University Press, 2003), 16.

52 Evans Chan, interview by Stefan Borsos, *CineAsia,* June-July 2001, http://www.evanschan. com/M_S_and_L/html/MainFrameset.html.
53 Ibid.
54 For a recent study of Hong Kong's government policy on land use and its impact on land shortage, the housing market, and the quality of living space, see Eddie C.M. Hui, Manfred C.M. Lam, and Vivian S.M. Ho, "Market Disequilibrium and Urban Land Shortage: Analysis of Policy and Patterns in Hong Kong," *Journal of Urban Planning and Development* 132, 2 (2006): 80-88.
55 Ibid., 122-41.
56 Lu, *Xianggang guishi,* 20.
57 Ahmed, *Cultural Politics,* 146.
58 Ibid., 148.
59 Ibid., 152.
60 Ibid., 155.

Chapter 2: Between Girls

1 Sara Ahmed, *The Cultural Politics of Emotions* (New York and London: Routledge, 2004), 206.
2 Ibid., 256.
3 Patricia Sieber, "Introduction," in *Red Is Not the Only Colour: Contemporary Chinese Fiction on Love and Sex between Women, Collected Stories,* ed. Patricia Sieber (Oxford: Rowman and Littlefield, 2001), 3.
4 Ibid. See also Tze-lan D. Sang's study of female same-sex love in Republican-era discourse and May Fourth fiction in *The Emergent Lesbian: Female Same-Sex Desire in Modern China* (Chicago: University Of Chicago Press, 2003), 127-60.
5 Sieber, *Red Is Not the Only Colour,* 5.
6 Ibid., 5-6, 14-15.
7 Chu Wei-cheng, "Linglei jingdian" [Alternative classics], in *Taiwan tongzhi: Xiaoshuo xuan* [Seleced *tongzhi* fiction from Taiwan], ed. Chu Wei-cheng (Taipei: Eryu, 2005), 16.
8 Ibid.
9 For a detailed account of how lesbian activism during this period signified itself through negotiating with the established feminist movement, see Sang, *The Emergent Lesbian,* 225-54.
10 Yau Ching, *Xingbie guangying: Xianggang dianying zhong de xing yu xingbie wenhua yanjiu* [Sexing shadows: Genders and sexualities in Hong Kong cinema] (Hong Kong: Hong Kong Film Critics Society, 2005), 135-38.
11 Ng Kar Man, "Friendship and Gender Construction: A Study of Young Women between Girlhood and Womanhood in Hong Kong" (M.Phil. thesis, University of Hong Kong, 2006).
12 Tuula Gordon and Elina Lahelma, "Who Wants to Be a Woman? Young Women's Reflections on Transitions to Adulthood," *Feminist Review* 78 (2004): 81, 95.
13 Judith Halberstam, *In a Queer Time and Place: Transgender Bodies, Subcultural Lives* (New York and London: New York University Press, 2005), 5.
14 Ibid., 153.
15 Linda Williams, "When the Woman Looks," in *Re-Vision: Essays in Feminist Film Criticism,* ed. Patricia Mellencamp, Mary Ann Doane, and Linda Williams (Frederick, MD: American Film Institute, 1983), 83-99.
16 Barbara Creed, "Horror and the Monstrous-Feminine: An Imaginary Abjection," *Screen* 27, 1 (1986): 44-54.
17 Linda Williams, "Learning to Scream," in *Horror: The Film Reader,* ed. Mark Jancovich (London and New York: Routledge, 2002), 164-68.
18 Carol J. Clover, "Her Body, Himself: Gender in the Slasher Film," *Representations* 20 (1987): 205-28.
19 Jay Prosser, *Light in the Dark Room: Photography and Loss* (Minneapolis: University of Minnesota Press, 2005), 1-2.
20 Susan Sontag, *On Photography* (London: Picador, 2001).
21 Linda Williams, *Hardcore* (Berkeley: University of California Press, 1999), 189-95.
22 Ibid., 194.

23 Mikita Brottman, *Offensive Films* (Nashville: Vanderbilt University Press, 2005), 79-95.

24 Prosser, *Light in the Dark Room,* 8.

25 Ann Cvetkovich, *An Archive of Feelings: Trauma, Sexuality, and Lesbian Public Culture* (Durham: Duke University Press, 2003), 90.

26 Harry M. Benshoff, *Monster in the Closet: Homosexuality and the Horror Film* (Manchester: Manchester University Press, 1997).

27 Anneke Smelik, "Bodies That Kill: Art Cinema and Its Murderous Girls in Love," *Textus* 13, 2 (2000): 449-68.

28 Harry M. Benshoff and Sean Griffin, *Queer Images: A History of Gay and Lesbian Film in America* (Oxford: Roman and Littlefield, 2006), 25-51.

29 See Yau, *Xingbie guangying,* 103-20; and Chou Wah Shan, *Tongzhilun* [On tongzhi] (Hong Kong: Xianggang Tongzhi Yanjiushe, 1995), 275-315.

30 For a discussion of *yiqi* as a form of masculine ideal, see Kam Louie, *Theorising Chinese Masculinity: Society and Gender in China* (Cambridge: Cambridge University Press, 2002), 32-35.

31 Esther M.K. Cheung, "The City That Haunts: The Uncanny in Fruit Chan's *Made in Hong Kong,*" in *Between Home and World,* ed. Esther M.K. Cheung and Chu Yiu-wai (Hong Kong: Oxford University Press, 2004), 366.

32 For a discussion of Chen Xue's importance as a queer author, see Fran Martin, *Situating Sexualities: Queer Representation in Taiwanese Fiction, Film and Public Culture* (Hong Kong: Hong Kong University Press, 2003), 119-40; and Lucifer Hung, *Ku'er zhaji: Suo'er ma sheng cheng* [Queer journal: Sodom the sanctuary] (Taipei: Yishufang, 1996), 102-6.

33 Yang Zhao, "He e zhi you?" [What's so bad about the bad woman?], preface to Chen Xue, *E nu shu* [Book of a bad woman] (Taipei: Ink Publishing, 2005), 115-25.

34 Chi Ta-wei, "Chen Xue yu xieshi zhuyi" [Chen Xue and realism], postscript to Chen Xue, *Hudie* [Butterfly] (Taipei: Ink Publishing, 2005), 186.

35 Biddy Martin, "Lesbian Identity and Autobiographical Difference," in *Life/Lines: Theorising Women's Autobiography,* ed. Bella Brodzki and Celeste Schenck (Ithaca: Cornell University Press, 1988), 77-103.

36 Chen, *Hudie,* 6.

37 A prominent example is the widely read *Crying and Laughing: Ah Po Narrating History,* a collection of interviews with women between the ages of 63 and 106 about their experiences in Hong Kong: see Ng Chun-Hung and Tsang Gar-Yin, eds., *Youhan youxiao: A Po koushu lishi* [Crying and laughing: Ah Poh narrating history] (Hong Kong: Association for the Advancement of Feminism, 1998).

38 Lucetta Yip Lo Kam, *Yueliang de saodong: Tata de chulian gushi, women de zishu* [Lunar desires: Her same-sex love, in her own words] (Hong Kong: Cultural Act Up, 2001).

39 Ibid., 6.

40 Day Wong, "Beyond Identity Politics: The Making of an Oral History of Hong Kong Women Who Have Same-Sex Desires," *Journal of Lesbian Studies* 10, 3-4 (2007): 29-48.

41 Ibid. I discuss these autobiographical projects in more detail in Chapter 5.

Chapter 3: Trans Formations

1 Sek Kei, *Shi Qi yinghua ji* [Collected reviews of Sek Kei], vol. 4 (Hong Kong: Subculture, 1999), 35.

2 Peter A. Jackson, "Pre-Gay, Post-Queer: Thai Perspectives on Proliferating Gender/Sex Diversity in Asia," *Journal of Homosexuality* 40, 3-4 (2001): 1.

3 Susan Stryker, "(De)Subjugated Knowledges: An Introduction to Transgender Studies," in *The Transgender Studies Reader,* ed. Susan Stryker and Stephen Whittle (New York: Routledge, 2006), 1-17.

4 Ibid., 7.

5 Ibid., 14.

6 Fran Martin and Josephine Ho, "Editorial Introduction: Trans/Asia, Trans/Gender," *Inter-Asia Cultural Studies* 7, 2 (2006): 185.

7 Ibid.

8 The studies have largely been results of the establishment of the Transgender Asia Research Network and the formation of the activist group TEAM (Transgender Equality and

Acceptance Movement); see Sam Winter, "Country Report – Hong Kong: Social and Cultural Issues," Transgender Asia Research Centre, http://web.hku.hk/~sjwinter/TransgenderASIA/ country_report_hk_social.htm; and Mark King, "Perceptions of MtF Transgendered Persons and Their Sexual Partners in Hong Kong: A Study of Social, Emotional, and Cognitive Sources of Biases," Transgender Asia Research Centre, http://web.hku.hk/~sjwinter/ TransgenderASIA/current_research_perceptions_of_mtf.htm. See also the works of Robyn Emerton cited below in note 11.

 9   "Gao 'mu' gui tongzhi yundong" [What the hell kind of *tongzhi* movement], People's Radio Hong Kong 1 (Wednesday, 10 to 11 p.m.), archived shows available at http://prhk2004. sinacool.com/hsu/000.html. One of the co-hosts, Lennie, keeps the blog "Xing? Wu Bie!" [Gender concern], which posts news clippings and also offers weekly phone-in and e-mail hotlines to answer readers' questions. See my discussion of the radio program as a form of queer self-inscription in Chapter 5.

10   Viviane Namaste, *Invisible Lives: The Erasure of Transsexual and Transgendered People* (Chicago: University of Chicago Press, 2000), 24-38.

11   Robyn Emerton, "Neither Here nor There: The Current Status of Transsexual and Other Transgender Persons under Hong Kong Law," *Hong Kong Law Journal* 34, 2 (2004): 247-77; and Robyn Emerton, "Finding a Voice, Fighting for Rights: The Emergence of the Transgender Movement in Hong Kong," *Inter-Asia Cultural Studies* 7, 2 (2006): 243-69.

12   Emerton, "Finding a Voice," 245.

13   Ibid., 265.

14   Ibid., 259.

15   Ibid., 248.

16   Ibid., 249.

17   Josephine Ho, ed., *Kua xingbie* [Trans] (Taipei: National Central University Centre for the Studies of Sexualities, 2003).

18   Josephine Ho, "Embodying Gender: Transgender Body/Subject Formations in Taiwan," *Inter-Asia Cultural Studies* 7, 2 (2006): 228-42.

19   TEAM, http://www.teamhk.org.

20   Jose Neil Cabañero Garcia, "Biaoyan, Bakla yu dongfang zhuyu yingshi, Bakla" [Performativity, Bakla, and the orientalist gaze], trans. Zhang Shuwen, in Ho, ed., *Kua xingbie,* 145-72.

21   Kate Bornstein, *My Gender Workbook* (New York and London: Routledge, 1997), 27.

22   Stryker, "(De)Subjugated Knowledges," 8-9.

23   Judith Halberstam, *In a Queer Time and Place: Transgender Bodies, Subcultural Lives* (New York and London: New York University Press, 2005), 49.

24   Winter, "Country Report."

25   Winter's factual mistakes are as follows: the film stars, but is not "made by," Lin Qingxia (Brigitte Lin); Dongfang Bubai does not "cross-dress" as a woman but rather undergoes a martial-arts-induced process of sex change; and Linghu Chong is a male, not female, character.

26   Jin Yong, *Xiao'ao jianghu* [The smiling, proud wanderer], vol. 4 (Hong Kong: Minghe She, 1980), 1690.

27   For a discussion of this historiographic "use" of the eunuch, see Samshasha, *Zhongguo tongxing'ai shilu* [History of homosexuality in China], rev. ed. (Hong Kong: Rosa Winkel Press, 1997), 348-49.

28   Jin, *Xiao'ao jianghu,* 1282.

29   Ibid., 1291.

30   Ibid., 1293.

31   Ibid., 1468.

32   For a discussion of the role of the hero-hermit in martial arts fiction, see Chen Pingyuan, *Qiangu wenren xiakemeng: Wuxia xiaoshuo leixing yanjiu* [The literati's chivalric dreams: Narrative models of Chinese knight-errant literature] (Taipei: Ryefield, 1995), 187-228.

33   Jin, *Xiao'ao jianghu,* 1690.

34   For an analysis of the relation between the decriminalization debates and the emergence of gay identity in the 1980s and 1990s, see Petula Sik-Ying Ho, "Policing Identity: Decriminalization of Homosexuality and the Emergence of Gay Identity in Hong Kong" (PhD thesis, Essex University, 1997).

35 For a detailed discussion of cross-dressing in the Chinese theatrical tradition, see Li Siu Leung, *Cross-Dressing in Chinese Opera* (Hong Kong: Hong Kong University Press, 2003).

36 The description of the film in the festival catalogue celebrates Dongfang Bubai's "ease with this newly acquired gender identity as a woman"; see the 2001 Netherlands Transgender Film Festival, http://www.transgenderfilmfestival.com/2001/_GB/article_swordsman. html.

37 Jay Prosser, *Second Skins: The Body Narratives of Transsexuality* (New York: Columbia University Press, 1998), 23.

38 Ibid., 32.

39 Chou Wah-Shan, *Tongzhilun* [On *tongzhi*] (Hong Kong: Xianggang Tongzhi Yanjiushe, 1995), 300.

40 Yau Ching, *Lingqi luzao* [Starting another stove] (Hong Kong: Youth Literary Book Store, 1996), 165.

41 Ibid., 166.

42 For a discussion of Anzieu's notion of the "self" in the context of the development of psychoanalytic theory, see Barbara Socor, *Conceiving the Self: Presence and Absence in Psychoanalytic Theory* (Madison and Connecticut: International Universities Press, 1997), 253-60.

43 Prosser, *Second Skins*, 65.

44 Ibid., 77.

45 Ibid.

46 Ibid., 84.

47 Leslie Feinberg, *Stone Butch Blues* (Milford, CT: Firebrand, 1992), 301.

48 Judith Halberstam, *Female Masculinity* (Durham: Duke University Press, 1998), 142-73.

49 Sek, *Shi Qi yinghua ji*, 39.

50 Shelly Kraicer, e-mail correspondence, 28 May 2002.

51 David Bordwell, *Planet Hong Kong: Popular Cinema and the Art of Entertainment* (Cambridge: Harvard University Press, 2000), 108-9.

52 Jillian Sandel, "A Better Tomorrow: American Masochism and Hong Kong Action Film," *Bright Lights Film Journal* 13 (1994): http://www.brightlightsfilm.com/31/hk_better1.html.

53 Mikel J. Koven, "My Brother, My Lover, My Self: Traditional Masculinity in the Hong Kong Action Cinema of John Woo," *Canadian Folklore* 19, 1 (1997): 55-68.

54 For an account of the homoerotic tradition in premodern Chinese literature and culture, see Kang Zhengguo, *Zhongshen fengyue jian: Xing yu zhongguo gudian wenxue* [Reviewing the erotic mirror: Sexuality and classical Chinese literature] (Taipei: Ryefield, 1996), 109-66.

55 Natalia Chan, *Shengshi bianyuan: Xianggang dianying de xingbie, teji yu jiuqi zhengzhi* [City on the edge of time: Gender, technology and 1997 politics in Hong Kong cinema] (Hong Kong: Oxford University Press, 2002), 41-42.

56 King, "Perceptions of MtF Transgendered Persons."

Chapter 4: In Queer Memory

1 For a detailed discussion of the political climate at the time of the protest, see Ray Yep, ed., *Yi Xianggang fangshi jixu ai guo: jiedu ershisan tiao zhengyi ji qiyi da youxing* [Patriotism Hong Kong style: Understanding the controversy of Article 23 and the 1 July 2003 protest] (Hong Kong: Synergy Net, 2003).

2 Ng Chun-Hung, "Women de shidai: Du Zhang Guorong" [Our era: In memorium – Leslie Cheung], *Xin bao* [Hong Kong economic journal], 4 July 2003.

3 Joanna Lee, "Bianyuan huo zhongxin yinxhao Xiangjiang miaobian" [Reflections of Hong Kong's changes through the margin and the centre], *Yazhou zhoukan* [Asia weekly], April 2003, http://lesliecheung.cc/memories/asiaweekly/asiaweekly2.htm.

4 Mathias Woo, "Xianggang liuxin wenhua de liliang" [The power of Hong Kong's popular culture], *Yazhou zhoukan* [Asia weekly], April 2003, http://lesliecheung.cc/memories/asiaweekly/asiaweekly6.htm.

5 "Zhang Guorong de wenhua biaoji: Jieshou yu kangju zhi jian" [Leslie Cheung's cultural legacy: Between acceptance and rejection], *Jingji ribao* [Economic times], 30 April 2003, http://lesliecheung.cc/memories/economictimes.htm.

6 Lam Pui-Li, "Ta yi tongku tixian zhenqing yanchu" [Painful experiences, authentic roles], *Yazhou zhoukan* [Asia weekly], April 2003, http://lesliecheung.cc/memories/asiaweekly/asiaweekly1.htm.

7 Wat Wing-Yin, "Tongzhi xin mingci – zhiai" [A new *tongzhi* term – beloved], *Kuai Zhoukan* [Express weekly], April 2003, http://lesliecheung.cc/memories/watwingyin.htm.

8 Gay Station BBS Forum, http://www.gaystation.com.hk/bbs/viewtopic.php?t=8300.

9 Natalia Chan, "Nansheng nuxiang, cihong tongti: Zhang Guorong de geshan wuying yu meijie lunshu" [Queering body and sexuality: Leslie Cheung's gender representation in Hong Kong popular music], *Meijie yixiang* [Envisage: Journal of Chinese media studies] 3 (2005): 144.

10 Tong Kar-Hei, "Lin Jianming xiang gege zhiqian" [Meg Lam apologized to Leslie Cheung], *Ming Pao Weekly*, 29 March 2004, http://www.mingpaoweekly.com/htm/20040329/mck2.htm.

11 Robert Urban, "Freddie Mercury and Queen: Past, Present, and Future Impressions," *AfterElton*, 16 February 2005, http://www.afterelton.com/music/2005/2/queen.html.

12 Natalia Chan, "Nansheng nuxiang," 136.

13 Ibid., 142-43.

14 See the large collection of commemorative articles on Leslie Cheung Cyberworld, http://lesliecheung.cc/memories/index.htm. A selection of these articles also appears in print in Leslie Cheung Cyberworld, ed., *The One and Only ... Leslie Cheung* (Hong Kong: City Entertainment, 2004), 64-83.

15 Natalia Chan, "Nansheng nuxiang," 136.

16 Natalia Chan, *Shengshi bianyuan: Xianggang dianying de xingbie, teji yu jiuqi zhengzhi* [City on the edge of time: Gender, technology, and 1997 politics in Hong Kong cinema] (Hong Kong: Oxford University Press, 2002), 9-42.

17 For an account of Cheung's admiration for Yam, see Natalia Chan, "Juedai fanghua: Zhang Guorong bu mie de yanhuo" [The legend: Leslie Cheung's undiminished legacy], *Xin Bao* [Hong Kong economic journal], 9 April 2003, http://lesliecheung.cc/memories/lokfung.htm.

18 Tan See-Kam, "The Cross-Gender Performances of Yam Kim-Fei, or The Queer Factor in Postwar Hong Kong Cantonese Opera/Opera Films," in *Queer Asian Cinema: Shadows in the Shade* (Binghamton, NY: Harrington Park Press, 2000).

19 For a discussion of Chan Bo-Chu's versatile cross-dressing practices, see Cheung Kit-Feng, *Wutai ouxiang: Cong Chen Baozhu dao Chen Baozhu* [Stage idol: From Chan Bo-Chu to Chan Bo-Chu] (Hong Kong: Hong Kong Arts Development Council, 2001), 93-114.

20 See my discussion of the film *Yin ± Yang: Gender in Chinese Cinema* in Chapter 3.

21 Verdy Leung and Zero Yiu, "Baibian yaonu de biaoyan zhengzhi: Mei Yanfong de mingxing wenben fenxi" [The politics of performance in the ever-changing monster girl: Textual analysis of Anita Mui's stardom], in *Xing zhengzhi* [Sexual politics], ed. Yau Ching (Hong Kong: Cosmos Books, 2006), 139-59.

22 For a discussion of Anthony Wong's "opaque" play with sexual identities, see Jeroen de Kloet, "Sonic Sturdiness: The Globalization of 'Chinese' Rock and Pop," *Critical Studies in Media Communication* 22, 4 (2005): 333.

23 Leslie Cheung and Anthony Wong, *Crossover,* CD (Hong Kong: Apex and Universal, 2002).

24 For queer art works inspired by the opera duo, see *Song of the Goddess* (Ellen Pao, 1993) and *Suet-Sin's Sisters* (Yau Ching, 1999). References to Yam's works in relation to sexual identity also appear in Stanley Kwan's *Still Love You after All These* (discussed in Chapter 1) and *Yin ± Yang: Gender in Chinese Cinema* (discussed in Chapter 3).

25 "Chen Baozhu muzi tongdai shouyan wutaiju, ti tongxing guanxi chengqing chuanyan" [Chan Bo-Chu and son perform on stage, responds to gossip about intimate female friend], *Tom.com Entertainment*, 27 March 2005, http://ent.tom.com/1306/1362/2005327-129402.html.

26 "Luowen you sanwei nang zhiji xiangban yisheng" [Roman Tam had three male companions in life], *Chinesewings.com*, 26 October 2002, http://news.chinesewings.com/cgi-bin/site/y.cgi?code=big5&id=20021026185668216.

27 "Huang Yaoming xin quxiang re caiyi" [Anthony Wong's sexual orientation prompts questions], *Wen Hui Bao* [Wen Wei Po], 25 May 2007, http://paper.wenweipo.com/2007/05/25/EN0705250006.htm.

28 Clare Whatling, *Screen Dreams: Fantasising Lesbians in Films* (Manchester and New York: Manchester University Press, 1997), 127.

29 Ibid., 119.

30 John Champagne and Elayne Tobin, "'She's Right Behind You': Gossip, Innuendo, and Rumour in the (De)Formation of Gay and Lesbian Studies," in *The Gay '90s: Disciplinary and Interdisciplinary Formations in Queer Studies*, ed. Carol Siegel, Thomas Foster, and Ellen E. Berry (New York and London: New York University Press, 1997), 54.

31 Gavin Butt, *Between You and Me: Queer Disclosures in the New York Art World, 1948-1963* (Durham and London: Duke University Press, 2005).

32 Chan Pak-Sang and Victor Leung, eds., *Dangnian qing: Zhang Guorong* [Interviews with Leslie Cheung] (Hong Kong: City Entertainment, 2003), 43.

33 "Zhang Guorong tan tongxinglian dianying" [Leslie Cheung on gay cinema], *Singdao Wanbao* [Singtao evening news], 17 April 1994; http://lesliecheung.cc/News/1994/17.4.94/17.4.94.htm.

34 "Zhang Guorong nuli nuqi" [Leslie Cheung's feminine air], *Xin Wanbao* [New evening news], 2 May 1992, http://lesliecheung.cc/News/1992/2.5.92/2.5.92.htm.

35 Chan and Leung, eds., *Dangnian qing,* 49.

36 One of the first critical discussions of the representation of the "sissy" in Hollywood cinema is the classic study by Vito Russo, *The Celluloid Closet: Homosexuality in the Movies* (New York: Harper Paperbacks, 1987); for a more recent study, see Harry M. Benshoff and Sean Griffin, *Queer Images: A History of Gay and Lesbian Film in America* (Oxford: Roman and Littlefield, 2006). For a critique of a similar phenomenon in Chinese-language films, see Chou Wah Shan, *Tongzhilun* [On *tongzhi*] (Hong Kong: Xianggang Tongzhi Yanjiushe, 1995), · 275-315.

37 Dennis Lin, "Sissies Online: Taiwanese Male Queers Performing Sissinesses in Cyberspaces," *Inter-Asia Cultural Studies* 7, 2 (2006): 270-88.

38 "Zhang Guorong yu shenmi ren xianglian" [Leslie Cheung in love with mystery person], *Xin Bao* [Hong Kong daily news], 31 July 1994, http://lesliecheung.cc/News/1994/31.7.94/31.7.94.htm.

39 "Zhang Guorong de banlu shi 'ta' hei shi 'ta'?" [Is Leslie Cheung's companion a 'he' or a 'she'?], *Dagong zhoukan* [Taikung magazine], January 2005, http://lesliecheung.cc/Magazine/1995/taikung95/interview/taikung95.htm.

40 Chan and Leung, eds., *Dangnian qing,* 53.

41 Ibid., 69.

42 Audrey Yue, "What's So Queer about *Happy Together?* A.K.A. Queer(N)Asian: Interface, Community, Belonging," *Inter-Asia Cultural Studies* 1, 2 (2000): 251-64.

43 Ibid., 258.

44 Christopher Doyle, *Don't Try for Me Argentina: Photographic Journal* (Hong Kong: City Entertainment, 1997), 56.

45 Ibid., 155.

46 Richard Corliss, "Forever Leslie," *Time Asia,* 7 May 2001, http://www.time.com/time/asia/arts/magazine/0,9754,108021,00.html.

47 Chinese Tongzhi 2000, http://groups.yahoo.com/group/tongzhi2000/.

48 Anson Mak, "Shi de, jinci shi xie Zhang Guorong" [Yes, this time it's about Leslie Cheung], *Xin Bao* [Hong Kong economic journal], 28 May 2001, http://www.aahsun.com/pdf/shin/shin3.jpg.

49 Anna Camilleri, "Jezebel to Joplin: Female Icons Re-Imagined," introduction to *Red Light: Superheroes, Saints, and Sluts,* ed. Anna Camilleri (Vancouver: Arsenal Pulp Press, 2005), 10.

50 Claire Hemmings, "Waiting for No Man: Bisexual Femme Subjectivity and Cultural Repudiation," in *Butch/Femme: Inside Lesbian Gender,* ed. Sally Munt (London: Cassell, 1998), 96.

51 Ibid., original emphasis.

52 Claire Hemmings, *Bisexual Spaces: A Geography of Sexuality and Gender* (New York and London: Routledge, 2002), 126.

53 Leslie Cheung, "Moon River," on *Leslie Cheung Live in Concert 97,* VCD (Hong Kong: Rock, 1997), disc 2, track 8.

54 For a discussion of literary representations, see Kang Zhengguo, *Chongshen fengyue jian: Xing yu zhongguo gudian wenxue* [Reviewing the erotic mirror: Sexuality and classical Chinese

literature] (Taipei: Ryefield, 1996), 109-66; for an exhaustive documentation of historical evidence, see Samshasha, *Zhongguo tongxing'ai shilu* [History of homosexuality in China], rev. ed. (Hong Kong: Rosa Winkel Press, 1997).

55 Shen Defu, *Bizhou zhai yutan* [More discussions from the study of the worn broom], quoted in Michael Szonyi, "The Cult of Hu Tianbao and the Eighteenth-Century Discourse of Homosexuality," *Late Imperial China* 19, 1 (1998): 8; discussed in Kang Zhengguo, *Chongshen fengyue jian*, 146; and in Samshasha, *Zhongguo tongxing'ai shilu*, 173.

56 Eve Kosofsky Sedgwick, *Touching Feeling: Affect, Pedagogy, Performativity* (Durham: Duke University Press, 2003), 7.

57 For an elaboration of the performative work of coming out, see Eve Kosofsky Sedgwick, *Epistemology of the Closet* (Berkeley: University of California Press, 1990), 4-5.

58 For a nuanced critique of gay marriage as a form of homonormativity, see Michael Warner, *The Trouble with Normal: Sex, Politics, and the Ethics of Queer Life* (Cambridge: Harvard University Press, 2000); and Lisa Duggan, *The Twilight of Equality? Neoliberalism, Cultural Politics, and the Attack on Democracy* (Boston: Beacon Press, 2004).

59 Judith Butler, *Undoing Gender* (New York and London: Routledge, 2004), 106, original emphasis.

60 Ibid., 117.

61 Chou Wah-Shan, "Homosexuality and the Cultural Politics of *Tongzhi* in Chinese Societies," *Journal of Homosexuality* 40, 3-4 (2001): 36.

62 Butler, *Undoing Gender*, 123.

63 "Tang Xuede zhiyou shengfen kan fuwen" [Daffy Tong mourns as "truest friend"], *Ming Pao Weekly*, 3 April 2003, http://www.mingpaoweekly.com/htm/20030403/maa1h.htm.

64 For the full text of the announcement, see Huang Weijia, "Tang Hede yi zhiai zhi ming wei gege zhisang" [Daffy Tong makes funeral arrangements as Cheung's beloved], *China Times*, 3 April 2003, http://intermargins.net/Criticism/Recreation%20Review/20030401.htm.

65 Rey Chow, "A Pain in the Neck, a Scene of 'Incest,' and Other Enigmas of an Allegorical Cinema in Tsai Ming-Liang's the River," *New Centennial Review* 4, 1 (2004): 123-42.

66 Leslie Cheung, "I Am What I Am," on *Passion Tour*, VCD (Hong Kong: Apex and Universal, 2001), disc 2, track 15. Technically, this was Cheung's last *filmed* performance and not literally his last because he gave a series of encore concerts during April 2000. Nonetheless, he also closed most of the encore concerts with this particular song.

67 "Shiwu nian lai pei xinsheng, Lin Xi peilu paidang xinyi 15" [Fifteen years of music, Lin Xi reveals partners' thoughts], *Apple Daily*, 6 April 2003, http://www.lesliecheung.cc/memories/linxi2.htm.

68 Leslie Cheung, "I Am What I Am," lyrics by Lin Xi, on *Big Heat*, CD (Hong Kong: Universal, 2000), track 14. Also quoted in Natalia Chan, "Nansheng nuxiang," 144-45.

69 Cheung, "I Am What I Am," on *Big Heat*, track 1.

70 Fran Martin, *Situating Sexualities: Queer Representation in Taiwanese Fiction, Film and Public Culture* (Hong Kong: Hong Kong University Press, 2003), 193.

71 Jenpeng Liu and Naifei Ding, "Reticent Poetics, Queer Politics," *Inter-Asia Cultural Studies* 6, 1 (2005): 30-55.

72 Martin, *Situating Sexualities*, 213-14.

73 Sedgwick, *Epistemology of the Closet*, 4-5.

Chapter 5: Do It Yourself

1 See my discussion of kinship terms in Chapter 4.

2 Sidonie A. Smith and Julia Watson, "Introduction," in *Women, Autobiography, Theory: A Reader*, ed. Sidonie A. Smith and Julia Watson (Madison: University of Wisconsin Press, 1998), 31.

3 Leigh Gilmore, *Autobiographics: A Feminist Theory of Women's Self-Representation* (Ithaca: Cornell University Press, 1994).

4 Jeanne Perreault, "Autography/Transformation/Asymmetry," in *Women, Autobiography, Theory*, ed. Smith and Watson, 190-96.

5 Arnaldo Cruz-Malavé and Martin Manalansan, "Dissident Sexualities/Alternative Globalisms," in *Queer Globalizations: Citizenship and the Afterlife of Colonialism*, ed. Arnaldo Cruz-

Malavé and Martin F. Manalansan IV (New York and London: New York University Press, 2002), 1-10.

6 Ibid., 2.

7 Ibid., 3.

8 Rosemary Hennessy, *Profit and Pleasure: Sexual Identities in Late Capitalism* (New York: Routledge, 2000).

9 Chris Berry, Fran Martin, and Audrey Yue, "Introduction: Beep – Click – Link," in *Mobile Cultures: New Media in Queer Asia*, ed. Chris Berry, Fran Martin, and Audrey Yue (Durham: Duke University Press, 2003), 1-18.

10 Ibid., 13-15.

11 Lucetta Yip Lo Kam, *Yueliang de saodong: Tata de chulian gushi – women de zishu* [Lunar desires: Her same-sex love, in her own words] (Hong Kong: Cultural Act Up, 2001), 5.

12 Ibid., 32-34.

13 Cheung Chau, a former fishing village that now thrives on tourism, is located around 10 km southwest of Hong Kong.

14 Discovery Bay is located on the northeastern coast of Lantau Island. It is a residential area reachable by ferry from several piers in the city centres.

15 Kam, *Yueliang de saodong*, 58.

16 Ibid., 101.

17 Ibid., 135.

18 Ibid., 44-45, 138-47, 182-87.

19 Ibid., 13-18, 71-73, 83-95.

20 Ibid., 61-70.

21 Ibid., 97-98.

22 Ibid., 112-13.

23 Ibid., 6.

24 Women's Coalition of Hong Kong, *Tamen de nuqing yinji: Xianggang hui ai shang nuren de nuren koushu lishi* [In the tracks of their love: Oral history of women who could fall in love with women in Hong Kong], http://oralhistory.wchk.org/.

25 Ibid., http://oralhistory.wchk.org/download.html.

26 Ibid., 18, original emphasis.

27 Ibid., 2.

28 Day Wong, "Beyond Identity Politics: The Making of an Oral History of Hong Kong Women Who Love Women," *Journal of Lesbian Studies* 10, 3-4 (2006): 29-48.

29 Ibid., 41.

30 Ibid., 39.

31 Ibid., 43, 46 note 7.

32 Chu Wei-cheng, "Linglei jingdian" [Alternative classics], in *Taiwan tongzhi xiaoshuo xuan* [Seleced *tongzhi* fiction from Taiwan], ed. Chu Wei-cheng (Taipei: Eryu, 2005), 26.

33 "Witnessing a New Queer Asia," *Persistent Vision* Conference, 2001, *Frameline: San Francisco Lesbian and Gay Film Festival,* San Francisco, 18 June 2001.

34 Anson Mak, *Shuangxing qingyu* [Bisexual desire] (Hong Kong: Hong Kong Christian Women's Association, 2000), 159-62.

35 Judith Halberstam, *Female Masculinity* (Durham: Duke University Press, 1998), 8.

36 "Gao 'mu' gui tongzhi yundong" [What the hell kind of *tongzhi* movement], People's Radio Hong Kong 1 (Wednesday, 10 to 11 p.m.), http://prhk2004.sinacool.com/hsu/000. html.

37 People's Radio Hong Kong, http://www.prhk.org.

38 Ibid.

39 All of the show's episodes are archived and available at http://prhk2004.sinacool.com/hsu/ 000.html.

40 See my discussion in Chapter 3.

41 Judith Halberstam, *In a Queer Time and Place: Transgender Bodies, Subcultural Lives* (New York and London: New York University Press, 2005), 163.

42 Ibid., 169-74.

Glossary

Chinese Names in Film, Cantonese Opera, and Fiction

English	Pinyin	中文
A Ho	A Hao	阿豪
A Tong	A Tong	阿童
A Yun	A Yun	阿潤
Anson	A Bao	阿寶
Bananna	Jiao	蕉
Bean Curd	Furu	腐乳
Brother Mark	Mark Ge	Mark 哥
Brother Shi	Shi Ge	石哥
Chan Kwok-Chan	Chen Guochan	陳國產
Chan Wing-Yan	Chen Yunren	陳永仁
Coke	Kele	可樂
Cookie	Bin	餅
Dongfang Bubai	Dongfang Bubai	東方不敗
Fengyi	Fengyi	鳳儀
Flavia	A Die	阿蝶
Fung Wai	Feng Wei	馮偉
Han Bin	Han Bin	韓賓
Hon	Han	漢
Ho-Nam	Haonan	浩楠
Jas	Baipi	白皮
Jin	Zhen Zhen	真真
Jiney	Qiqi	琪琪
Lang Kim-Sum	Leng Jianxin	冷劍心
Linghu Chong	Linghu Chong	令胡沖
Mei-Ling	Meiling	美玲
Mimi	Wenwen	雯雯
Ming	Ming	明
Murial	Wuhao	武皓
Princess Cheung Ping	Changping gongzhu	長平公主
Princess Ping Yeung	Pingyang gongzhu	平陽公主
Sammi	Xinmei	心眉
Sissy	Si	絲
Sister Thirteen	Shisan mei	十三妹
Tong	Tang	唐
Wei-Ming	Weiming	維明

English	Pinyin	中文
Xiao Jie	Xiao Jie	小潔
Xiao Ye	Xiao Ye	小葉
Xiao Zhe	Xiao Zhe	小哲
Yilin	Yilin	儀霖
Ying Ying	Yingying	盈盈
Yuddy	Yuzai	郁仔
Yue Lingshan	Yue Lingshan	岳靈珊

Other Chinese Personal Names

English	Pinyin	中文
Ah Lik	A Li	阿力
Bak Suet-Sin	Bai Xuexian	白雪仙
Chan Bo-Chu	Chen Baozhu	陳寶珠
Chan Fai Young	Chen Huiyang	陳輝陽
Cheng, Albert	Zheng Jinghan	鄭經翰
Cheung, Leslie	Zhang Guorong	張國榮
Ho Check Chong	He Zecang	何澤蒼
Lam, Edward	Lin Yihua	林奕華
Law Ka	Luo Ka	羅卡
Lin, Bridgette	Lin Qingxia	林青霞
Lin Xi	Lin Xi	林夕
Mo, Teresa	Mao Shunjun	毛舜均
Mui, Anita	Mei Yanfang	梅艷芳
Sek Kei	Shi Qi	石棋
Siu Chou	Xiao Cao	小曹
Tam, Roman	Luo Wen	羅文
Tat Ming Pair	Da Ming Yi Pai	達明一派
Tong, Daffy	Tang Hede	唐鶴德
Tsang, Eric	Ceng Zhiwei	曾志偉
Wai Wai	Weiwei	瑋瑋
Wong Yuk-Man	Huang Yuming	黃毓民
Wong, Anthony	Huang Yaoming	黃耀明
Wong, Faye	Wang Fei	王菲
Yam Kim-Fai	Ren Jianhui	任劍輝
Yuen, Anita	Yuan Yongyi	袁詠儀
Zhang Fengyi	Zhang Fengyi	張豐藝

Chinese Place Names

English	Pinyin	中文
Central	Zhonghuan	中環
Chek Lap Kok Airport	Chilie jiao jichang	赤鱲角機場
Cheung Chau	Chang zhou	長洲
Discovery Bay	Yujing huan	愉景灣
Kai Tak Airport	Qide jichang	啓德機場
Lamma Island	Nanya dao	南丫島
Lantau Island	Gaosheng xiyuan	高陞戲院
Ko Shing Theatre	Dayu shan	大嶼山
Sheung Wan	Shanghuan	上環
Tin Shui Wei	Tianshuiwei	天水圍
Tonkin Street	Dongjing jie	東京街
Western District	Xihuan	西環

Chinese Terms and Phrases

Phrases and terms in pinyin	中文
aiguo aigang	愛國愛港
baohuang dang	保皇黨
gao "mu" gui tongzhi yundong	搞乜鬼同志運動
gou pengyou gou yiqi	夠朋友夠義氣
hansu	含蓄
huanxingren	換性人
kanpo chaotuo	看破超脫
kuaxingren	跨性人
ku'er	酷兒
lidao	離島
pingchang xin	平常心
qidi	契弟
qixiong	契兄
qixiongdi	契兄弟
renyao	人妖
shengxian	聖象
tongzhi	同志
wuxin	無心
xiangxue	相學
xiaoyuan xiaoshuo	校園小說
xuelian	學聯
yanggang	陽剛
yinmou	陰謀
yinrou	陰柔
yumou	預謀
zhiai	摯愛
zhiyou	摯友

Bibliography

English-Language Sources

Aaron, Michele. *New Queer Cinema: A Critical Reader*. Edinburgh: Edinburgh University Press, 2004.

Abbas, Ackbar. *Hong Kong: Culture and the Politics of Disappearance*. Minneapolis: University of Minnesota Press, 1997.

–. "Hong Kong: Other Histories, Other Places." In *Between Home and World: A Reader in Hong Kong Cinema*, ed. Esther M.K. Cheung and Chu Yiu-wai, 273-96. Hong Kong: Oxford University Press, 2004.

Ahmed, Sara. *The Cultural Politics of Emotions*. New York and London: Routledge, 2004.

Benshoff, Harry M. *Monster in the Closet: Homosexuality and the Horror Film*. Manchester: Manchester University Press, 1997.

Benshoff, Harry M., and Sean Griffin. *Queer Images: A History of Gay and Lesbian Film in America*. Oxford: Roman and Littlefield, 2006.

Berry, Chris. "The Sacred, the Profane, and the Domestic in Cui Zi'en's Cinema." *Positions: East Asia Cultures Critique* 12, 1 (2004): 195-201.

–. "Staging Gay Life in China." *Jump Cut: A Review of Contemporary Media* 42 (1998): 84-89.

–, Fran Martin, and Audrey Yue. "Introduction: Beep – Click – Link." In *Mobile Cultures: New Media in Queer Asia*, ed. Chris Berry, Fran Martin, and Audrey Yue, 1-18. Durham: Duke University Press, 2003.

Betsky, Aaron. *Queer Space: Architecture and Same-Sex Desire*. New York: William Morrow, 1997.

Bordwell, David. *Planet Hong Kong: Popular Cinema and the Art of Entertainment*. Cambridge: Harvard University Press, 2000.

Bornstein, Kate. *My Gender Workbook*. New York and London: Routledge, 1997.

Brottman, Mikita. *Offensive Films*. Nashville: Vanderbilt University Press, 2005.

Bullock, Denise. "Lesbian Cruising: An Examination of the Concept and Methods." *Journal of Homosexuality* 47, 2 (2004): 1-31.

Butler, Judith. *Bodies That Matter: On the Discursive Limits of Sex*. New York: Routledge, 1993.

–. *Undoing Gender*. New York and London: Routledge, 2004.

Butt, Gavin. *Between You and Me: Queer Disclosures in the New York Art World, 1948-1963*. Durham and London: Duke University Press, 2005.

Califia, Patrick. *Sex Changes: The Politics of Transgenderism*. San Francisco: Cleis Press, 2003.

Camilleri, Anna. *I Am a Red Dress: Incantations on a Grandmother, a Mother, and a Daughter*. Vancouver: Arsenal Pulp Press, 2004.

–. "Jezebel to Joplin: Female Icons Re-Imagined." Introduction to *Red Light: Superheroes, Saints, and Sluts*, ed. Anna Camilleri, 9-14. Vancouver: Arsenal Pulp Press, 2005.

Champagne, John, and Elayne Tobin. "'She's Right Behind You': Gossip, Innuendo, and Rumour in the (De)Formation of Gay and Lesbian Studies." In *The Gay '90s: Disciplinary and Interdisciplinary Formations in Queer Studies,* ed. Carol Siegel, Thomas Foster, and Ellen E. Berry, 51-82. New York and London: New York University Press, 1997.

Chan, Evans. Interview by Stefan Borsos, *CineAsia,* June-July 2001, http://www.evanschan.com/M_S_and_L/html/MainFrameset.html.

Cheung, Esther M.K. "The City That Haunts: The Uncanny in Fruit Chan's *Made in Hong Kong.*" In *Between Home and World: A Reader in Hong Kong Cinema,* ed. Esther M.K. Cheung and Chu Yiu-wai, 352-68. Hong Kong: Oxford University Press, 2004.

Cheung, Esther M.K., and Chu Yiu-wai, eds. *Between Home and World: A Reader in Hong Kong Cinema.* Hong Kong: Oxford University Press, 2004.

Chisholm, Dianne. "The City of Collective Memory," *GLQ: Journal of Lesbian and Gay Studies* 7, 2 (2001): 195-243.

Chou Wah-Shan. "Homosexuality and the Cultural Politics of *Tongzhi* in Chinese Societies." *Journal of Homosexuality* 40, 3-4 (2001): 27-46.

Chow, Rey. *Ethics after Idealism: Theory-Culture-Ethnicity-Reading.* Bloomington: Indiana University Press, 1998.

–. "A Pain in the Neck, a Scene of 'Incest,' and Other Enigmas of an Allegorical Cinema in Tsai Ming-Liang's *The River.*" *New Centennial Review* 4, 1 (2004): 123-42.

–. *Writing Diaspora: Tactics of Intervention in Contemporary Cultural Studies.* Bloomington: Indiana University Press, 1993.

Chu Wei-cheng. "Queer(Ing) Taiwan and Its Future: From an Agenda of Mainstream Self-Enlightenment to One of Sexual Citizenship?" Paper presented at Sexualities, Genders, and Rights in Asia: 1st International Conference of Queer Asian Studies, Bangkok, Mahidol University, 7-9 July 2005.

Clover, Carol J. "Her Body, Himself: Gender in the Slasher Film." *Representations* 20 (1987): 205-28.

Corlett, William. *Community without Unity: A Politics of Derridean Extravagance.* Durham: Duke University Press, 1989.

Corliss, Richard. "Forever Leslie." *Time Asia,* 7 May 2001, http://www.time.com/time/asia/arts/magazine/0,9754,108021,00.html.

Creed, Barbara. "Horror and the Monstrous-Feminine: An Imaginary Abjection." *Screen* 27, 1 (1986): 44-54.

Cruz-Malave, Arnaldo, and F. Martin Manalansan IV. "Dissident Sexualities/Alternative Globalisms." In *Queer Globalizations: Citizenship and the Afterlife of Colonialism,* ed. Arnaldo Cruz-Malavé and F. Martin Manalansan IV, 1-10. New York: New York University Press, 2002.

–, eds. *Queer Globalizations: Citizenship and the Afterlife of Colonialism.* New York: New York University Press, 2002.

Cvetkovich, Ann. *An Archive of Feelings: Trauma, Sexuality, and Lesbian Public Culture.* Durham: Duke University Press, 2003.

Dasgupta, Romit. "The Film *Bishonen* and Queer(N)Asia through Japanese Popular Culture." In *Popular Culture, Globalization and Japan,* ed. Matthew and Rumi Sakamoto Allen, 56-74. New York: Routledge, 2006.

de Kloet, Jereon. "Sonic Sturdiness: The Globalization of 'Chinese' Rock and Pop." *Critical Studies in Media Communication* 22, 4 (2005): 321-38.

Désert, Jean-Ulrick. "Queer Space." In *Queers in Space: Communities, Public Places, Sites of Resistance,* ed. Gordon Brent Ingram, Anne-Marie Bouthilette, and Yolanda Retter, 17-26. Seattle: Bay Press, 1997.

Doyle, Christopher. *Don't Try for Me Argentina: Photographic Journal.* Hong Kong: City Entertainment, 1997.

Duggan, Lisa. *The Twilight of Equality? Neoliberalism, Cultural Politics, and the Attack on Democracy.* Boston: Beacon Press, 2004.

Emerton, Robyn. "Finding a Voice, Fighting for Rights: The Emergence of the Transgender Movement in Hong Kong." *Inter-Asia Cultural Studies* 7, 2 (2006): 243-69.

–. "Neither Here nor There: The Current Status of Transsexual and Other Transgender Persons under Hong Kong Law." *Hong Kong Law Journal* 34, 2 (2004): 247-77.

–. "Time for Change: A Call for the Legal Recognition of Transsexual and Other Transgender Persons in Hong Kong." *Hong Kong Law Journal* 34, 3 (2004): 516-55.

Feinberg, Leslie. *Stone Butch Blues*. Milford, CT: Firebrand, 1992.

–. *Trans Liberation: Beyond Pink or Blue*. Boston: Beacon Press, 1999.

Garber, Marjorie. *Vested Interests: Cross-Dressing and Cultural Anxiety*. New York: Routledge, 1997.

–. *Vice Versa: Bisexuality and the Eroticism of Everyday Life*. New York: Simon and Schuster, 1996.

Gilmore, Leigh. *Autobiographics: A Feminist Theory of Women's Self-Representation*. Ithaca: Cornell University Press, 1994.

Gordon, Tuula, and Elina Lahelma. "Who Wants to Be a Woman? Young Women's Reflections on Transitions to Adulthood." *Feminist Review* 78 (2004): 80-98.

Halberstam, Judith. *Female Masculinity*. Durham: Duke University Press, 1998.

–. *In a Queer Time and Place: Transgender Bodies, Subcultural Lives*. New York and London: New York University Press, 2005.

Hall, Donald E., and Maria Pramaggiore, eds. *Representing Bisexualities: Subjects and Cultures of Fluid Desire*. New York and London: New York University Press, 1996.

Harvey, David. *The Condition of Postmodernity: An Enquiry into the Origins of Cultural Change*. Oxford: Blackwell, 1991.

Hemmings, Claire. *Bisexual Spaces: A Geography of Sexuality and Gender*. New York and London: Routledge, 2002.

–. "Waiting for No Man: Bisexual Femme Subjectivity and Cultural Repudiation." In *Butch/Femme: Inside Lesbian Gender*, ed. Sally Munt, 90-100. London: Cassell, 1998.

Hennessy, Rosemary. *Profit and Pleasure: Sexual Identities in Late Capitalism*. New York: Routledge, 2000.

Ho, Josephine. "Embodying Gender: Transgender Body/Subject Formations in Taiwan." *Inter-Asia Cultural Studies* 7, 2 (2006): 228-42.

Ho, Petula Sik-Ying. "Policing Identity: Decriminalization of Homosexuality and the Emergence of Gay Identity in Hong Kong." PhD thesis, Essex University, 1997.

Huang Tsung-yi. "Hong Kong Blue: Flâneurie with the Camera's Eye in a Phantasmagoric Global City." *JNT: Journal of Narrative Theory* 30, 3 (2000): 385-402.

Hui, Eddie C.M., Manfred C.M. Lam, and Vivian S.M. Ho. "Market Disequilibrium and Urban Land Shortage: Analysis of Policy and Patterns in Hong Kong." *Journal of Urban Planning and Development* 132, 2 (2006): 80-88.

Ingram, Gordon Brent. "Marginality and the Landscapes of Erotic Alien(N)ation." In *Queers in Space: Communities, Public Places, Sites of Resistance*, ed. Gordon Brent Ingram, Anne-Marie Bouthilette, and Yolanda Retter, 27-52. Seattle: Bay Press, 1997.

–, Anne-Marie Bouthilette, and Yolanda Retter, eds. *Queers in Space: Communities, Public Places, Sites of Resistance*. Seattle: Bay Press, 1997.

Jackson, Peter A. "Pre-Gay, Post-Queer: Thai Perspectives on Proliferating Gender/Sex Diversity in Asia." *Journal of Homosexuality* 40, 3-4 (2001): 1-25.

King, Mark. "Perceptions of MtF Transgendered Persons and Their Sexual Partners in Hong Kong: A Study of Social, Emotional, and Cognitive Sources of Biases." Transgender Asia Research Centre, http://web.hku.hk/~sjwinter/TransgenderASIA/current_research_perceptions_of_mtf.htm.

Kong, Travis. "Queering Masculinity in Hong Kong Movies." In *Masculinities and Hong Kong Cinema*, ed. Laikwan Pang and Day Wong, 57-80. Hong Kong: Hong Kong University Press, 2005.

Koven, Mikel J. "My Brother, My Lover, My Self: Traditional Masculinity in the Hong Kong Action Cinema of John Woo." *Canadian Folklore* 19, 1 (1997): 55-68.

Leap, William L., and Tom Boellstorff, eds. *Speaking in Queer Tongues: Globalization and Gay Language*. Urbana and Chicago: University of Illinois Press, 2003.

Leung Ping-Kwan. "Urban Cinema and Cultural Identity of Hong Kong." In *Between Home and World: A Reader in Hong Kong Cinema*, ed. Esther M.K. Cheung and Chu Yiu-wai, 369-98. Hong Kong: Oxford University Press, 2004.

Li Siu Leung. *Cross-Dressing in Chinese Opera*. Hong Kong: Hong Kong University Press, 2003.

Lin, Dennis. "Sissies Online: Taiwanese Male Queers Performing Sissinesses in Cyberspaces." *Inter-Asia Cultural Studies* 7, 2 (2006): 270-88.

Liu Jenpeng, and Ding Naifei. "Reticent Poetics, Queer Politics." *Inter-Asia Cultural Studies* 6, 1 (2005): 30-55.

Louie, Kam. *Theorising Chinese Masculinity: Society and Gender in China*. Cambridge: Cambridge University Press, 2002.

Martin, Biddy. "Lesbian Identity and Autobiographical Difference." In *Life/Lines: Theorising Women's Autobiography,* ed. Bella Brodzki and Celeste Schenck, 77-103. Ithaca: Cornell University Press, 1988.

Martin, Fran. *Situating Sexualities: Queer Representation in Taiwanese Fiction, Film and Public Culture*. Hong Kong: Hong Kong University Press, 2003.

–, and Josephine Ho. "Editorial Introduction: Trans/Asia, Trans/Gender." *Inter-Asia Cultural Studies* 7, 2 (2006): 185-87.

Massad, Joseph. "Re-Orientating Desire: The Gay International and the Arab World." *Public Culture* 14, 2 (2002): 361-85.

Namaste, Viviane. *Invisible Lives: The Erasure of Transsexual and Transgendered People*. Chicago: University of Chicago Press, 2000.

Ng Kar Man. "Friendship and Gender Construction: A Study of Young Women between Girlhood and Womanhood in Hong Kong." M. Phil. thesis, University of Hong Kong, 2006.

Ong Aihwa. *Flexible Citizenship: The Cultural Logics of Transnationality*. Durham: Duke University Press, 1998.

Perreault, Jeanne. "Autography/Transformation/Assymetry." In *Women, Autobiography, Theory: A Reader,* ed. Sidonie A. Smith and Julia Watson, 190-96. Madison: University of Wisconsin Press, 1998.

Pramaggiore, Maria. "Epistemologies of the Fence." In *Representing Bisexualities: Subjects and Cultures of Fluid Desire,* ed. Donald E. Hall and Maria Pramaggiore, 1-7. New York and London: New York University Press, 1996.

–. "Straddling the Screen: Bisexual Spectatorship and Contemporary Narrative Film." In *Representing Bisexualities: Subjects and Cultures of Fluid Desire,* ed. Donald E. Hall and Maria Pramaggiore, 272-97. New York and London: New York University Press, 1996.

Prosser, Jay. *Light in the Dark Room: Photography and Loss*. Minneapolis: University of Minnesota Press, 2005.

–. *Second Skins: The Body Narratives of Transsexuality*. New York: Columbia University Press, 1998.

Rose, Chloe Brushwood, and Anna Camilleri, eds. *Brazen Femme: Queering Femininity*. Vancouver: Arsenal Press, 2002.

Rushbrook, Dereka. "Cities, Queer Space, and the Cosmopolitan Tourist." *GLQ: Journal of Lesbian and Gay Studies* 8, 1-2 (2002): 183-206.

Russo, Vito. *The Celluloid Closet: Homosexuality in the Movies*. New York: Harper Paperbacks, 1987.

Sandel, Jillian. "A Better Tomorrow: American Masochism and Hong Kong Action Film." *Bright Lights Film Journal* 13 (1994): http://www.brightlightsfilm.com/31/hk_better1.html.

Sang Tze-Lan D. *The Emerging Lesbian: Female Same-Sex Desire in Modern China*. Chicago: University Of Chicago Press, 2003.

Santiago, Silviano. "The Wily Homosexual (First – and Necessarily Hasty – Notes)." In *Queer Globalizations: Citizenship and the Afterlife of Colonialism,* ed. Arnaldo Cruz-Malavé and Martin F. Manalansan IV, 13-19. New York and London: New York University Press, 2002.

Sedgwick, Eve Kosofsky. *Epistemology of the Closet*. Berkeley: University of California Press, 1990.

–. *Touching Feeling: Affect, Pedagogy, Performativity*. Durham: Duke University Press, 2003.

Sieber, Patricia. "Introduction." In *Red Is Not the Only Colour: Contemporary Chinese Fiction on Love and Sex between Women, Collected Stories,* ed. Patricia Sieber, 1-35. Oxford: Rowman and Littlefield, 2001.

Signorile, Michelangelo. *Queers in America: Sex, the Media, and the Closets of Power*. 3rd ed. Madison: University of Wisconsin Press, 2003.

Skeldon, Ronald. "Hong Kong in an International Migration System." In *The Hong Kong Reader: Passage to Chinese Sovereignty*, ed. Ming K. Chan and Gerard A. Postiglione, 21-52. Armonk, NY: M.E. Sharpe, 1996.

Smelik, Anneke. "Bodies That Kill: Art Cinema and Its Murderous Girls in Love." *Textus* 13, 2 (2000): 449-68.

Smith, Sidonie A., and Julia Watson. "Introduction: Situating Subjectivity in Women's Autobiographical Practices." In *Women, Autobiography, Theory: A Reader*, ed. Sidonie A. Smith and Julia Watson, 3-52. Madison: University of Wisconsin Press, 1998.

–, eds. *Women, Autobiography, Theory: A Reader*. Madison: University of Wisconsin Press, 1998.

Socor, Barbara. *Conceiving the Self: Presence and Absence in Psychoanalytic Theory*. Madison and Connecticut: International Universities Press, 1997.

Sontag, Susan. *On Photography*. London: Picador, 2001.

Straayer, Chris. *Deviant Eyes, Deviant Bodies*. New York: Columbia University Press, 1996.

Stryker, Susan. "(De)Subjugated Knowledges: An Introduction to Transgender Studies." In *The Transgender Studies Reader*, ed. Susan Stryker and Stephen Whittle, 1-17. New York: Routledge, 2006.

Szonyi, Michael. "The Cult of Hu Tianbao and the Eighteenth-Century Discourse of Homosexuality." *Late Imperial China* 19, 1 (1998): 1-25.

Tan See-Kam. "The Cross-Gender Performances of Yam Kim-Fei, or The Queer Factor in Postwar Hong Kong Cantonese Opera/Opera Films." In *Queer Asian Cinema: Shadows in the Shade*, 201-11. Binghamton, NY: Harrington Park Press, 2000.

Turner, Mark. *Backward Glances: Cruising the Queer Streets of New York and London*. London: Reaktion Books, 2003.

Urban, Robert. "Freddie Mercury and Queen: Past, Present, and Future Impressions." *AfterElton.com*, 16 February 2005, http://www.afterelton.com/music/2005/2/queen.html.

Vaid, Urvashi. *Virtual Equality: The Mainstreaming of Gay and Lesbian Liberation*. New York: Anchor, 1996.

Warner, Michael. *The Trouble with Normal: Sex, Politics, and the Ethics of Queer Life*. Cambridge: Harvard University Press, 2000.

Whatling, Clare. *Screen Dreams: Fantasising Lesbians in Films*. Manchester and New York: Manchester University Press, 1997.

Williams, Linda. *Hardcore*. Berkeley: University of California Press, 1999.

–. "Learning to Scream." In *Horror: The Film Reader*, ed. Mark Jancovich, 164-68. London and New York: Routledge, 2002.

–. "When the Woman Looks." In *Re-Vision: Essays in Feminist Film Criticism*, ed. Patricia Mellencamp, Mary Ann Doane, and Linda Williams, 83-99. Frederick, MD: American Film Institute, 1983.

Winter, Sam. "Country Report – Hong Kong: Social and Cultural Issues." Transgender Asia Research Centre, http://web.hku.hk/~sjwinter/TransgenderASIA/country_report_hk_social.htm.

Wong, Day. "Beyond Identity Politics: The Making of an Oral History of Hong Kong Women Who Love Women." *Journal of Lesbian Studies* 10, 3-4 (2006): 29-48.

–. "(Post-)Identity Politics and Anti-Normalization: (Homo) Sexual Rights Movement." In *Remaking Citizenship in Hong Kong: Community, Nation and the Global City*, 195-214. London and New York: Routledge/Curzon, 2004.

Yue, Audrey. "What's So Queer about *Happy Together*? A.K.A. Queer(N)Asian: Interface, Community, Belonging." *Inter-Asia Cultural Studies* 1, 2 (2000): 251-64.

Chinese-Language Sources

Cao Minwei (曹民偉). *You gannai fengliu: Xianggang bainian qingse shi* (有咁耐風流：香港百年情色史) [Hong Kong erotic history]. Hong Kong: Lok Man, 2004.

Chan, Natalia (洛楓). "Juedai fanghua: Zhang Guorong bu mie de yanhuo" (絕代芳華：張國榮不滅的煙火) [The legend: Leslie Cheung's undiminished legacy]." *Xin Bao* (信報) [Hong Kong economic journal], 9 April 2003, http://lesliecheung.cc/memories/lokfung.htm.

–. "Nansheng nuxiang, cihong tongti: Zhang Guorong de geshan wuying yu meijie lunshu" (男生女相，雌雄同體：張國榮的歌衫舞影與媒介論述) [Queering body and sexuality: Leslie Cheung's gender representation in Hong Kong popular music]. *Meijie yixiang* (媒介擬想) [Envisage: journal of Chinese media studies] 3 (2005): 134-46.

–. *Shengshi bianyuan: Xianggang dianying de xingbie, teji yu jiuqi zhengzhi* (盛世邊緣：香港電影的性別、特技與九七政治) [City on the edge of time: Gender, technology, and 1997 politics in Hong Kong cinema]. Hong Kong: Oxford University Press, 2002.

Chan Pak-Sang (陳柏生) and Victor Leung (梁維康), eds. *Dangnian qing: Zhang Guorong* (當年情：張國榮) [Interviews with Leslie Cheung]. Hong Kong: City Entertainment, 2003.

Chang, Eileen (張愛玲). *Qingcheng zhi lian* (傾城之戀) [Love in a fallen city]. Taipei: Crown, 1991.

"Chen Bao Zhu muzi tongdai shouyan wutaiju, ti tongxing guanxi chengqing chuanyan" (陳寶珠母子同台首演舞台劇，提同性關係澄清傳言) [Chan Bo-Chu and son perform on stage, responds to gossip about intimate female friend]. *Tom.com Entertainment*, 27 March 27, http://ent.tom.com/1306/1362/2005327-129402.html.

Chen Pingyuan (陳平原). *Qiangu wenren xiakemeng: Wuxia xiaoshuo leixing yanjiu* (千古文人俠客夢：武俠小說類形研究) [The literati's chivalric dreams: Narrative models of Chinese knight-errant literature]. Taipei: Ryefield, 1995.

Chen Xue (陳雪). *E nu shu* (惡女書) [Book of a bad woman]. Taipei: Ink Publishing, 2005.

–. *Hudie* (蝴蝶) [Butterfly]. Taipei: Ink Publishing, 2005.

Cheung Kit-Feng (張結鳳). *Wutai ouxiang: Cong Chen Baozhu dao Chen Baozhu* (舞台偶象：從陳寶珠到陳寶珠) [Stage idol: From Chan Bo-Chu to Chan Bo-Chu]. Hong Kong: Hong Kong Arts Development Council, 2001.

Chi Ta-wei (紀大偉). "Chen Xue yu xieshi zhuyi" (陳雪與現實主義) [Chen Xue and realism]. Postscript to *Hudie* (蝴蝶) [Butterfly], by Chen Xue (陳雪), 186. Taipei: Ink Publishing, 2005.

–. "Ku'er lun: Sikao dangdai Taiwan ku'er yu ku'er wenxue" (酷兒論：思考當代台灣酷兒與酷兒 文學) [On ku'er: Thoughts on *ku'er* and *ku'er* literature in contemporary Taiwan]. In *Ku'er kuanghuan jie* (酷兒狂歡節) [Queer carnival], ed. Chi Ta-wei (紀大偉), 9-28. Taipei: Meta Media, 1997.

Chou Wah Shan (周華山). *Tongzhilun* (同志論) [On *tongzhi*]. Hong Kong: Xianggang Tongzhi Yanjiushe, 1995.

Chu Wei-cheng (朱偉誠). "Linglei jingdian" (另類經典) [Alternative classics]. In *Taiwan Tongzhi xiaoshuo xuan* (臺灣同志小說選) [Selected *tongzhi* fiction from Taiwan], ed. Chu Wei-cheng (朱偉誠), 9-35. Taipei: Eryu, 2005.

–. "Tongzhi · Taiwan: Xonggongmin, guozu jiangou huo gongmin shehui" (同志·台灣：性公民、國族建構或公民社會) [Queer(ing) Taiwan: Sexual citizenship, nation building, or civil society]. *Nuxue xuezhi: Funu yu xingbei yanjiu* (女學學誌：婦女與性別研究) [Journal of women's and gender studies] 15 (2003): 115-51.

Garcia, Jose Neil Cabañero. "Biaoyan, Bakla yu dongfang zhuyu yingshi" (表演，Bakla 與東方主義的凝視) [Performativity, Bakla, and the Orientalist gaze]. Trans. Zhang Shuwen (張淑紋). In *Kua xingbie* (跨性別) [Trans], ed. Josephine Ho (何春蕤), 145-72. Taipei: National Central University Centre for the Studies of Sexualities, 2003.

Ho, Josephine (何春蕤), ed. *Kua xingbie* (跨性別) [Trans]. Taipei: National Central University Centre for the Studies of Sexualities, 2003.

"Hu Jintao: Yiguo shi lianzhi de qianti" (胡錦濤：一國是兩制的前題) [Hu Juntao: One country is the precondition of two systems]. *BBC Chinese.com*, 1 July 2007, http://news.bbc.co.uk/chinese/trad/hi/newsid_6250000/newsid_6258000/6258048.stm.

Huang Weijia (王維佳). "Tang Hede yi zhiai zhi ming wei gege zhisang" (唐鶴德以摯愛之名為哥哥治喪) [Daffy Tong makes funeral arrangements as Cheung's beloved]. *China Times* (中國時報), 3 April 2003, http://intermargins.net/Criticism/Recreation%20Review/20030401.htm.

"Huang Yaoming xin quxiang re caiyi" (黃耀明性取向惹猜疑) [Anthony Wong's sexual orientation prompts questions]. *Wen Hui Bao* (文匯報) [Wen Wei Po], 25 May 2007, http://paper.wenweipo.com/2007/05/25/EN0705250006.htm.

Hung, Lucifer (洪凌). *Ku'er zhaji: Suo'er ma sheng cheng* (酷異劄記：索爾瑪聖城) [Queer journal: Sodom the sanctuary]. Taipei: Yishufang, 1996.

Jin Yong (金庸). *Xiao'ao jianghu* (笑傲江湖) [The smiling, proud wanderer]. Vol. 4. Hong Kong: Minghe She, 1980.

Kam, Yip Lo Lucetta (金曄路), ed. *Yueliang de saodong: Tata de chulian gushi – women de zishu* (月亮的騷動：她她的初戀故事– 我們的自述) [Lunar desires: Her same-sex love, in her own words]. Hong Kong: Cultural Act Up, 2001.

Kang Zhengguo (康正果). *Chongshen fengyue jian: Xing yu zhongguo gudian wenxue* (重審風月鑑：性與中國文學) [Reviewing the erotic mirror: Sexuality and classical Chinese literature]. Taipei: Ryefield, 1996.

Lai, J.J. (賴正哲). *Qu gongsi shangban: Xin gongyuan de nan tongzhi de qingyu kongjian* (去公司上班：新公園的男同志空間) [Going to work in the office: Homosexual space in New Park]. Taipei: Nushu wenhua, 2005.

Lam Pui-Li (林沛理). "Ta yi tongku tixian zhenqing yanchu" (他以痛苦體驗真情演出) [Painful experiences, authentic roles]. *Yazhou zhoukan* (亞洲週刊) [Asia weekly], April 2003, http://lesliecheung.cc/memories/asiaweekly/asiaweekly1.htm.

Lee, Bono (李照興). "Nanyadao de bianyuan shenhua" (南丫島的邊緣神話) [Lamma Island's legends of marginality]. In *Xianggang 101: Aihen Xianggang de yilingyi ge liyou* (香港101：愛恨香港的101個理由) [Hong Kong 101: One hundred and one reasons to love and hate Hong Kong], ed. Bono Lee (李照興) and Fan Tsang (曾凡), 70-73. Hong Kong: Crown, 2001.

Lee, Joanna (李正欣). "Bianyuan huo zhongxin yinxhao Xiangjiang miaobian" (邊緣或中心映照香江變貌) [Reflections of Hong Kong's changes through the margin and the centre]. *Yazhou zhoukan* (亞洲週刊) [Asia weekly], April 2003, http://lesliecheung.cc/memories/asiaweekly/asiaweekly2.htm.

Leslie Cheung Cyberworld, ed., *The One and Only ... Leslie Cheung*. Hong Kong: City Entertainment, 2004.

Leung Ping-Kwan (也斯). *Xianggang wenhua* (香港文化) [Hong Kong culture]. Hong Kong: Hong Kong Arts Centre, 1995.

Leung, Verdy (梁偉怡), and Zero Yiu (饒欣凌). "Baibian yaonu de biaoyan zhengzhi: Mei Yanfong de mingxing wenben fenxi" (百變妖女的表演政治: 梅艷芳的明星文本分析) [The politics of performance in the ever-changing monster girl: Textual analysis of Anita Mui's stardom]. In *Xing zhengzhi* (性政治) [Sexual politics], ed. Yau Ching (游靜), 139-59. Hong Kong: Cosmos Books, 2006.

Li Yinhe (李銀河). *Tongxinglian ya wenhua* (同性戀亞文化) [The homosexual subculture]. Beijing: Jinri Zhonghua Chubanshe, 1998.

–, and Wang Xiaobo (王小波). *Tamen de shijie* (他們的世界) [Their world]. Hong Kong: Cosmos Books, 1993.

Long Yingtai (龍應台). "Xianggang ni wang nali qu?" (香港你往那裡去?) [Hong Kong: Where are you going?]. *Ming Pao* (明報), 9 November 2004, A4.

Longtin (朗天). *Hou jiuqi yu Xianggang dianying* (後九七與香港電影) [Post-97 and Hong Kong cinema]. Hong Kong: Hong Kong Film Critics Society, 2003.

Loo, John (盧劍雄), ed. *Huaren tongzhi xin dupin* (華人同志新讀本) [New reader on Chinese tongzhi]. Hong Kong: Worldson, 1999.

Lu Wei-Luan (盧瑋鑾). *Xianggang gushi: Geren huiyi yu wenxue sikao* (香港故事：個人回憶與文學思考) [Hong Kong stories: Personal memories and literary reflections]. Hong Kong: Oxford University Press, 1996.

Luowen you sanwei nan zhiji xiangban yisheng" (羅文有三位男知己相伴一生) [Roman Tam had three male companions in life]. *Chinesewings.com,* 26 October 2002, http://news.chinesewings.com/cgi-bin/site/y.cgi?code=big5&id=20021026185668216.

Mak, Anson (麥海珊). "Shi de, jingci shi xie Zhang Guorong" (是的，今次是寫張國榮) [Yes, this time it's about Leslie Cheung]. *Xin bao* (信報) [Hong Kong economic journal], 28 May 2001, http://www.aahsun.com/pdf/shin/shin3.jpg.

–. *Shuangxing qingyu* (雙性情慾) [Bisexual desire]. Hong Kong: Hong Kong Christian Women's Association, 2000.

Ng Chun-Hung (吳俊雄). "Women de shidai: Du Zhang Guorong" (我們的時代：悼張國榮) [Our era: In memorium – Leslie Cheung]. *Xin bao* (信報) [Hong Kong economic journal], 4 July 2003, http://lesliecheung.cc/memories/leungfoon.htm.

–, and Cheung Chi-Wai (張志偉), eds. *Yuedu Xianggang puji wenhua, 1970-2000* (閱讀香港普及文化, 1970-2000) [Reading Hong Kong popular cultures, 1970-2000]. Hong Kong: Oxford University Press, 2002.

–, and Tsang Gar-Yin (曾嘉燕), eds. *Youhan youxiao: A Po koushu lishi* (又喊又笑：阿婆口述歷史) [Crying and laughing: Ah Poh narrating history]. Hong Kong: Association for the Advancement of Feminism, 1998.

Ng Kit-Fan (吳潔芬). "Chunsui de guodu" (純粹的國度) [A pure world]. In *Ta ta ta ta di gushi* (他他她她的故事) [His-his her-her stories], ed. John Loo (盧劍雄), 206-57. Hong Kong: Worldson, 1996.

Pun, Lawrence (潘國靈). "Wei he yao yiben Wang Jiawei zhuanlun?" (為何要一本王家衛專論?) [Why a critical anthology on Wong Kar-Wai?]. In *Wang Jiawei de yinghua shijie* (王家衛的影畫世界) [The cinema of Wong Kar-Wai], ed. Lawrence Pun (潘國靈) and Bono Lee (李照興), v-vii. Hong Kong: Joint Publishing, 2004.

Roan Ching-yueh (阮慶岳). *Chugui kongjian: Xuyi tongzhi cheng* (出柜空間：虛擬同志城) [Queer space cha cha cha]. Taipei: Meta Media, 1998.

Samshasha (小明雄). *Zhongguo tongxing'ai shilu* (中國同性愛史錄) [History of homosexuality in China]. Rev. ed. Hong Kong: Rosa Winkel Press, 1997.

Sek Kei (石琪). *Shi Qi yinghua ji* (石琪影話集) [Collected reviews of Sek Kei]. Vol 4. Hong Kong: Subculture, 1999.

"Shiwu nian lai pu xinsheng, Lin Xi peilu paidang xinyi 15" (年來代譜心聲林夕披露拍檔心意) [Fifteen years of music, Lin Xi reveals partners' thoughts]. *Apple Daily* (蘋果日報), 6 April 2003, http://www.lesliecheung.cc/memories/linxi2.htm.

"Tang Hede zhiyou shengfen kan fuwen" (唐鶴德摯友身份刊訃聞) [Daffy Tong mourns as "truest friend"]. *Ming Pao Weekly* (明報周刊), 3 April 2003, http://www.mingpaoweekly.com/htm/20030403/maa1h.htm.

Tong Kar-Hei (唐嘉晞). "Lin Jianming xiang gege zhiqian" (林健明向哥哥致歉) [Meg Lam apologized to Leslie Cheung]. *Ming Pao Weekly* (明報周刊), 29 March 2004, http://www.mingpaoweekly.com/htm/20040329/mck2.htm.

Wang Zhihong (王志宏). "Taibei Xingongyuan de qingyu dituxue: Kongjian zaixian yu tongxinglian rentong" (臺北新公園的情慾地圖學：空間再現與同性戀認同) [The erotic geography of New Park: Homosexual identification and spatial emergence]. *Taiwan shehuiyanjiu jikan* (台灣社會學季刊) [Taiwan journal of sociology] 22 (1996): 195-218.

Wat Wing-Yin (屈穎妍). "Tongzhi xin mingci – zhiai" (同志新名詞 – 摯愛) [A new *tongzhi* term – beloved]. *Kuai zhoukan* (快週刊) [Express weekly], April 2003, http://lesliecheung.cc/memories/watwingyin.htm.

Women's Coalition of Hong Kong. *Tamen de nuqing yinji: Xianggang hui ai shang nuren de nuren koushu lishi* (她們的女情印記：香港會愛上女人的女人口述史) [In the tracks of their love: Oral history of women who could fall in love with women in Hong Kong]. http://oralhistory.wchk.org/.

Woo, Mathias (胡恩威). *Xianggang fengge* (香港風格) [Hong Kong style]. Hong Kong: TOM Publishing, 2005.

–. "Xianggang liuxing wenhua de liliang" (香港流行文化的力量) [The power of Hong Kong's popular culture]. *Yazhou zhoukan* (亞洲週刊) [Asia weekly], April 2003, http://lesliecheung.cc/memories/asiaweekly/asiaweekly6.htm.

Yang Zhao (楊照). "He e zhi you?" (何惡之有?) [What's so bad about the bad woman?]. Preface to *E nu shu* (惡女書) [Book of a bad woman], by Chen Xue (陳雪), 115-25. Taipei: Ink Publishing, 2005.

Yau Ching (游靜). *Bu keneng de jia* (不可能的家) [The impossible home]. Hong Kong: Youth Literary Book Store, 2000.

–. *Lingqi luzao* (另起爐灶) [Starting another stove]. Hong Kong: Youth Literary Book Store, 1996.

–. *Xingbie guangying: Xianggang dianying zhong de xing yu xingbie wenhua yanjiu* (性別光影：香港電影中的性與性別文化研究) [Sexing shadows: Genders and sexualities in Hong Kong cinema]. Hong Kong: Hong Kong Film Critics Society, 2005.

Yep, Ray (葉健民), ed. *Yi Xianggang fangshi jixu ai guo: Jiedu ershisan tiao zhengyi ji qiyi da youxing* (以香港方式繼續愛國：解讀二十三條爭議及七一大遊行) [Patriotism Hong Kong style: Understanding the controversy of Article 23 and the 1 July 2003 protest]. Hong Kong: Synergy Net, 2003.

"Zhang Guorong de banlu shi 'ta' hei shi 'ta'?" (張國榮的伴侶是「他」還是「她?) [Is Leslie Cheung's companion a 'he' or a 'she'?]. *Dagong zhoukan* (大公周刊) [Taikung magazine], January 2005, http://lesliecheung.cc/Magazine/1995/taikung95/interview/taikung95.htm.

"Zhang Guorong de wenhua biaoji: Jieshou yu kangju zhi jian" (張國榮的文化標記：接受與抗拒之間) [Leslie Cheung's cultural legacy: Between accep-tance and rejection]. *Jingji ribao* (經濟日報) [Economic times], 30 April 2003, http://lesliecheung.cc/memories/economictimes.htm.

"Zhang Guorong tan tongxinglian dianying" (張國榮談同性戀電影) [Leslie Cheung on gay cinema]. *Singdao Wanbao* (星島晚報) [Singtao evening news], 17 April 1994, http://lesliecheung.cc/News/1994/17.4.94/17.4.94.htm.

"Zhang Guorong yu shenmi ren xianglian" (張國榮與神秘人相戀) [Leslie Cheung in love with mystery person]. *Xin Bao* (新報) [Hong Kong daily news], 31 July 1994, http://lesliecheung.cc/News/1994/31.7.94/31.7.94.htm.

"Zhang Guorong nuli nuqi" (張國榮「女裡女氣」·) [Leslie Cheung's feminine air]. *Xin Wanbao* (新晚報) [New evening news], 2 May 1992, http://lesliecheung.cc/News/1992/2.5.92/2.5.92.htm.

Filmography

20-30-40. Directed by Sylvia Chang (張艾嘉). Hong Kong: Era Films, 2004.

A Better Tomorrow (英雄本色). Directed by John Woo (吳宇森). Hong Kong: Mei Ah, 1986.

Ab-Normal Beauty (死亡寫真). Directed by Oxide Pang (彭順). Hong Kong: Universe, 2004.

All's Well That Ends Well (家有喜事). Directed by Clifton Ko (高志森). Hong Kong: Mei Ah, 1992.

Beyond Our Ken (公主復仇記). Directed by Pang Ho-Cheung (彭浩翔). Hong Kong: Mei Ah, 2004.

Bishonen (美少年之戀). Directed by Yonfan (楊凡). Hong Kong: Fa Sun Film, 1998.

Butterfly (蝴蝶). Directed by Yan Yan Mak (麥婉欣). Hong Kong: Panorama, 2004.

Days of Being Wild (阿飛正傳). Directed by Wong Kar-Wai (王家衛). Hong Kong: Kino, 1990.

The East Is Red (東方不敗：風雲再起). Directed by Ching Siu-Tung (程小東). Hong Kong: Mei Ah, 1993.

East Palace West Palace (東宮西宮). Directed by Zhang Yuan (張原). Hong Kong: Joy Sales, 1996.

The Eye (見鬼). Directed by Danny Pang (彭發) and Oxide Pang (彭順). Hong Kong: Applause Pictures, 2002.

The Eye 2 (見鬼 2). Directed by Danny Pang (彭發) and Oxide Pang (彭順). Hong Kong: Applause Pictures, 2004.

Farewell My Concubine (霸王別姬). Directed by Chen Kaige (陳凱歌). Hong Kong: Tomson, 1993.

Golden Chicken 2 (金雞 2). Directed by Samson Chiu (趙良駿). Hong Kong: Applause Pictures, 2003.

Happy Together (春光乍洩). Directed by Wong Kar-Wai (王家衛). Hong Kong: Jet Tone, 1997.

He's a Woman She's a Man (金枝玉葉). Directed by Peter Chan (陳可辛). Hong Kong: Fotto Mobile, 1994.

Ho Yuk: Let's Love Hong Kong (好郁). Directed by Yau Ching (游靜). Hong Kong: Made-in-China Productions, 2002.

Hu-Du-Men (虎渡門). Directed by Shu Kei (舒琪). Hong Kong: Mei Ah, 1996.

Infernal Affairs (無間道). Directed by Andrew Lau (劉偉強) and Mak Siu-Fai (麥兆輝). Hong Kong: Media Asia Films, 2002.

Infernal Affairs 2 (無間道 2). Directed by Andrew Lau (劉偉強) and Mak Siu-Fai (麥兆輝). Hong Kong: Media Asia Films, 2003.

Infernal Affairs 3 (無間道 3). Directed by Andrew Lau (劉偉強) and Mak Siu-Fai (麥兆輝). Hong Kong: Media Asia Films, 2003.

The Intimates (自梳). Directed by Jacob Cheung (張之亮). Hong Kong: Mei Ah, 1997.

Island Tales (有時跳舞). Directed by Stanley Kwan (關錦鵬). Hong Kong: Golden Scene, 2000.

The Killer (喋血雙雄). Directed by John Woo (吳宇森). Hong Kong: Media Asia, 1989.

Koma (救命). Directed by Law Chi-Leung (羅志良). Hong Kong: Filmko, 2004.

Love and Sex amongst the Ruins (人間色相). Directed by Cheung Chi-Sing (張志誠). Hong Kong: Media Asia, 1996.

The Map of Sex and Love (情色地圖). Directed by Evans Chan (陳耀成). Hong Kong: River-drive, 2001.

Midnight Fly (慌心假期). Directed by Jacob Cheung (張之亮). Hong Kong: Filmko, 2001.

Portland Street Blues (洪興十三妹). Directed by Raymond Yip (葉偉文). Hong Kong: Ever-wide, 1998.

Rouge (胭脂扣). Directed by Stanley Kwan (關錦鵬). Hong Kong: Deltamac, 1987.

Song of the Goddess (似是故人來). Directed by Ellen Pao (鮑藹倫). Hong Kong: Videotage, 1993.

Spacked Out (無人駕駛). Directed by Lawrence Lau (劉國昌). Hong Kong: Mei Ah, 2000.

Speechless. Directed by Monica Lee (李韻恬). Hong Kong: InD Blue, 2004.

Still Love You after All These (念你如昔). Directed by Stanley Kwan (關錦鵬). Hong Kong: Arc Light Films, 1997.

Suet-Sin's Sisters (白雪仙的妹妹). Directed by Yau Ching (游靜). Hong Kong: Hong Kong Arts Centre and Videostage, 1999.

Swordsman 2 (笑傲江湖 2：東方不敗). Directed by Ching Siu-Tung (程小東). Hong Kong: Mei Ah, 1992.

Tempting Heart (心動). Directed by Sylvia Chang (張艾嘉). Hong Kong: Media Asia, 1999.

Visible Secrets (幽靈人間). Directed by Ann Hui (許鞍華). Hong Kong: Media Asia Films, 2001.

Yin ± Yang: Gender in Chinese Cinema (男生女相：中國電影的性別). Directed by Stanley Kwan (關錦鵬). Hong Kong: British Film Institute, 1996.

Discography

Cheung, Leslie (張國榮). "I Am What I Am" (我). Lyrics by Lin Xi (林夕). On *Big Heat* (大熱), CD, track 14. Hong Kong: Universal, 2000.

–. "I Am What I Am" (我). On *Passion Tour* (熱情演唱會), VCD, disc 2, track 15. Hong Kong: Apex and Universal, 2001.

–. "Moon River" (月亮代表我的心). On *Leslie Cheung Live in Concert 97* (張國榮跨越97演唱會), VCD, disc 2, track 8. Hong Kong: Rock, 1997.

Wong, Faye (王菲). "Undercurrents" (暗湧). Lyrics by Lin Xi (林夕). Music by Chan Fai Young (陳輝陽). On *Best of Faye Wong, 89-97* (王菲精選, 89-97), CD, disc 1, track 2. Hong Kong: Cinepoly Records, 1998.

Wong, Anthony (黃耀明). "Undercurrents" (暗湧). Lyrics by Lin Xi (林夕). Music by Chan Fai Young (陳輝陽). Arrangement by Keith Leung (梁基爵). On *Hold You Tight: Original Motion Picture Soundtrack* (愈快樂愈墮落電影原聲帶), CD, track 11. Hong Kong: Polygram, 1998.

Index

Printed and bound in Canada by Friesens

Set in Stone by Artegraphica Design Co. Ltd.

Copy editor: Robert Lewis

Proofreader: Dianne Tiefensee